CAMBRIDGE STUDIES IN LINGUISTICS

General Editors : W. SIDNEY ALLEN, B. COMRIE, C. J. FILLMORE,
E. J. A. HENDERSON, F. W. HOUSEHOLDER, R. LASS, J. LYONS,
R. B. LE PAGE, F. R. PALMER, R. POSNER, J. L. M. TRIM

Quantity in historical phonology
Icelandic and related cases

In this series

QUANTITY IN HISTORICAL PHONOLOGY

Icelandic and related cases

KRISTJÁN ÁRNASON

CAMBRIDGE UNIVERSITY PRESS

CAMBRIDGE

LONDON   NEW YORK   NEW ROCHELLE

MELBOURNE   SYDNEY

Published by the Press Syndicate of the University of Cambridge
The Pitt Building, Trumpington Street, Cambridge CB2 1RP
32 East 57th Street, New York, NY 10022, USA
296 Beaconsfield Parade, Middle Park, Melbourne 3206, Australia

First published 1980

Printed in Malta by Interprint Ltd

British Library Cataloguing in Publication Data
Árnason, Kristján
Quantity in historical phonology. – (Cambridge
studies in linguistics; 30 ISSN 0068–676x).
1. Icelandic and Old Norse languages –
Phonology, Historical 2. Icelandic languages
– Phonology, Historical
I. Title II. Series
439'.69'15   PD2240   79–41363

ISBN 0 521 23040 3

To the memory of my father, Árni Kristjánsson
Minningu föður míns, Árna Kristjánssonar, helga ég þetta rit

Acknowledgments

This book originated as a PhD thesis in the Department of Linguistics, the University of Edinburgh (1977), and Roger Lass, my supervisor, gave me not only the strongest scholarly support, but also invaluable moral encouragement. Others who were friendly enough to comment on the work during that stage were Professor David Abercrombie, John Anderson, Gillian Brown, Hermann Pálsson, Hreinn Benediktsson and Stefán Karlsson. During the revision of the text for publication, Professor W. Sidney Allen has given me generous advice and suggested improvements, and he and other editors have helped to improve my English style. I wish to express gratitude to all these people. Finally, I want to thank my wife, Guðrún Ágústsdóttir, for the help, especially in typing and retyping the various versions of the manuscript.

Reykjavík   K.Á.
February 1980

Contents

Contents

1 *Introduction*

1.1 **Purpose**

This study has, broadly speaking, a twofold purpose: it is primarily intended to shed some light on the phonological status of length and quantity in Icelandic and to consider its development from about 1200 to the present day and, secondly, it is hoped that the problems discussed raise theoretical issues of current interest in general linguistics, more particularly historical linguistics and phonology. As a side effect it is my hope that what follows (in particular chapter 3) may create a useful framework for a more general study of the history of quantity and other prosodic features in the other Scandinavian and Germanic languages.

Chapter 2 is a discussion of the question of how to deal with length and quantity in Modern Icelandic. An analysis is proposed where vowel length is seen as predictable on the basis of stress and syllabification, in such a way that if more than one consonant follows the vowel within the same syllable, the vowel is short, otherwise it is long. Vocalic length is thus determined by syllabic quantity which in turn is defined by stress. The syllabification that is proposed defines the stressed syllable as 'final-maximalistic' in that as many consonants as possible are assigned to the coda of the syllable. In particular it is suggested that some sort of phonotactic constraint prevails that forbids syllables ending in a sequence of a /p/, /t/, /k/ or /s/ followed by a /v/, /j/ or /r/. This, it is suggested, accounts for the fact that forms like *nepja* [nɛːpʰja] 'cold weather', have long vowels in spite of the fact that two consonants follow. Several theoretical questions are touched on in connection with the discussion of the Icelandic data. Among these are the status of the concept of the syllable in phonological theory, and the concept of strength of consonants and the idea of a hierarchy of strength in consonants. In §§2.6 and 2.7, problems are raised which seem to demand some qualifications as to the scope and ontological status of the proposed analysis.

Chapter 3 gives short summaries of the histories of quantity in other

1

Germanic languages. It is emphasised that the development of quantity and length in Faroese, Norwegian and Swedish seems to be very similar to that in Icelandic, whereas the developments in Danish and the West Germanic languages, though similar in many respects, are basically different. The most important difference between Icelandic, Faroese, Norwegian and Swedish, on the one hand, and Danish, English and German, on the other, is that in the latter vowel length can (except for a few dialects, e.g. Scots and Upper Austrian) be said still to be free in spite of the changes that took place and 'aimed at' making it predictable. In §3.8, a modest attempt is made at bringing these phenomena into a still wider context by considering briefly similar phenomena in Latin and Greek.

Chapter 4 deals with the development in Icelandic in more detail. It begins (§4.2) by summarising what is known about Icelandic in about 1200 and then moves on (§4.3) to try to trace the changes that were to affect the Old Icelandic structure. Much of the chapter is devoted to the evaluation of metrics as evidence about the quantity structure of the language. Particular attention is paid to the evidence given by *dróttkvætt*- and *rímur*-poetry from the periods dealt with.

Chapter 5 is devoted to the problem of 'explaining' the changes that led to the reorganisation of quantity that is usually termed the Icelandic 'quantity shift' (Danish: *kvantitetsomvæltningen*, Icelandic: *hljóðdvalarbreytingin*). This change was that length, having been 'free' in vowels in Old Icelandic, came to be determined by the context in the way described in chapter 2. It is suggested that stress was crucially involved in the change (or changes) and that the result was to produce a unit, central in the phonology of Modern Icelandic, the 'stressed syllable'. Among the theoretical questions touched on are the problem of what can be called an explanation in historical linguistics and what sort of metatheoretical demands should be made on statements in general, and in historical linguistics in particular, in order that they may be called scientific statements or explanations. Closely connected with this, the concept of 'cause of a linguistic change' is discussed. A third theoretical problem dealt with is the idea of 'historical conspiracies' (cf. Lass 1974), and the idea that changes may aim at a certain structure.

Chapter 6 deals with the question of how, in general, durational phenomena are to be treated in phonological descriptions and how they can function in phonological systems. Relevant issues here are, for instance, the relation between long vowels and diphthongs and the question of whether vocalic length can (in certain cases) be analysed as vowel gemination. Also important is the relation between syllabic quantity and segmental length and the question of whether (or when) length can be 'inherent' to segments. Connected with these is the question of how dichotomous vowel systems like those split by length are organised in relation to one another. In the light of this discussion, some afterthoughts are added concerning the structure of Old Icelandic and Modern Icelandic.

1.2 Phonological creed alias theoretical background

Although this study is not intended as a thesis for or against any particular theory in phonology, it seems only proper that I reveal a few of my feelings concerning some current issues in phonological theory. Although the background for the discussion in the following chapters is the paradigm of generative phonology, there are a number of reservations that I have to make concerning much of this type of phonology as it has been practised in the last decade or two. I thoroughly agree with those who maintain that many of the regularities that have been incorporated into 'phonology', in works like Chomsky & Halle (1968) and S. Anderson (1974), do not belong in phonology at all. My reservations may recall those expressed in works like Linell (1974) and Derwing (1973), although the motivation for my creed may be slightly different from the force behind Linell's and Derwing's criticisms of generative phonology. Their main argument is the psychological implausibility of abstract morpheme-invariants like/ re = duke/ for the common core in *reduce* and *reduction*. Although I agree with this, it seems to me (as both Derwing and Linell admit) that a case can be made for some sort of common denominator for the [rədjúːs] of *reduce* and the [rədʌk] of *reduction*. The point is that the motivation for it is by no means phonological, but something else, either semantic, or morphological, or both. That is, somewhere in their grammar (their 'competence') most speakers probably have some 'device' that represents the fact that the forms *reduce* and *reduction* are related, but that device is, I think, not phonological. The most important reason for their being seen as having something in common is the fact that they are semantically and morphologically related.

Let us have a look at a few pairs in Icelandic which can be said to show a morphophonemic alternation between [ou] (orthographic *ó*) and [ai], (orthographic *æ*). A number of forms show inflectional alternations:

(a) *fór – færi – færum* 'went'   (indicative sg. vs
                                           subjunctive sg. vs
                                         subjunctive pl.)

    tók – tæki – tækjum 'took'   (indicative sg. vs
                                           subjunctive sg. vs
                                         subjunctive pl.)

    stór – stærri – stærstur 'big'   (positive vs comparative
                                           vs superlative)

Other forms seem to show derivational regularity:

(b) *óp* 'a cry'   *æpa* 'to cry'
    hól 'praise, compliment'   *hæla* 'to praise'
    blóð 'blood'   *blæða* 'to bleed'

Lastly we have the following forms:

(c) *skór* 'a shoe'   *skæri* 'scissors'
    sól 'sun'   *sæla* 'happiness'
    dós 'a tin'   *dæsa* 'to sigh'

We now ask ourselves whether we should, in the spirit of 'orthodox' generative phonology (of the Chomsky & Halle (1968) type), set up underlying forms from which the alternants with [ou] and [ai] can both be derived. First of all, why should we want to do this? In the case of the inflecting forms, the answer would be that forms with the same 'lexical meaning' show regular alternations between [ou] and [ai] according to morphological environment. In the second set of examples, there is a similar alternation occurring in a derivational paradigm, [ou] in the nouns, but [ai] in the verbs. If these data had been handled by Chomsky & Halle (1968), they would have at least seriously considered the possibility of deriving the alternating forms in question from underlying invariant morphemes. But the point is that, given this data, the motivation is not phonological at all, but semantic and morphological. The only place where phonological considerations (i.e. things to do with phonic substance and linguistic structure directly related to it) can conceivably be brought forward is in the forms, *færi*, *tæki* and *stærri*, where the [ai]-vowel is followed by a front vowel in the ending. [ai] is more 'frontish' than [ou] (if that can mean anything). But this does not work for *færum* and *stærstur* (it might for *tækjum*, since it has a palatal: [tʰaiːcʰʏm] following the vowel), nor for *æpa*, *hæla* and *blæða*. In the last set of examples, we have the same sort of alternations in the stem vowels, but no semantic similarity between the forms. What is to be done here? I am sure that no generative 'phonologist' would suggest that these pairs be derived from a common underlying 'phonological' form. Why? Because they are not semantically related. So, the less *semantic* motivation there is for setting up morpheme invariants, the less likely the generative 'phonologist' is to want to set up abstract 'systematic phonemic' forms.

In the battle against this generative-phonologist 'straw-man' I have implied something that many linguists might not want to subscribe to, namely that it is possible to distinguish clearly between what is phonological and what is not. This, of course, is one of the basic riddles in modern linguistic theory. No attempt will be made here to find conclusive answers, but a few remarks are in order, if only to try to provide some sort of background for what follows.

It seems clear that some processes and regularities that are detected in speakers' linguistic output are more easily related to what are termed 'phonetic facts' than others. The regularity that palatals and no velars occur in front of a front high vowel like [i] can be fairly directly related to a process of coarticulation, whereas the alternation between [ou] and [ai] in the forms above can only be explained phonetically by going back at least to Old Icelandic and probably all the way to Proto-Nordic. This phonetic perspective can in many cases then be used to give marks to regularities as to their phoneticness, but it is doubtful whether this scale is categorial. New regularities are likely to be the most phonetic ones, and older ones are likely to have environments the transparency of which is partially a function of their age (cf. Árnason 1978a). Since the age scale is infinite, the historically based phoneticness scale will be infinite too.

It is, of course, possible that functional or psychological perspectives will make it possible to postulate the existence of categories like morphological, morphophonological, and phonological, but it may seem just as likely that the difference between these should be considered to be scalar, rather than categorial.

Attempts like those made within so-called 'natural generative phonology' to establish a categorisation by formal criteria such as the 'True Generalization Condition' suggested in Hooper (1976a:13) leave a host of unanswered questions as to the status of the various morphophonemic regularities that are excluded by the above mentioned constraint.

I will not delve into this problem here, but only state the belief that to call regularities like the spirantisation of the stop in *corrode* before the suffix *-ive* (Chomsky & Halle 1968:229) phonological is stretching the phonetic scale absurdly far, but that there are still regularities that do not fall into the category of 'natural phonological rules' but still show properties similar to many that do, and thus have important features in common with them.

Other current problems in phonology will be mentioned when the context warrants it. One is the fundamental question of the status of phonology in relation to other parts of the linguistic system. Is it 'interpretive' or does it have its own axioms? Although most statements in what follows are phrased in the metalanguage of interpretive generative phonology, that does not mean that I necessarily believe that framework to be optimal or even the best of those available at present. It is partly a convenience to use generative phonology as a frame of reference because of its present status as the predominant paradigm. There are several factors which may seem to support the view that phonology is independent. One is the lack of isomorphism between morphological and syntactic units (sentences, morphemes, etc.) on the one hand, and phonological units (intonation groups, words, syllables) on the other (cf. Fudge 1969:259). The fact that it is possible to form a phonological construct that sounds native in a language without its necessarily having any meaning seems to suggest the existence of an autonomous phonology. Probably the most difficult task facing autonomous phonologists is that of describing a way of mapping syntactic (or grammatical) structures onto phonological ones.

The problem of 'psychological reality' of phonological entities is of course a basic one, and it has received special attention in recent years because of the attacks that have been made on orthodox generative phonology, on the grounds that it is psychologically absurd. This is a problem that I will largely avoid, since my approach is basically historical, and historical changes are easily looked at from a supra-individual viewpoint, where questions concerning psychological reality are only indirectly relevant. There is, however, good reason to touch on this problem, especially since it seems to me that some clarification of the issue can be gained by considering the nature of generalisations in historical linguistics in relation to generalisations made in synchronic linguistics.

It is of course no coincidence that many of the most extreme solutions proposed within orthodox generative phonology look much like historical analyses. The similarity in argumentation and results between generative phonology and internal reconstruction is emphasised by Lass (1977), and he points out that internal reconstruction is in its origin a 'kind of bastard child by extension of the older comparative method' (p.3). Since most solutions in generative phonology are basically founded on the same principles as internal reconstruction, which in turn derives (perhaps 'illegitimately') from the comparative method devised in the nineteenth century, it comes as no surprise that the results are far from being psychologically plausible. The argumentation is abstract and panchronic in nature (a sort of logic is involved) and there is no reason to expect the results to have any psychological reality for real-life speakers of the languages analysed in this way. The gap between generative analysis and what can seem *a priori* to be sensible guesses about psychological entities is thus only natural, and probably unbridgeable.

Where this leaves generative phonology is another question. It is not necessary to throw it out as useless simply on the grounds that it is unfit for producing pictures of speakers' linguistic competences. It may still be useful synchronically in clarifying various aspects of the norm, or it may simply be looked on as a good (or bad) way of accounting for (explaining) linguistic regularities without it being necessary to reify its accounts as psychological entities or processes.

1.3 An overview of Icelandic phonology

A considerable amount of work has been done on Modern Icelandic phonology. General handbooks of Icelandic include Einarsson (1945) and Kelly & Kress (1972). General treatments of the phonology are to be found in Malone (1952), Haugen (1958), and the vowel phonology in particular is treated in, for example, Benediktsson (1959:301-2) and Steblin-Kamenskij (1960). Generative treatment of aspects of Icelandic phonology is to be found in S. Anderson (1969, 1972a, 1974). Works dealing specifically with quantity are: Malone (1953), Benediktsson (1963a), Garnes (1973), Kjartansson (1974), Árnason (1975), Orešnik & Pétursson (1977). Among phonetic studies of Icelandic may be mentioned: Ófeigsson (1920-4), Einarsson (1927), Bergsveinsson (1941), Guðfinnsson (1946, 1964), and Pétursson (1974). An important phonetico-phonological study of quantity in Modern Icelandic is to be found in Garnes (1974a), where results from various experiments are reported and commented on.

I will not produce commentaries on any of these works, although the discussion that follows will occasion references to them. Instead, I will try to give a reasonably clear and unbiased account of the most important features of Modern Icelandic phonology for the convenience of those who are not familiar with the data. Evidently some prejudices of mine will affect the following account, since I do not pay attention to all analyses proposed by all scholars, but I hope I am not presenting a minority view.

Vowels

Modern Icelandic has thirteen vowel phonemes, represented in a 'phonemicised' broad IPA transcription in table 1. There is no

TABLE 1. *Vowel Phonemes of Modern Icelandic*

Monophthongs		Diphthongs
/i/ /u/		/ɛi/ /œy/ /au/ /ou/
/ɪ/ /ʏ/		/ai/
/ɛ/ /œ/ /ɔ/		
/a/		

distributional difference between the dipthongs and the monophthongs; both can occur short or long (according to the rule described in chapter 2), so they can be said to form an integrated system of steady state and moving or 'dynamic' (Steblin-Kamenskij 1960:42) vowels. The quality of the vowels varies somewhat according to whether they are long or short (cf. §5.5, and Garnes 1974b). When the non-high monophthongs /ɪ/, /ʏ/, /ɛ/, /œ/, /ɔ/ and /a/ combine with a following [j], (which can in most of these cases be analysed as deriving from a velar fricative by palatalisation), they form in most dialects diphthongal allophones ('combinatorial diphthongs'): [ɪi], [ʏi], [ɛi], [œi], [ɔi] and [ai]. These diphthongs are entirely predictable from the environment, and are therefore not to be considered as phonemes, and few people do indeed consider them as such. This phonemic analysis is isomorphic with the analysis underlying the orthography, each of the phonemes having a separate symbol or digraph: /i/–*í*, /ɪ/–*i*, /ɛ/–*e*, /ʏ/–*u*, /œ/–*ö*, /u/–*ú*, /ɔ/–*o*, /a/–*a*, /ɛi/–*ei*, /œy/–*au*, /au/–*á*, /ou/–*ó*, /ai/–*æ*.

Consonants

A phonological analysis of the Icelandic consonants poses much more complicated problems than the analysis of the vowels, and no attempt will be made here to solve them all. I will only give a brief summary of the main facts.

Stops. There can be said to be two groups of stops in Modern Icelandic, distinguished in traditional Icelandic grammar by the terms 'hard' (*hörð lokhljóð*) and 'soft' (*lin lokhljóð*). I will follow this tradition and use the orthographic symbols in their phonemic representation. Here we meet the first unclear point: it is disputable whether palatals: [cʰ], [ɟ̊] should be represented as separate phonemes or just allophones of velars (see Árnason 1978a for a discussion of this problem). I choose here, more or less arbitrarily, to look on them as allophones of velars. Ignoring the problems of the palatals, then, the stop phonemes can be said to be the following:

Hard: /p/   /t/   /k/
Soft: /b/   /d/   /g/

The hard/soft distinction is very important in Modern Icelandic phonology. In initial position, the hard stops are aspirated in all dialects, and the soft ones unaspirated. Both are voiceless in all environments (and in that respect the notation used above is perhaps slightly misleading). In medial position between vowels, and between a vowel and /j, v, r/, there is a dialect difference. In the north only the hard consonants occur in this environment, but in the south only soft ones. Thus *taka* 'take' is [tʰaːkʰa] in the north, but [tʰaːka] or [tʰaːɡa] in the south. In accordance with this the southern variety is called 'soft speech' (*linmæli*), and the northern variety is called 'hard speech' (*harðmæli*). In Praguean terms the 'hardness' opposition is neutralised in this position, in the north in favour of the hard phoneme, but in the south in favour of the soft one. Following an initial /s/, the hard stops lose their aspiration (or only soft ones occur): *spara* [spaːra] 'save'. This is true of all dialects. In other medial positions the hard/soft distinction can be said to prevail in all dialects. If hard stops follow liquids or nasals, the latter are devoiced: *heilt* [hɛi̥lt] 'whole' (neuter) (cf. *heil* [hɛiːl] 'whole' fem.), *fantur* [fantʏr] 'villain', etc. There are exceptions to this in some northern dialects. When the hard stops are geminated according to the spelling, or they precede /l, n, m/, they are 'preaspirated' (cf. §2.3): *vakka* [vahka] 'walk to and fro' (as opposed to *vagga* [vaɡːa], [vakːa] 'a cradle') *vakna* [vahkna] 'wake up' (intrans.) (as opposed to *vagna* [vaɡna] 'cart', acc.pl.). Here (as a matter of prejudice as far as this presentation is concerned) I choose to follow the spelling in my phonological analysis, but there are various arguments in support of this (see Árnason 1977b, Þráinsson 1978). I would thus analyse *vakka*, *vagga* *vakna* and *vagna* phonologically as /vakka/, /vagga/, /vakna/ and /vagna/ and set up a preaspiration rule to derive the appropriate phonetic forms (see pp. 23–6).

Fricatives. The phonological analysis of fricatives is no less problematic than that of the stops. The phonetic forms that occur are:

f θ ç x s

v ð j ɣ

Of these /f/, /v/, /j/, /s/ are undisputably phonemic. [θ] and [ð] are in complementary distribution, so there is good reason to assign them to the same phoneme, call it /θ/ (or, according to Icelandic writing, /þ/). In the velar and palatal region, there is considerable confusion. It is arguable that [ç] is a separate phoneme from [j], since it is in a minimal opposition with it in pairs like *hjón* [çou:n] 'a married couple' vs *Jón* [jou:n] 'John', but some might suggest that [ç] should be analysed phonologically as /hj/ (see below).

The phonological status of [x] and [ɣ] is not immediately clear. They alternate with each other morphophonemically, and [ɣ] alternates with [g̊], and [x] alternates with [kʰ], and to make things still more complicated, [ɣ] sometimes alternates with [j] (see §2.4.4 for some discussion of this).

Nasals and liquids. The following nasal and liquid sounds are to be found in Icelandic- *m, n, ɲ, ŋ, l* and *r*. Of these there are both voiced and voiceless varieties, and it seems most natural to derive the voiceless ones from underlying voiced phonemes. The voiceless varieties are usually predictable from the surroundings, as in the examples mentioned above: voiceless in front of hard stops (*heil* [hɛi:l] – *heilt* [hɛilt] 'whole', *væn* [vai:n] – *vænt* [vaint] 'nice' (fem. vs neuter)). The only place where there is doubt as to whether voicelessness of a nasal or a liquid is predictable is in initial position in forms like *hnota* [nɔ:tʰa] 'nut' where there is on the surface a minimal opposition with [n] as in *nota* [nɔ:tʰa] 'to use', but here it might be suggested that the voicelessness derives from an underlying /h/, which can only occur initially. This would, then, be in agreement with the analysis of [ç] as underlying /hj/. I will not commit myself on this issue, but for the sake of the exposition I will assume that the voiceless alternants are allophones but not separate phonemes. This does not affect the validity of other comments made here on Modern Icelandic phonology.

In connection with the nasals, there is still a comment to be made on palatals and velars. In general, [ɲ] is confined to palatal environments: *lengi* [lɛiɲɟɪ] 'for long', and [ŋ] to velar environments: *langur* [lauŋg̊ʏr] 'long' (adj.), whereas [n] appears in other environments. This could be taken to suggest an analysis of velar and palatal nasals as allophones of the dental one. However, there are to be found minimal pairs distinguished

by a velar vs dental nasal: *lengd* [lɛiŋd̥] 'length' vs *leynd* [lɛ ind̥] 'secrecy',
but a case can be made, admittedly on morphological grounds, for an
underlying /g/ between the nasal and the dental in *lengd*: cf. *langur*
[lauŋɡ̊ʏr] 'long'.

A final note on [h]. As in most other Germanic dialects [h] (basically
realised phonetically as voicelessness) occurs in initial position, as in *hata*
[haːtʰa] or [aaːtʰa] 'to hate'. It seems reasonable to call this a separate
phoneme (with a very defective distribution). If initial [ç], [l̥], [r̥], [n̥] are
considered to be derived from /hj/, /hl/ etc., /h/ occurs initially in front of
vowels, liquids, nasals and /j/, but if these segments are separate
phonemes, the distribution of /h/ is limited to prevocalic initial position
(see below pp. 23–6 on the relation between /h/ and preaspiration).

2 *Quantity and stress in Modern Icelandic*

2.1 Some preliminary remarks

I shall preface the investigation of Modern Icelandic with a brief discussion of the theoretical equipment available for the analysis of the data and of some other points that are essential for an adequate discussion of the problems raised.

I shall try, in what follows, to make a distinction between three technical terms: 'duration', 'length' and 'quantity'. The term 'duration' will be used in a sense similar to that proposed by Lehiste (1970:42, for example), i.e. as meaning physically measured length of segments. All segments will have some duration whether the degree of that duration is linguistically significant or not. The two other terms will be used to refer to phonologically relevant duration, a distinction being made between 'segmental length' and 'syllabic quantity' (cf. Allen 1973). It is theoretically possible for segmental length either to be structurally 'inherent' in the segments or to be a function of the environment, and here syllabic quantity may play a role. Syllabic quantity is governed by the rules that determine the duration of the syllable as a whole. The difference between Old Icelandic and Modern Icelandic, from the point of view of the present investigation, can be said to be that in Old Icelandic, segmental length was more independent of syllabic quantity than it is in Modern Icelandic. In Modern Icelandic segmental length is derivable from syllabic quantity in stressed syllables: stressed syllables are all long or 'heavy' and the distribution of segmental length follows simply statable rules: long vocalism + short consonantism or short vocalism + long consonantism. In Old Icelandic, however, syllabic quantity was determined by segmental length, since a short vowel followed by a short consonant formed a short or 'light' syllable, but a long vowel always formed a long or 'heavy' one. At the segmental level, length in Modern Icelandic is syntagmatic, but previously was paradigmatic.

The concept of stress will be central to the present discussion since

12

there is a close connection between stress, quantity and length in Icelandic. There are some well-known problems connected with the use of the term 'stress' in linguistic discussion. It has been found difficult to find simply definable phonetic correlates of stress in many cases; its function is often complicated, and it often has complex relations with other parts of the phonological system within which it operates. I shall make little attempt to clarify any of these problems but simply start out by making a few (to me) sensible assumptions in order to set up some sort of framework for the following discussion. (Since my discussion is more or less confined to Icelandic I shall not claim that the constructs that I use will be applicable with the same ease in other contexts. I still hope, of course, that what I have to say will shed some light on phenomena in other languages and that these 'Icelandic constructs' can somehow be related to a general theory of language.)

I shall assume that a central unit can be set up as a part of the phonological system of Modern Icelandic which I shall call the 'stressed syllable'. This is a phonological unit whose relation to phonetic phenomena is not necessarily isomorphic, although in many cases it seems that it is relatively easy to relate this phonological unit to things that *a priori* would seem, say, plausible as production units. For example, the monosyllable *hest* would be described in my phonological analysis as consisting of one phonological stressed syllable, this being the unit, for example, defining the length of the segments. It does not seem implausible to maintain that when this word occurs utterance-finally or is pronounced in isolation, the phonological boundaries will coincide with the boundaries of a production unit which could be described as a phonetic syllable. It is not clear whether such a simple relation prevails in other environments, such as the case of the disyllabic *hestur* which will be described below in §2.2 as having the stressed syllable *hest* + the unstressed syllable *ur*. It is possible that, in actual production, many speakers will use the [t]-sound as a release for the following syllable, which is not in full accordance with the phonological proposal mentioned. It is also unclear what the relation between this phonological unit and auditory units, i.e. units used in speech perception, would be, since little is yet known about these phenomena.

It will be assumed in what follows that stress is a phonological category that has at least two types of function. One can talk about *marked* (or contrastive) stress and *unmarked* (or lexical) stress. The latter defines the stress pattern of words when they appear as tonics (are in focus) in sentences or when cited in isolation. (This unmarked pattern may be modified when the words are in non-focal position in sentences, for example so that the vocalism of the normally stressed syllable is reduced.) The marked stress pattern can be used to put contrastive emphasis on parts of utterances. Sequences that are normally unstressed can receive contrastive stress, and there seems to be little limit to where it can appear. It can even occur on inflectional endings. The phonological manifestation of both types of stress seems to be similar. For example *mann*INUM '(from) the man' with a contrastive stress on the second (normally unstressed) syllable is realised with a long [ɪː] in the second syllable followed by [n], parallel to the long [ɪː] in *hinum* [hɪːnʏm] (the independent form of the definite article, dat.sg.) with the normal stress on the first syllable. One could thus say that, from the phonological point of view, marked and unmarked stress are the same, the difference being in the function. Each main-stress peak has associated with it a pattern of secondary stresses, which is basically that every second syllable to the right of the peak has a secondary stress. Complications in this simple pattern arise in the case of compounds where the stress patterns of more than one word are conflated to form more complicated structures. Also, when contrastive stress falls in places other than the normally stressed first syllables, the stress pattern is reshaped, and a secondary stress of some sort remains in the place where the non-contrastive stress would have fallen. (I return to these matters in §2.5.)

2.2 Length and quantity

As has already been mentioned, lexical, non-contrastive stress appears on the first syllable of every non-compound word in Modern Icelandic and a secondary stress on every second one counting from the second one onwards. Examples illustrating this (the number 1 above a syllable represents 'primary stress' and 2 represents 'secondary stress'; if no number appears above a syllable it means that that syllable has 'no stress') are *táka* 'take' and *ǽtla* 'be going to' for disyllabics and *álmanàk* 'calendar' and *álmanàkanna̋* 'calendar' (gen. pl.) for polysyllabics. My main concern here will be syllables carrying primary stress, where there can be said to be a simple rule governing the length of segments.

It can be said that all primary stressed syllables (henceforth simply called stressed syllables) have the same quantity. They are long or heavy, whereas the unstressed ones are light. Long vowels or long consonants only occur in stressed syllables. (As mentioned above, lexically unstressed syllables can take contrastive stress, and then the distribution of segmental length becomes similar to that of the lexically stressed ones.)

Stressed syllables can be divided into three types (cf. Benediktsson 1963a and references):

(1) (a) C_0VCC ... (possibly more than two Cs)

    (b) $C_0V:C$

    (c) $C_0V:$

i.e. the rhyme (cf. Fudge 1969) can be a short vowel followed by two or more consonants (type (a)) or a long vowel followed by one (type (b)) or no (type (c)) consonant. (In this discussion a syllabification is presumed that will be justified later. This is not essential since the description can easily be rephrased in terms of segments, for example by defining the type (b) as a vowel and silence, etc. The syllable can then be taken at this stage as a convenient heuristic term to be defined more precisely later. Another assumption, not justified at this stage, is that long consonants in forms like *vinna* [vɪnːa] can be analysed as geminates, i.e. a sequence of two identical consonants.)

Examples illustrating the length distribution are:

(2) (a) *hestur* [hɛsdʏr] 'horse'

       vinna [vɪnːa] 'work'

    (b) *tapa* [tʰaːpʰa]([tʰaːba]) 'loose'

       tala [tʰaːla] 'talk'

    (c) *ný* [niː] 'new'

       te [tʰɛː] 'tea'

       búa [buː(w)a] 'to live'

The phonological analysis of these data has been a matter of dispute for some time (see e.g. Bergsveinsson 1941; Malone 1952, 1953; Haugen 1958, Benediktsson 1963a, Garnes 1973, 1974a; Kjartansson 1974; Árnason 1975, 1977a). Scholars have looked at pairs like *man* [maːn] 'slave', 'remember' (1p.sg.pres.) and *mann* [manː] 'man' (acc.) and made the observation that sequences like [man] and [maːnː] are impossible in Modern Icelandic. The fact that there are no stressed VC or V:C: rhymes has led to the conclusion that length cannot be free or distinctive in both consonants and vowels, because then we would expect a four-way distinction in stressed syllables between V:C, V:C:, VC and VC:. This can be taken as generally agreed upon. (Malone (1952) held the view that length was distinctive both in consonants and vowels, but he later (1953) abandoned it.) What has been a matter of dispute is whether phonological length should be assigned to vowels or consonants or indeed whether it should be determined at some higher level. The four types of solutions proposed so far for the pair *man – mann* can be summed up as follows (cf. Benediktsson 1963a):

(3) (a) /maːn/ vs /manː/ (Malone 1952)

 (b) /maˈn/ vs /manˈ/ (Malone 1953; Haugen 1958)

 (c) /maːn/ vs /man/ (Bergsveinsson 1941; Garnes 1973, 1974a)

 (d) /man/ vs /manː/ (Benediktsson 1963a, Árnason 1975, 1977a)

As already mentioned, solution (a) seems uneconomical, since a system with length in both vowels and consonants will most naturally generate four combinations of vowel + consonant and two types of open syllable (V:$ and V$).

In solution (b), proposed by Malone (1953) and elaborated by Haugen (1958), length is abstracted from the individual segments and made a part of what Haugen calls the 'accent' of the syllable, the place of length being the distinguishing mark between *man* and *mann*.[1] This solution seems to take care of the gaps in the distribution of length just mentioned and makes an attempt to account for the relationship between stress and length. Still, it has some problems connected with it. In the pair *man – mann*, a distinction is made by the placement of length alone, i.e. it is free to occur either on the nucleus or the coda. But this is only the case in a limited number of forms, namely the forms in (1a) which are described above as having geminates following the stressed vowel (*vinna*) and which have corresponding forms with a long vowel and a following consonant: *vina* [vɪːna] 'friends' (gen.pl.). In forms with heterogeneous consonantism following the vowel (cf. *hestur*), the distribution is no longer free since the length cannot fall on the vowel. Conversely, in sequences with no consonant following the vowel, the length has to fall on the vowel. Thus, in order to give a complete account of the distribution of length and explain its defective distribution, the accent analysis needs some qualification.

In the case of forms like *ný* [niː] these qualifications do indeed seem natural, since the only place for length to fall would be the vowel; but in the case of forms like *hestur* there seem to be some complications. No one segment can be said to take the length. It cannot fall on the vowel, and there is no long consonant like that of *vinna*. If this is so, we might want to assume that the durational part of the 'accent' is carried jointly by, say, the two consonants following the vowel, which would bring us out of the sphere of segmental length and into the sphere of syllabic quantity.

There is perhaps some justification for maintaining that length is carried by the [s] in forms like *hestur* in the fact that this segment tends to be slightly longer than for example the initial [s] in *saga* 'story' or the one following the long vowel in *vasa* [vaːsa] 'pocket' (acc.). The term 'half length' has sometimes been used to refer to this. In Stetsonian terms this might be taken as suggesting that the arrest of the stressed syllable falls on the consonant immediately following the vowel. This would not be unlikely to have a lengthening effect on the consonant, but it is doubtful whether this could be said to be the same phonological phenomenon as the length of the vowel in *man* and the length of the consonant in *mann*. I will return to this later.

The arguments that have been advanced in support of solution (3c) are based on phonetic evidence in some sense. Sveinn Bergsveinsson (1941; and in a discussion in Benediktsson 1963a) resorts to something which he calls 'Dehnbarkeit' of segments: 'Der Unterschied der zwei Normen (i.e. long–short) bei den Konsonanten ... ist nicht so ausgeprägt wie bei den Vokalen' (1941:84). By 'Dehnbarkeit' I imagine Bergsveinsson means the ability to be lengthened; and as a consequence of the vowels having more 'Dehnbarkeit' than the consonants, their length vs shortness is more 'prominent' (ausgeprägt) than that of consonants. It is not immediately clear what bearing observations of this sort should have on the phonological analysis. I will deal with this after describing briefly an experiment reported on in Garnes (1974a) which led her to the acceptance of solution (3c). The experiment tested the responses of native Icelandic speakers to synthetic tokens made out of e.g. the sounds corresponding to Icelandic *í* [i] and *s* [s]. The length of the segments was varied systematically, and the subjects were told to identify the sound sequences as either *ís* 'ice' (nom.) or *íss* 'ice' (gen.). The result of this experiment was that the judgements of the speakers were almost solely based on the length of the vowel (Garnes 1974a:224–69; see also Árnason 1975). The argument is, then, that since speakers use the duration of vowels to distinguish between the stimuli, vowel length must be 'distinctive' and pairs like *ís–íss*; *man–mann* are to be analysed phonologically as /iːs/ vs /is/ and /maːn/ vs /man/ respectively. This would then entail a phonological rule lengthening consonants after short vowels, and the length of the consonants would then be 'predictable' and not 'distinctive'. We notice that the term 'distinctive' is used in this (somewhat hypothetical) argument for phonemic vowel length in Icelandic in two different senses. In its first sense it means roughly: 'used by the hearer to distinguish, or rather to try to find out to what form in his language the noise he hears best corresponds'. In the second sense 'distinctive' is used as meaning 'the opposite of predictable'.

We have here an interesting ambiguity in the term 'distinctive' which can cause much confusion, not only in the discussion of this particular problem, but also of some fundamental issues in modern phonology. The concept of phonemic units, fundamental to present-day phonological theory, derives from two insights. One is that not all phonetic substance is relevant to the same degree: some things are 'distinctive', others 'redundant'. The other is that it is economical for the linguist, and presumably also for the speaker to isolate certain properties of the occurring linguistic signs and consider them as basic, and to derive other properties from these 'underlying' ones by the use of simple rules. It is usually assumed, explicitly or implicitly, that these two central considerations – one based on the idea of distinctive function and the other based on economy and simplicity – will converge to form, optimally, a well-motivated system of phonemic (distinctive) underlying units and a set of allophonic rules that will give a coherent model of the linguistic system in question. There is, however, good reason to suspect that this will not always be the case. The concept of distinctive function and the concept of simplicity as usually applied in linguistic argumentation belong to two different spheres and may lead to different results. The concept of simplicity is, as we saw in chapter 1, semi-logical and was first applied in linguistics in the historical–comparative method, whereas the concept of distinctiveness belongs to the description of linguistic behaviour. Each of these concepts has its own associated problems. The features that are used by speakers may vary from one situation to another, and the concept of simplicity may often seem to be quite remote from the actual raw data of individuals using language. Thus, it is relatively easy to avoid the uncomfortable consequences of Garnes' experiment by suggesting that perhaps the speakers will not always behave in the same way outside the experimental situation, which can hardly be said to be typical of language use. The reference of the term 'distinctive', in its most natural sense, must be very contingent; what functions as distinctive in one situation will not necessarily do so in another. The concept of simplicity has its own problems that are only too clearly reflected in some of the absurdities that have come up in some generative phonologies. (Perhaps one should say that the absurdity lies in the ontological status some of the authors assign to their underlying forms as 'psychologically real'.)

It is thus possible to use other considerations than the concept of distinctiveness when forming a model of a phonological system, and it is not permissible to use the terms predictable and distinctive interchangeably, since 'predictable' is a formal notion and 'distinctive' a functional one. One could maintain that vocalic length is distinctive and predictable without contradicting oneself. The fact that vocalic length was distinctive in Garnes' experiment can simply be said to be due to the fact that when words like *ís* and *íss* are pronounced in isolation, the [i]-sound is likely to be more prominent (perhaps in a sense similar to Bergsveinsson's term 'ausgeprägt') than the [s]-sound and therefore used by the speakers to decide what is going on.

Finally, it may be added that the question of predictability or distinctiveness may indeed look quite different from the point of view of the speaker *qua* producer of the noise.

The evaluation of Garnes' experiment as evidence of phonological structure touches on another central problem in linguistics, which is that it is not always clear what conclusions can be drawn about linguistic structure, whatever its ontological status in fact is, from experimental data involving linguistic behaviour of speakers. This is so, in general, because there are always more things than 'linguistic structure' involved when speakers perform tasks like the ones in Garnes' experiment. The speaker's 'knowledge' of the structure of his language is not necessarily the same as the strategies he uses when making judgements like those measured by Garnes. The fact that it seems to be possible to avoid experimental evidence like this may lead one to become sceptical of its value in linguistic argumentation, or perhaps, conversely, lead one to become sceptical of linguistic arguments and constructs, since it can be very difficult to test them by experiment. In fact, I think (or hope) that behavioural experiments and linguistic argumentation are by no means incompatible, but it seems often very difficult to formulate a linguistic argument and then an experiment which could be used to test its validity in such a way that it is clear that the variables of the experiment can be unambiguously related to unique phenomena in a proposed underlying linguistic structure.

It may be added (see Árnason 1978b), that linguistic concepts do not seem to be equally open to testing by means of behavioural experiments. This is so because the concepts have different backgrounds. Terms like 'distinctive' have a highly functional flavour, whereas 'underlying' (unpredictable) is more formal and specific to the system it works in. It has, in generative phonology, a status similar to the terms 'paradigmatic' or 'systemic' as used in other schools of linguistics. It is evident that the more functional the concepts are, the easier it will be to devise experiments to test their value, and the more formal and more abstract they are, the more difficult it will be to test them. It seems easier to conceive an experiment that would test, for example, whether something is an interrogative sentence than it is to think of an experiment that would test whether something is a subordinate clause. The general question arises as to whether functional and formal constructs should be mingled in one system or perhaps be kept separate from each other in linguistic argumentation.

Of the analyses summarised in (3), solution (d) remains to be considered. The arguments in favour of this analysis are presented in Benediktsson (1963a) and in somewhat more detail in Árnason (1975). The basic argument is morphophonemic; it is maintained that the morphology becomes hopelessly complicated if any of the other analyses mentioned in (3) is adopted. Icelandic shows morphophonemic alternation between long and short vowels; we can take the two strong neuter nouns *hús* 'house' and *vor* 'spring' as examples:

(4) *hús* [huːs] (nom. sg.)　　*vor* [vɔːr]
　　húss [husː] (gen. sg.)　　*vors* [vɔr̥s]

The genitival ending is -*s*, and when it is added to a stem ending in a consonant, the vowel automatically becomes short. If the phonological analysis for the pair *hús* – *húss* were /huːs/ vs /hus/, as it would be if alternative (3c) were adopted, the morphological analysis would work something like this:

(5) (a) Length is phonemic in vowels and predictable in consonants.

　　(b) The length of the vowel distinguishes lexically between the nom. and gen. of the word *hús*.

　　(c) The genitival marker for *hús* is the vowel shortness as opposed to the length in the nominative.

However, conclusion (5c) seems unfortunate, since, if *vor* and *hús* are to belong to the same declensional class, the genitive marker for *vor* would be the shortness of the vowel and the -*s* in *vors* would have to be predicted for this form by some strange morphophonemic rule.

Solution (3b) is open to the same criticism as (3c). In (3b) *hús* and *húss* would be phonologically /huʹs/ and /husʹ/, and the genitive would be marked by the place of the accent, and the same strange morphophonemic rule would have to predict the -*s* in *vors*.

The argumentation in favour of (3d) is entirely different from that in favour of (3c). It presupposes that the phonological analysis can be motivated by considerations of the simplicity of the morphological analysis. This seems perfectly legitimate in a paradigm like orthodox transformational generative phonology, where morphological information is, it seems, partly coded in phonological terms, and it would seem desirable to have the relation between morphology and phonology as simple as possible. But it is also possible to seek support for solution (3d) on more phonological grounds. If we were to devise a system for generating the phonological structures of Icelandic in a type of 'generative phonotactics' (cf. Fudge 1969), it would be simpler to account for vowel length in terms of the following consonantism than the other way around. This is so because (in spite of minor qualitative differences) it is possible in every case to find a short vowel of the same or similar quality corresponding to any long vowel, and vice versa: long [aiː] has a corresponding short [ai] and long [iː] a corresponding short [i], whereas, for example, 'long' [st] as in *hestur* has no corresponding short [st]. It is thus very simple to assume that a vocalic quality is determined for every nucleus and then its length predicted on the basis of the shape of the coda. It seems that predicting the shape of the coda on the basis of the shape of the nucleus will be more cumbersome, since a long consonantism can be much more varied in its segmental composition than a long nuclear vocalism. It seems that the phonotactics will be simpler if it is assumed that the consonantism defines the length of the vocalism, since the possible combinations in the coda will in any case have to be described independently of the question of length and quantity. The quantity of the coda is, partly at least, determined by its segmental composition, whereas length can be superimposed as an independent variable on any vocalic quality.

I will not make a choice at this stage between the types of solutions described above, but it seems that (3d) has certain advantages, particularly in the framework of 'interpretive generative phonology'. In a way this would then be in spite of the results of Garnes' experiment, which seem to suggest that vowels can, in some cases at least, carry a heavier burden of distinctive function than the consonants.

I will therefore make my point of reference the analysis proposed by Benediktsson (1963a) and adopted in Árnason (1975, 1977a). It has the further advantage of creating a useful framework for the historical changes to be investigated in chapter 4. I will refer to the length rule in

Modern Icelandic as a rule defining the length of vowels in stressed syllables as a function of the following consonantism: *vowels are short before two or more consonants, but long otherwise.*

There is an exception to the length rule, which should be mentioned now. This is that before sequences in which the first consonant is a member of the set /p, t, k, s/ and the second of the set /v, j, r/ vowels are long:

(6) *nepja* [nɛːpʰja], [nɛːbja] 'cold weather'
 vitja [vɪːtʰja], [vɪːdja] 'attend to'
 sœkja [saiːcʰa], [saiːja] 'to fetch'
 Esja [ɛːsja] name of a mountain
 (upp)götva [ɡœːtfa], [ɡœːdva] 'to discover'
 skrökva [sɡrœːkfa], [sɡrœːɡva] 'to tell a lie'
 depra [dɛːpra], [dɛːbra] 'sadness'
 titra [tʰɪːtra], [tʰɪːdra] 'to shiver'
 sykra [sɪːkra], [sɪːɡra] 'to put sugar on'
 Esra [ɛːsra] a man's name
 tvisvar [tfɪːsvar] 'twice'

The sequence /pv/ does not occur, probably prevented by a phonotactic constraint. I will come later to the problem of how to deal with this exception.

Except for those just mentioned, then, every sequence of two or more consonants is preceded by a short vowel. This is unlikely to be a coincidence, and is probably an aspect of the same rule that gives short vowels in front of long consonants. This fact suggests an analysis of the long consonants as underlying clusters of two identical ones. This seems to be very plausible. Consider for example the above-mentioned pair *hús – húss* as compared with *vor – vors*. The genitive marker is evidently -*s*, and the difference between the nominative and genitive of *hús* is best described as the absence vs presence of a second /s/ : /hus/ – /huss/. A low-level rule is perhaps needed to eliminate the boundary between the first and the second element of the cluster, if one is conceivable (see Lehiste 1970 :44). There are of course examples where there is no morphological support for the analysis of long consonants as clusters of two identical ones, for example *koss* 'a kiss', *kunna* 'to know how to', but it seems to be reasonable, in the absence of any evidence to the contrary, to analyse these examples in the same manner: /koss/, /kunna/. It may be mentioned in passing that this is exactly what Icelandic orthography does, as can be seen from the examples, but the arguments put forward in favour of the present analysis are independent of that.

I can think of one fact which could possibly be considered to contradict the analysis of long consonants as clusters. In words with long consonants in their stems, for example verbs like *kyssa* 'kiss' and *kenna* 'teach' or adjectives like *viss* 'certain', when a consonantal inflectional ending is added to the stem, the consonant loses its length, or, in our terms, one of the consonants of the cluster is deleted: *kyssti* [cʰɪsdɪ] (past, 1, 3p. sg.), *visst* [vɪstʰ] (neuter). This cannot be dealt with simply by a phonological constraint prohibiting clusters of three consonants in these surroundings, since there are stems, having clusters of non-identical consonants, which keep their clusters intact: *herma* – *hermdi*, [hɛrmd̥ɪ], not *[hɛrd̥ɪ] or *[hɛmdɪ]. There are, however, stems with consonant clusters which show behaviour which might be considered to be an aspect of the same phenomenon as appears in *kyssa – kyssti* and *kenna – kenndi*. In verbs like *verpa* 'lay eggs' and adjectives like *skarpur* 'sharp', the addition of the inflectional morpheme -*t* causes a considerable weakening of the /p/ or rather its morphophonemic variant [f], so that there is hardly any sign of it, maybe only a slight rounding of the [r]. The following are variant phonetic realisations of *verpa* in the past tense, *verpti* and *skarpur* in the neuter, *skarpt*: [vɛr̥fd̥ɪ], [vɛr̥Φd̥ɪ], [vɛr̥ʷd̥ɪ]; [sg̊ar̥ftʰ], [sg̊ar̥ʷtʰ], [sg̊ar̥tʰ] The first instances of each show the effects of a general rule, which turns clusters of two unvoiced stops into clusters of fricative + stop, but the other forms show at least a tendency to get rid of the clusters of three consonants by deleting the one in the middle. There is a difference of style between the three forms, the first being the most careful speech, and the others less so. A similar phenomenon is to be found in verbs with stems in /-ng/, for example *hengja* [hɛiɲ̊ja] 'hang' (trans.), [hɛiɲd̥ɪ] (past), where there is in most dialects of Modern Icelandic no sign of the stem-final /g/, except for the place of articulation of the nasal. A number of examples of this kind could be cited. If there is a rule eliminating some (but certainly not all) clusters of three consonants, the /sst/ and /nnt/ etc. can easily be included among those.

2.3 Preaspiration

Before moving on to a more detailed discussion of the phonology of length and quantity in Modern Icelandic, a note on preaspiration is in order; apart from being of interest as a phonological phenomenon, particularly because of its rarity in the languages of the world, preaspiration may be connected with length and quantity both from the synchronic and the historical point of view.

Icelandic preaspiration, as the term implies, has often been seen as some sort of inverse of (post)aspiration (cf. e.g. Guðfinnsson 1946). The voiceless gap between the vowel and the following consonantism in forms like *hnakkur* 'saddle', *tappi* 'cork', *detta* 'fall', *epli* 'apple', *kukl* 'witchcraft', *vopn* 'weapon' and *vakna* 'to wake up' (intrans.) has been seen as similar or related to the aspiration on the /t/ in *tala* [tʰaːla].

Until recently there was room for some disagreement concerning the phonetic characteristics of the preaspiration, particularly its duration in relation to other phenomena in its environment, but it now seems to be accepted that a transcription of the type [nahkʏr], [tʰahpɪ], [dɛhta], [ɛhplɪ], [kʏhkl], [vɔhpn] and [vahkna] (earlier adopted by Ófeigsson 1920–4; Einarsson 1927; Malone 1952) is preferable to the one used by Guðfinnsson (1946) with the preaspiration represented by a superscript [ʰ] and a (full or half) length mark on the following stops: [naʰkːʏr], [ɛʰpːlɪ] etc. Recent phonetic studies, for example Pétursson (1974:188–9) and Garnes (1973), have established that the stop segments in *hnakkur* etc. are short, i.e. shorter for example than the intervocalic stop in *lögga* [lœ̊ɡ̊ːa] ([lœkːa]) and that the preaspiration takes up a considerable part of the time of the syllable (word) as a whole. These facts lead Pétursson (1974:186) to the conclusion that the preaspiration is an instance of the phoneme /h/ which also occurs in initial position in forms like *hús* and *hestur*, and has the same or similar phonetic characteristics as the preaspiration: voicelessness ('spread glottis') and a vocal tract configuration appropriate to the adjacent vowel. Þráinsson (Thráinsson) (1978:21) similarly says that 'phonetic considerations and quantity relations seem to make it unavoidable to consider preaspiration a segment', although he maintains that an analysis of preaspiration as an instance of /h/ is unacceptable phonologically. A similar view is expressed in Árnason (1977b). There are several phonological or morphophonemic processes that seem to suggest that the preaspiration is intimately connected with the stop segments that necessarily follow it, and that an analysis of it as an underlying phoneme would lead to the loss of otherwise natural generalisations.

However preaspiration is to be handled phonologically, it deserves special mention in connection with the length rule, since the environment of the length rule is the postnuclear consonantism, and that is precisely where preaspiration develops. Indeed, it has been suggested by Allen

(1973:70) that preaspiration developed through a '*voiceless* lengthening' (italics his) of the vowel in forms like *brattur* [brahtʏr] that arose to compensate for a shortening of the historically long plosive. Furthermore, the preaspiration being describable as a voiceless vowel or a 'non-articulated' consonant has a special status among phonetic segments and could conceivably be maintained either to belong to the vocalic nucleus or the consonantal coda.

Þráinsson argues for an analysis according to which preaspiration is formed by a rule which deletes the supralaryngeal features of the first of two identical 'hard' stops (containing in Þráinsson's terminology the features + spread glottis, − slack vocal cords, − constricted glottis, + stiff vocal cords). If it is assumed that the length rule precedes the rule forming the preaspiration, there is no problem, since the double underlying consonant in, say, *hnakkur* will define the environment for a short vowel. But certain objections can be voiced against Þráinsson's suggestion that preaspiration is formed on underlying geminates in all cases. There is no direct motivation for underlying geminates in forms like *vatn* and *epli*, and yet these forms have preaspiration. Here Þráinsson assumes that a lengthening takes place that feeds the preaspiration rule. This, one might want to connect with the 'half length' of segments like the [s] in *hestur*, but, as we will see below (pp. 36–7), there is some reason to believe that this half length or 'tenseness' is in fact conditioned by the shortness of the vowel. And indeed one might wonder whether the primary feature or (part of) the conditioning factor of the preaspiration is not rather the shortness of the vowel (cf. Allen's idea of compensatory lengthening). It seems worth considering at least whether an explanation (historical or synchronic) is possible in terms of the contact between the short vowel and the following consonantism. It is an interesting fact that for most dialects of Modern Icelandic (excluding those that have voiced *l*, *m*, *n* or *ð* before /p, t, k/) it can be said that if a 'hard' stop follows the vowel, any consonantal element that intervenes between it and the short vowel must be a voiceless 'continuant' (n̥, n̥, ŋ̊, m̥, l̥, r̥, s, f, θ, x or h). One may wonder whether this is a coincidence. Forms like *seint* [sɛin̥t] 'late', *samt* [sam̥t] 'yet', *heilt* [hɛil̥t] 'whole', *svart* [svar̥t] 'black', *hest* [hɛst] 'horse', *oft* [ɔft] 'often', *maðk* [maθk] 'worm', *slakt* [sdlaxt] 'slack', *datt* [daht] 'fell', all have following the vowel a period of voiceless friction of some sort, which is 'arrested' by a stop.

I will leave open the question of how to deal with preaspiration, if only because I shall not give a complete synchronic analysis of the length phenomena for reasons I hope will become clear as we move on. But it seems likely that preaspiration will, in a grammar operating with ordered rules, most appropriately by (intrinsically) ordered after the operation of the length rule. (This, I suspect, will reflect the chronological order of the historical changes in question.) This would make it possible to utilise the shortness of the vowel, the output of the length rule, in the definition of the preaspiration rule. Or, since the environment of the length rule is still transparent in most cases, one could, as Þráinsson does, define it in terms of the consonantism as occurring on hard geminates.

A similar analysis is suggested in Árnason (1977b), only here the consonantal environment is defined in a slightly more complicated way as geminated hard stops or hard stops followed by *l*, *m*, or *n*.

2.4 Syllable, length and quantity

2.4.1 The syllable in phonology. As can be seen from the useful survey given in Awedyk (1975), both phonetic and phonological considerations have led people to set up the syllable as a unit in linguistic theory. In phonetics they have looked at the syllable as a unit of speech production (Stetson) or tried to define it in acoustic terms as based on variation in sonority, each syllable having a sonority peak (Jespersen). Others, like de Groot (1926), have wanted to look at the concept more as an abstract entity having correlates in speech production, acoustic substance, or speech perception. One of the most important points for phonology is the usefulness of a concept of this type to account for the distribution of segments and the variation that can be seen in the function of (smaller) phonological units like segments or features, according to syllabic environment. The fact that /gʌlp/ *gulp* and /plʌg/ *plug* are permissible sequences in English, but not /glpʌ/, /plgʌ/, /lpgʌ/, /gʌpl/ and a host of others, can be accounted for by setting up a definition of a phonological unit that determines the way segments are related syntagmatically. One can say, for example, that the English syllable can have a coda consisting of the sequence /lp/ but not the sequence /pl/. Another case where the syllable can be a useful unit in phonology is when some phonological process seems to operate within a domain larger than segment and smaller than word. It may serve 'as a unit of stress placement, or of tone placement, or of the timing of vowel length' (Pike 1947:90). Recently, the need has been felt to incorporate a concept of the syllable into the theoretical mechanism of generative phonology in order to make it possible to account for various phonological processes (Hooper 1972; Vennemann 1972; Kahn 1976). In Hooper (1976a:179–242) an attempt is made to incorporate a theory of syllable structure into a framework of 'natural generative phonology'.

It seems essential, in a discussion of the syllable, that the phonetic and the phonological arguments in its favour (or disfavour) should be clearly distinguished. The phonetic arguments in the main relate to linguistic behaviour (production, perception) or to the actual physical build-up of the linguistic signal (acoustics), whereas formal criteria like the distribution of segments have a different sphere of reference, whose reality is much more difficult to establish. The difference between phonological and phonetic considerations may lead to the conclusion that two types of units should be talked about: phonetic syllables and phonological syllables.

I choose here to approach the problem of the syllable in the following way: it is possible to set up a trichotomy and, in the first place, to talk about *phonological syllables*, which are abstract theoretical constructs, motivated by formal arguments based on things like the distribution of phonological units (segmental or suprasegmental); in the second place it might seem sensible to talk about *production units*, which could be described as 'comfortable chunks of utterance'; and in the third place one might talk about *perception units*, 'handy chunks for use in the process of analysing the speech signal'.

The definition of phonological syllables given above may seem inadequate to those who argue that it should also have a psychological basis and be a unit in the minds of speakers that can be easily related to the behavioural units of production and perception. We may keep this possibility open while bearing in mind that this is not necessary for carrying on a sensible discussion in a historical context like the present one, and that it is perhaps premature to postulate anything about 'psychological reality' in our present state of ignorance.

In the present discussion, the term 'syllable' will be used in the formal sense described above, and it is hoped that, in theory at least, some sort of mapping can be established between it and production units and perception units of the sort mentioned above.

2.4.2 Exceptions to the length rule, syllabification. I will now look at the exceptions to the length rule listed under (6) in §2.2. As stated there, vowels are long before sequences of two consonants of which the first is from the set /p, t, k, s/ and the second from the set /v, j, r/. One has to ask whether there is a natural explanation for this.

It has been suggested by Vennemann (1972:7) and Garnes (1975a:156–8) that this apparent exception to the length rule can be explained in terms of syllable structure. They propose a syllabification which treats the forms *nepja, vitja, sækja, Esja, (upp)götva, skrökva, depra, titra, sykra, Esra* and *tvisvar* differently from other forms having intervocalic sequences of more than one consonant. Garnes calls upon a 'sonority hierarchy', proposed by Zwicky (1972), to help to define the environments of a syllabification rule which gives the desired results. She proposes that the forms with a short vowel be syllabified so that a syllable boundary falls between the two consonants, leaving a consonant following the vowel within the same syllable; the forms with a long vowel she proposes to syllabify so that the syllable boundary falls immediately after the vowel. This would give a syllabification like *vak–ka* 'walk to and fro', *vak–na* 'wake up' (intrans.), *hes–tur* 'horse' for the short vowel forms, as opposed to *ve–kja* 'wake up' (trans.), *va–kra* 'good for riding' (acc.masc.pl.) *E–sja* etc. for the long vowel forms. Vennemann uses a strength hierarchy with /v, j, r/ as the 'weakest' of Modern Icelandic consonants and /p, t, k, s/ as the strongest to get the same results.

In recent treatment of the role of the syllable in phonology (J. Anderson 1969, 1975; Fudge 1969; Pulgram 1970; Hooper 1972, 1976a, b; Vennemann 1972; Anderson & Jones 1974; Basbøll 1974; Kahn 1976) much of the discussion has centred around syllabification; that is, how longer sequences (words) are divided up into syllables. In accordance with claims that the syllable is universal (cf. Pulgram 1970) attempts have been made to devise rules or principles of syllabification which are (explicitly or implicitly) claimed to have universal application. It should be noted, however, that even though the syllable is a linguistic universal it does not necessarily follow that there exists a universal principle of syllabification that could be applied to all languages. It is quite possible that syllabification rules are language-specific even though the syllable is a universal unit, just as at least some rules for the expansion of NPs are language-specific even though the noun phrase itself is probably universal.

We can distinguish two ways of approaching the problem of syllabification. One is to define syllabification rules in terms of segments. Hooper, for example, states (1972:535) a rule to the effect that a syllable boundary should automatically fall between two 'non-sonorant' (i.e.

containing the feature [− sonorant]) segments. Another way is to make use of the so-called 'law of initials' and 'law of finals'. Here it is assumed, the syllable being a unit in phonotactics, that the sort of sequences occurring initially in words can be used in determining what are possible onsets in syllables, thereby giving clues as to how to syllabify. Similarly, the set of clusters occurring word-finally could be used to define what are possible codas. A statement typical of this principle is Pulgram's basic principle that all syllables are open, provided this does not lead to onsets which are not permitted word-initially. We may, for the purposes of this discussion of Icelandic, call the first the 'segmental approach' and the second the 'phonotactic approach'. There is a theoretical difference in the claims made by these approaches which will be discussed later.

Returning to Modern Icelandic, it seems that Garnes' proposal (as well as that of Vennemann 1972) is based on the 'segmental' approach, i.e. according to her principle, if a voiceless obstruent is followed by a segment which has sonority (in Zwicky's sense) which is greater than or equal to that of /r/, then the syllable boundary falls in front of the obstruent, but if the segment following the obstruent has less sonority, the syllable boundary falls between the two segments: *va–ka* 'to be awake' *va–kra*, *ek–la* 'lack', *vak–na*, *vak–ka*. The lateral /l/ has less sonority than /r/ in Zwicky's hierarchy, and the breaking-point lies, according to Garnes, between these two, as far as Icelandic syllabification is concerned. There are specific problems with this analysis for Icelandic. Apart from the fact that the principle, as it stands, does not take care of forms like *biðja* [bɪðja] 'ask', *telja* [tʰɛlja] 'count', *blaðra* [blaðra] 'balloon' and *gulra* [ɣʏlra] 'yellow' (gen.pl.), which have short vowels and should then be syllabified *bið–ja, tel–ja, blað–ra* etc., Garnes is forced to set up underlying forms for *j* and *v* which are otherwise unmotivated. She proposes to analyse them as underlying glides /y/ and /w/ in order to put them in the right place in the sonority spectrum, whereas they are usually realised as fricatives, which, according to Zwicky, are less sonorant than *l*, *n* and *m*. Even if we accept Garnes' dubious assumption that Zwicky's sonority hierarchy is valid on a very abstract systematic phonemic level, Garnes' proposal has the gross disadvantage of setting up underlying segments which invariably turn up as something else on the surface; if we allow this, it will become very hard to find a reasonable way of restricting the form of abstract phonological representations (cf. Kiparsky 1968b).

I shall return to Vennemann's proposal later in this section, but first I will consider the problem from the 'phonotactic' point of view, prefacing this with a few remarks about alternative hypotheses within that general framework. J. Anderson (1975:10) distinguishes between what he calls the 'maximalist' vs 'minimalist' views. Pulgram's principle mentioned above is what Anderson would call 'final minimalistic', according to which as few segments as are allowed to stand word-finally after the vowel occurring in the syllable are assigned to the coda of each syllable. This would mean, for example, that a form like *cider* will be syllabified *ci–der*, since the vowel of the first syllable can stand word-finally without any following consonant. The 'initial minimalistic' view would be to assign as few segments as allowed by the phonotactic rules of the language to the onset of the syllable. Anderson (and implicitly Anderson & Jones 1974) proposes what he calls the 'maximalist view', according to which as many segments as possible (according to the phonotactic principle) are assigned both to the onset and coda of each syllable, and overlap is allowed for. According to this, the form *debit* would be syllabified like this: $[_1\text{de}[_2\text{b}]_1\text{it}]_2$, where the brackets numbered 1 and 2 mark the limits of the first and the second syllable respectively. In this case the segment /b/ belongs simultaneously to both the first and the second syllable. (I find the terms 'maximalistic' and 'minimalistic', as Anderson uses them, somewhat confusing, since it could be said that, for example, 'initial minimalistic' can mean exactly the same as 'final maximalistic'. That is, if you assign as few segments as possible to the onset of the following syllable and there is no overlap and nothing left over, you automatically assign as many segments as possible to the coda of the preceding syllable. Perhaps Anderson's principle could be called the 'overlap principle' to avoid confusion.)

It is now interesting to see whether we can use the phonotactic method to give us the syllabification we want for creating a simple environment for the length rule in Icelandic. If we start by looking at the examples *hestur* [hɛstʏr] 'horse' (short vowel) and *dysja* [dɪːsja] 'to bury' (long vowel) we may ask whether, for example, the 'final minimalistic principle' proposed by Pulgram can help us. According to this, as few segments as possible are assigned to the first syllable. We see immediately that this does not work, since /st/ and /sj/ are both permissible word-initially in Icelandic: *standa* 'stand' and *sjá* 'see', and [ɛ] and [ɪ] can stand finally: [ɛ] in *te* [tʰɛː] 'tea' and [ɪ] in the name of the letter *i*; *hestur* and *dysja* should then both be syllabified in the same way: *he–stur* and *dy–sja*. If, on the other hand, we assume that Modern Icelandic should be syllabified 'final-maximally', we seem to be getting somewhere. According to this principle, we should assign as many segments as possible to the coda of the first syllable. We can show that /st/ is a permissible word-final cluster: *hest* 'horse' (acc.), *ást* 'love' etc., whereas /sj/ is not. This is particularly clear in the inflection of *dys* [dɪːs] 'grave', which is derivationally related to the verb *dysja* 'to bury'. The genitive singular is formed by adding the ending *-ar* to the stem, and then /j/ appears: *dysjar* [dɪːsjar]. The /j/ of the stem /dɪsj/ is evidently prevented from appearing in the endingless nominative by a phonotactic constraint forbidding the sequence /sj # /. According to a final maximalistic principle, then, we get *hest–ur* vs *dys–ja* (the /s/ is assigned to the first syllable in *dysja*, since /s/ can appear word-finally after a vowel). If we look at the other exceptions to the length rule, we see that they will all be syllabified in the same way as *dysja* by the final maximalistic principle: *nep–ja, vit–ja, sæk–ja, Es–ja, (upp)göt–va, skrök–va, dep–ra, tit–ra, syk–ra, Es–ra, tvis–var.*

But we have not solved the problem. Let us look at the forms *biðja* [b̥ɪðja] 'to ask', *tefja* [tʰɛvja] 'to delay' and *stöðva* [stœðva] 'to stop', which have short first vowels. If we were to syllabify these forms according to the final maximalistic view, we would get *bið–ja, tef–ja* and *stöð–va*, since [ðj], [vj], and [ðv] are not permissible word-final clusters in Icelandic. So we see that these forms, having a short vowel, get the same syllabification as *dysja* with a long vowel. This indicates that the final maximalistic principle cannot help us to get a syllabification in terms of which we can simplify the length rule.

We have still one alternative within the phonotactic framework, namely Anderson & Jones' (1974) overlap principle. This could perhaps help us to differentiate between *dysja* etc. on the one hand and *biðja, tefja* and *stöðva* on the other. We then notice that [ðj], and [ðv] are not permissible word-initially.[2] According to the overlap principle *dysja* would be syllabified [₁dy[₂s]₁ja]₂, since /sj/ is permissible word-initially, but *biðja* and *stöðva* would be syllabified [₁bið]₁ [₂ja]₂ and [₁stöð]₁ [₂va]₂, since [ðj] and [ðv] are neither permissible word-finally nor word-initially, and must then belong to different syllables without any overlap. The fact that /s/ in *dysja* constitutes an overlap could then perhaps be utilised in the length rule, since evidently single intervocalic consonants will also constitute an overlap between two syllables as in *mana* [maːna] 'to egg on': [₁ma[₂n]₁a]₂. But this does not solve our problem either. Forms like *venja* [vɛnja] 'habit', *temja* [tʰɛmja] 'to domesticate', *velja* [vɛlja] 'to choose', *berja* [b̥ɛrja] 'to hit', with short vowels, have intervocalic sequences which are impermissible word-finally, but permissible word-initially: *njóta* 'to enjoy', *ljótur* 'ugly', *rjómi* 'cream'; they should then fall in the same category as /sj/ according to the phonotactic overlap principle, i.e. be syllabified $[_1\text{ve}[_2\text{n}]_1\text{ja}]_2$ etc. with the /n/ etc. forming an overlap exactly like the /s/ in *dysja*.

The phonotactic approach, therefore, apparently cannot offer a simple explanation for the exceptional behaviour of the sequences /pj/, /kj/, /pr/, /kr/ etc. This might lead to scepticism as to whether the syllable has anything to do with the distribution of vowel length, or it might make one sceptical of the value of the phonotactic principle.

Let us try to clarify a couple of points at this stage. Firstly, we are dealing with stressed 'syllables', and it is conceivable that a non-final stressed syllable is allowed to 'absorb' a longer postvocalic consonant sequence than a final one so that the set of word-final codas is not the same as the set of word-medial codas. Secondly, we may observe that in order for the phonotactic principle to be valid as a discovery procedure for finding the 'right' syllabification, an assumption must be made that phonotactic constraints in word-initial and word-final positions in a language can be defined independently of the concept syllable in that language. (A part of the definition of the concept syllable must be an account of syllabification.) But this is self-contradictory, since behind the phonotactic principle lies an assumption that the syllable is a unit of phonological organisation; and maintaining that the syllable defines what can occur initially in words and then assuming that what occurs initially determines syllabification (defines the syllable) is of course circular. Thus the 'phonotactic principle' has no independent significance and is only a useful heuristic that can give clues as to how one should define the phonological syllable. Whatever the status of our 'phonotactic principle', the fact is of course that the ultimate definition of phonotactic regularities must be given in terms of the units that are the actual building blocks of the syllable, i.e. the actual segments and/or prosodies that constitute it. (It makes sense to say that the syllable defines the organisation of smaller phonological units or to say that the organisation of phonological units into larger units defines these larger units (syllables, words etc.), but there is *a priori* no reason to assume that the organisation of phonological units in one type of environment (word-finally for example) is always exactly the same as in some other type of environment (word-medially).)

If we turn back to the Icelandic examples and say, for example, that *Esja* is to be syllabified *Es–ja* and *hestur* is to be syllabified *hest–ur* and we do so because the sequences /sj/ and /st/ show different behaviour with respect to phonotactic constraints in that /st/ can occur word-finally, but /sj/ cannot, we have in fact not given an explanation, but only pushed the solution one step away from us. We have not explained why these sequences behave differently. In fact it seems that statements concerning phonotactics and syllable structure are essentially statements as to the behaviour of segments and other phonological units when combining with other units of the same 'rank' to form larger units, and any real explanation of the segments' behaviour is most probably to be sought in the 'nature' of the segments themselves. (Of course one might say that part of their nature is the way they behave.)

From the point of view of 'generative phonotactics' (cf. Fudge 1969; Sampson 1970), the explanation of why certain phonological structures but not others should occur is essentially an explanation of why certain sequences of segments and not others are to be generated by the phonological system, and more generally why there seem to be constraints concerning the shape of syllables themselves.

2.4.3 Why the syllable? In view of the problems that seem to face us in making use of the syllable in this account of the length rule in Icelandic, one might wonder whether it should be brought into the discussion at all. There are two basic reasons (or one two-part reason) for doing so. We seem to have something which we can call the environment of the length rule, and it would be nice if we could make it more 'respectable', for example by maintaining that the unit has some significant status in the phonology of the language. The double gain made if we were able to maintain that the length rule is connected with something we could call the syllable would be that our descriptive mechanism would conceivably be simpler (since the definition would be needed independently of our length rule) and that we might be able to maintain that we had been able to say something about the nature of the length rule, its relation to something that we believe exists and would like to be able to call the syllable in Icelandic. The latter type of motivation would, of course, if valid, be much more respectable, but all the more difficult to give any substance to.

Part of the motivation for our wanting to bring the term syllable into the picture derives from the historical perspective of this discussion. As will be shown in chapter 4, Old Icelandic had free vowel length. This created variation in what we call syllabic quantity. That is, units could be formed that most probably varied in their actual duration and probably had different phonological status according to their composition. Heavy and light syllables had, for example, different functions in poetry. Forms like *fat* 'a piece of clothing', with a short vowel and a single consonant could not form a metrical ictus by themselves, whereas *fát* 'confusion' and *fatt* 'erect' (neuter) with, respectively, a long vocalism and a long consonantism, could. The difference in metrical function seems to justify a phonological distinction between two types of units. The term phonological syllable immediately presents itself. (A definition in terms of morphemes would not work, since *fátt* 'few' (neuter) will have to be analysed as bimorphemic: *fá + tt*, the *tt* functioning as a neuter morph whereas *sátt* 'agreement' is best analysed as monomorphemic. Also, there exist in Old Icelandic polysyllabic morphemes like *endemi*, (*endimi*) 'something unique'.)

As time advanced, a change took place in the function of units like *fat*, so that they became able to carry a metrical ictus by themselves. It seems reasonable to assume that this was due to a change in the shape of the unit, giving it the same metrical value as *fát* and *fatt* and *fátt*. It seems reasonable to describe this change at least to some extent in terms of a unit like the syllable. And, as I have said before, the difference between Old Icelandic and Modern Icelandic can be described in terms of different laws of syllabic quantity.

It may be added that in traditional accounts the so-called 'quantity shift' consisted not only of a lengthening of vowels in originally light syllables, but also of a shortening of vowels in 'hypercharacterised' syllables (see below). This can be seen as having the result that *fátt* came to have the same quantity as *fatt* and *fát* originally had, and as *fat* came to have after the lengthening of its vowel. Thus it can be said that the lengthening in *fat* and the shortening in *fátt* aimed at a uniform syllable quantity. To give a simple and insightful account of these phenomena without the use of the concept syllable seems to be much more difficult.

We have already seen that there are many theoretically possible ways of syllabifying disyllabic forms with intervocalic sequences of more than one consonant. In forms like *hestur* there are mathematically three options open for each form: (i) *he–stur, E–sja, bi–ðja*; (ii) *hes–tur, Es–ja, bið–ja*; (iii) *hest–ur, Esj–a, biðj–a*, not to mention the alternatives that become available if one allows for overlap between syllables. From the point of view of the simplicity of the length rule, a syllabification like *hest–ur, biðj–a* and *Es–ja* seems to be optimal. If this were acceptable, the length rule could be stated simply as a lengthening of vowels in stressed syllables that end in no more than one consonant and/or shortening of vowels in syllables that end in two or more consonants. It could be stated like this:

$$V \longrightarrow \bar{V} / \_\_ C^1 \$$$

and/or

$$V \longrightarrow \check{V} / \_\_ C_2 \$$$

Let us, then, tentatively suggest that the forms are to be syllabified in the way described above. The principle would be that two consonants following a stressed vowel are assigned to the preceding syllable, except when the two consonants in question are /p, t, k, s/ + /v, j, r/, in which case only the first member of the sequence is assigned to the preceding syllable. If only one consonant follows, it is by the same token assigned to the preceding syllable. This syllabification can perhaps be called final-maximalistic in some sense, since as many consonants as allowed by some constraint are assigned to the coda of the syllable.

The main advantage of this syllabification (if it can be called syllabification at all) is that the environment of the length rule, if defined in this way, will be exactly the same in monosyllables and polysyllables, whereas if we were to adopt the syllabification suggested by Garnes (1975a) and Venneman (1972), where the syllable boundary falls before one intervocalic consonant (as well as /p, t, k, s,/ + /v, j, r/), the length rule cannot be stated as simply. In the latter case the rule will have to be in two parts. One part would account for monosyllabic forms like *hest, nes* 'cape,' where the vowel is short if followed by two or more consonants, but long if followed by one or no consonant within the same syllable. Another part of the length rule will have to account for the length in polysyllabic forms like *hestur, nesi*, where the vowel is short if one (or more) cosyllabic consonant(s) follow(s), but long if the syllable is open, i.e. if no consonant follows within the same syllable.

The most obvious disadvantage of the syllabification suggested here is that it does not follow the 'law of finals' (cf. e.g. Vennemann 1972; J. Anderson 1975), since the syllabification of *grenja* and *biðja* (*biðj–a*, *grenj–a*) gives syllables that end in clusters that are not permissible word-finally in the language. And if this law (as well as the law of initials) is a universal constraint, this syllabification should of course be viewed with scepticism.[3]

A weaker claim would be that what we are suggesting is not syllabification, but merely a delimitation of the domain of the length rule. But then, of course, we will have to ask ourselves what exactly this unit is.

If it is not a syllable, then what is it? The question immediately turns into another one: whether this unit can have some other function in the phonology of Modern Icelandic, whether, for example, some other rules seem to be defined in terms of it. If this turns out to be the case, we may feel justified in giving this unit a major status in the phonology of Icelandic. I will therefore investigate the question of whether there are other things in the phonology of Modern Icelandic which would become more easily explainable in terms of a syllabification of the sort suggested above.

In forms like *hestur, grenja, biðja* etc. the consonant following the (short) vowel is often said to be half-long (cf. Ófeigsson 1920–4: XVIII–XIX; Guðfinnsson 1946:68–9): [hɛsˑtʏr], [ġrɛnˑja], [bɪðˑja]. There seems to be some justification for this. I have, for example, made spectrograms of my own speech in the utterance *þessi hestur*, which show that the [s] in *hestur* is considerably longer than any other consonant segment in the utterance except the long [sː] in *þessi*, which is again noticeably longer than the one in *hestur*. Although the term 'half-long' seems to be quite appropriate for this phenomenon on the evidence mentioned above, I am not sure that there are not additional features that characterise consonants in these environments; one should perhaps use some more meaningless term, 'tense' for example. If we now look at the distribution of this phenomenon, we see that it must be predicted by things similar to those that affect the length rule. The consonants are half-long or 'tense', if they follow a short vowel and precede a consonant. The distribution of this 'tenseness' is independent of whether the word is monosyllabic or polysyllabic; that is, we have *hest* [hɛsˑt], *vans* [vanˑs] and *glaðs* [glaðˑs] with 'tense' consonants just as in *hestur, gleðja* and *grenja*. It is very tempting to try to explain the distribution of these 'tense' consonants in terms of their place in the syllable (cf. Hoard 1971), but we then once again face the fact that this 'tensing' takes place regardless of whether the consonant appears in a monosyllable or in a polysyllabic word. This makes it impossible to capture this phenomenon in a simple way with a syllabification like the one proposed by Vennemann (1972) and Garnes (1975a). Not only are the consonants 'tense' before another consonant, regardless of whether that other consonant is word-final or not (which would make the environment for a conceivable 'tensing' rule defined in terms of Garnes–Vennemann syllabification vary according to whether the forms were monosyllabic or polysyllabic), but also the [s] in forms like *nes* [nɛːs] would be in the same syllabic environment as the [s] in *hestur* (both closing a syllable), but with a difference in 'tenseness'. This demonstrates that if the 'tenseness' of consonants is to be explained in terms of syllable structure, this syllable structure cannot be the one proposed by Vennemann and Garnes. But if we adopt the syllabification proposed here, the environment will always be the same, namely, when a postvocalic consonant is followed by another consonant within the same syllable, the former is 'tensed'.

However, once again we have no guarantee that this 'tenseness' of consonants has anything to do with syllabification. Furthermore, even if we grant that it does do so, the argument is rather weak as independent evidence for the syllabification we are proposing, precisely because the distribution of 'tense' consonants seems to be related to the distribution of short vowels. It is, as we have seen, quite conceivable that the 'tenseness' of the consonant is governed by the same general rule as assigns length and shortness to vowels.

Another feature could perhaps be taken as evidence for the syllabification proposed here, with as many consonants as possible belonging to the first syllable: preaspiration. As is shown in §2.3, the 'hard' stops /p, t, k/ are preaspirated when geminated or in front of *l, n* and *m*. Here, the preceding vowel is always short: *epli* [ɛhplɪ], *vatn* [vahtn], *rytmi* [rɪhtmɪ] 'rhythm' etc. If we look at the environment where preaspiration occurs, we see that it occurs independently of whether the clusters are word-final or intervocalic. In this respect the preaspiration shows the same behaviour as the length rule and 'tensing' of consonants, and it evidently cannot be sensitive to a syllabification like the one suggested by Vennemann and Garnes, since then in monosyllables the preaspiration would occur on *p, t, k* if followed by another cosyllabic *p, t, k, l, n, m,* but in polysyllabics it would be triggered by a heterosyllabic consonant following.

In this case, as in the others, it is of course possible that the preaspiration rule is not sensitive to syllabification at all; but if a syllabification has something to do with preaspiration, it must be one that treats /vatn-/ in both *vatnið* 'the water' and *vatn* 'water' in the same way, and our 'maximalistic' syllabification is such a syllabification. As a weak argument for the case that preaspiration has got something to do with syllabification I could cite compounds like *litlaus* [lɪːtlœyːs] 'colourless' (from *litur* 'colour' and *laus* 'free (of), without') and *saknæmur* [saːknaiːmʏr] 'peccable' (from *sök* (gen. *sakar*) 'guilt', and *næmur* 'susceptible (to)'). In these forms, even though the /t/ and /k/ precede /l/

and /n/ respectively, preaspiration does not occur. This is evidently because there is an internal word boundary between the two parts of the compounds. This internal boundary can be taken to imply a syllable boundary, and if we state the preaspiration rule so that it cannot apply across a syllable boundary, these exceptions are automatically accounted for. But the trouble is that there are other ways of explaining why the preaspiration does not occur. We notice that the morphs *lit-* and *sak-*, and also the second parts of the compounds, have long vowels. This can be taken to show that the constituents are semi-independent words that have gone through all phonological processes, including the length rule and the preaspiration rule (which does not have any effect on the forms *lit-* and *sak-*), before being amalgamated into compound words by some special weakening of the word boundary. In that case the forms *lit-* and *sak-* become just regular monosyllables. (I will return to compounds shortly.)

In summary, we can say that there is some evidence that the length rule is connected with syllabification. We have also seen some evidence for considering this syllabification 'final maximalistic' in a special sense rather than of the type proposed by Vennemann (1972) and Garnes (1975a). It can be described in the following way:

(7) If a stressed vowel is followed by one consonant, assign the consonant to the preceding syllable, and if the vowel is followed by two consonants, assign both to the preceding syllable, unless the first consonant is one of the set /p, t, k, s/ and the second of the set /v, j, r/. In the latter case the syllable boundary is to be set between the two consonants.[4]

2.4.4 'Strength' of consonants. I have suggested a syllabification which makes the length rule very simple. Apart from the question of whether this syllabification should be preferred over another, for example the syllabification proposed by Vennemann (1972), and Garnes (1975a), there is another question left unanswered: why should the sequences /p, t, k, s/ + /v, j, r/ behave differently from other intervocalic sequences of two consonants? This can in part be dealt with independently of which of the alternative ways of syllabifying is adopted, since in any case /p, t, k, s/ + /v, j, r/ will be exceptional.

As mentioned above, Garnes proposes an explanation in terms of a sonority hierarchy. We saw that this explanation is problematic, since it entails underlying forms for /v/ and /j/ that seem otherwise unmotivated.

Vennemann proposes a hierarchy of a slightly different sort, which he defines in terms of what he calls the 'strength of Modern Icelandic consonants'. He proposes a tentative scale of consonant strength (1972:6):

1	2	3	4	5	6	7	8	
								strength
v	r	l	m	f	s	p	t	
j			n	b		k		
				d				
				g				

(This scale is evidently incomplete, since it does not mention the fricatives [θ], [ð] and [ɣ].)

As can be seen from the diagram, Vennemann considers /v/, /j/ and /r/ to be the 'weakest' of Modern Icelandic consonants. It is not self-evident how the weakness or strength of consonants should be defined. Vennemann wants to explain what he means on phonological grounds and, for example, cites as evidence for the weakness of /r/ that it seems to be more susceptible to assimilation to or reduction by following consonants. He mentions that /r/ is always (i.e. in all dialects) devoiced in front of /p/, /t/ and /k/, but /l/, /n/ and /m/ only sometimes (i.e. in some dialects). He also mentions that only /r/ is weakened or lost before /s/ and some other consonants or consonant sequences (but e.g. /n/, /l/, /m/ remain). Vennemann is probably referring to pronunciations like [vɛstfɪskʏr] of orthographic *vestfirskur* 'from the western fjords', more formal [vɛstfɪrskʏr]. It is not true that only /r/ disappears or weakens in this environment, because pronunciations like [ɛ̃skʏr] for orthographic *enskur* 'English', more formal [ɛnskʏr] are quite frequent. (Perhaps it is possible to maintain that the nasalisation left on the vowel is a sign of the greater strength of /n/ than /r/, but of course there are no signs of a 'rhotacisation' caused by /r/ anywhere else in the phonology, whereas nasalisation is a very natural process in Icelandic, and probably in any language. So the /r/ does not have as good a chance of leaving any trace after it when it disappears as /n/ does.)

As a sign of the weakness of /j/ and /v/, Vennemann mentions that they tend not to occur in front of [i] and [u] respectively. But this could just as well be caused by a phonotactic restriction that forbids a sequence of two segments that are too much alike. A restriction of the same type probably forbids sequences of a stop + homorganic nasal in initial position: /pm/, /tn/, /kŋ/ are not allowed word-initially in Icelandic, and similarly a stop + homorganic fricative does not occur word-initially.

Attempts at substantiating a theory of a universal hierarchy of consonantal strength are described by Hooper (1976a:201–7). It is suggested that a tendency for a consonant to assimilate to a neighbouring consonant is a sign of the former's weakness relative to the other's strength. Thus Hankamer & Aissen (1974, referred to in Hooper 1976a:203) report on assimilations in Pali, where, for example, 'underlying' /ng/ gives [gg], but underlying /ny/ gives [nn]. This is taken to show a relative hierarchy of strength: /g/ ⟶ /n/ ⟶ /y/. These and other factors lead Hooper to suggest the following universal strength hierarchy (1976a:206):

glides	liquids	nasals	voiced continuant	voiceless continuant, voiced stop	voiceless stop
1	2	3	4	5	6

There seems, however, to be a need for some further investigation into the relationship of the concept of strength to factors observable in assimilatory processes. For one thing, we would rarely expect assimilation of a vowel to a preceding or a following stop: [op] ⟶ [pp] is not a very likely phonological process. This shows that there is no direct relation between the concept of strength hierarchy as conceived by Hooper and assimilatory processes. On the strength scale, [p] is in the strongest category, but [o] as a vowel would presumably be in the weakest category. It is, as we have seen, possible to call the preaspiration in Icelandic a case of partial assimilation of the following consonantism to the preceding vowel: [ɔpp] ⟶ [ɔ̥p]. This would, if taken seriously, indicate an order of strength: stop ⟶ vowel. Examples of assimilations that go counter to the hierarchy mentioned above are found in the prehistory of Icelandic. *ðl* assimilates to *ll* in forms like *frilla* 'a (female) lover', cf. *friðill* 'a (male) lover' and *lþ* to *ll* in *gull* 'gold', cf. Gothic *gulþ*; *hollr* 'healthy', cf. Gothic *hulþs*. *nþ* assimilates to *nn* in *tǫnn* 'tooth', cf. Gothic *tunþus* and *finna* 'find', cf. Gothic *finþan*. This would suggest a strength relation: fricative ⟶ lateral, nasal. True, there are also a number of processes that fit into the hierarchy scale, such as *sR* ⟶ *ss* in *lauss* (< *lausR*) and *ðt* ⟶ *tt* in *blítt* (< *blíð* + *t*), but since there are obviously some contradictory processes, one should be suspicious of those that fit. One may wonder whether the concept of hierarchy as relevant to phonotactics can be related in a simple way with assimilatory processes like those we have seen. It is not uncommon for assimilation to take place across syllable boundaries, and it seems that the basic force of assimilation can be defined independently of the syllable, although of course the assimilations that take place may be moulded by syllable structure in certain cases.

One might, then, suggest that in trying to substantiate theories concerning strength of segments it is more profitable to stay within the realm of phonotactics and concentrate on the distributional behaviour of the segments (cf. Sigurd 1955). It is, for example, interesting to note that initial clusters of /j/ + /l/, /n/ or /m/ do not exist (*/jl/, */jn/, */jm/), whereas /j/ following /l/, /n/, /m/ is natural: *ljótur* 'ugly', *njóta* 'enjoy', *mjólk* 'milk'. This could perhaps be interpreted as showing that /j/ has a tendency to stand nearer the vowel than /l, n, m/, when co-occurring with them. Similarly, final clusters like /lr/, /nr/, /mr/ hardly occur (/mr/ occurs word-finally in forms like *kumr*, which are derived secondarily from verbs like *kumra* 'to bleat', forming an action name of the same meaning, cf. §2.6), whereas /rl/, /rn/, /rm/ are regular: *harm* 'sorrow' (acc.), *Karl* 'Charles', *barn* 'child'. (It must be admitted that in most dialects of Icelandic the clusters /rn/ and /rl/ have become [rdn] and [rdl] or [dn] and [dl] respectively, but there are still some dialects which retain the older pronunciation [rn] and [rl].) It seems, then, that /r/ tends to stand closer to the vowel than /l/, /n/ or /m/.

In the light of this, one could perhaps make the generalisation that /r/ and /j/ have a greater adherence (cf. Sigurd 1955) or more sonority (cf. Hooper 1976b) or are 'weaker' than /l/, /n/, /m/. I have not been able to find similar arguments for the 'weakness' of /v/.

If one could establish a hierarchy among the consonants, either along the lines suggested here or along those suggested by Vennemann and Hooper, or both, the fact that /p, t, k, s/ + /v, j, r/ show exceptional behaviour as intervocalic sequences could perhaps be explained as some sort of a consequence of their being at opposite ends of a strength scale. This can perhaps be made more plausible if we say that the tendency of /j/, /r/ (and, we hope, /v/ too) to stand next to the vowel in a syllable prevents forms like *vekja* and *Esja* being syllabified in a way that would leave a segment of the 'strongest' type between it and the vowel nucleus, so only one consonant is assigned to the first syllable. The phonemes /l/, /n/, /m/ show more independence and allow /p, t, k, s/ to stand between them and the vowel nucleus, and the forms *vakna, ekla* etc. are syllabified *vakn–a, ekl–a* etc., and this is why they have preaspiration and a short vowel. The fact that *venja* and *biðja, stöðva, viðra* etc. have short vowels can be explained as a consequence of the fact that /n/ and [ð] (and presumably /m/, /v/, /l/ etc. too) do not have so much strength as to forbid a syllabification *venj–a, biðj–a, stöðv–a,* i.e. /j/, /v/ and /r/ can tolerate them between themselves and the nuclear vowel.

If this bears some relation to the facts, we can restate the syllabification principle (7) and make it look more natural. If we say that /p, t, k, s/ have a degree of strength equal to or greater than the index *j* and /v, j, r/ have a degree of strength less than or equal to the index *i*, the principle may be restated in the following way:

(8) If a vowel bearing primary stress is followed by one consonant, assign the consonant to the preceding syllable, and if the vowel is followed by two consonants, assign both to the preceding syllable, if it does not result in a coda where a consonant of strength greater than or equal to the index *j* intervenes between the nuclear vowel and a consonant of strength less than or equal to the index *i*.

Another possible way of explaining the exceptional behaviour of /p, t, k, s/ + /v, j, r/ is to look for segmental features in them which could be used in a syllabification rule. To do this properly would of course mean setting up a distinctive feature system for the Icelandic consonant system as a whole, and it would go beyond the scope of this study to do so. I would, however, like to mention very briefly some facts that may indicate that a solution along these lines is also possible. The central question is whether we can make /p, t, k, s/ and /v, j, r/ form natural classes of some sort. If we can, for example, justify some common feature or features for /v, j, r/ on independent grounds, we will feel confident that they form a natural class. As mentioned above, /j/ and /v/ are phonetically most like voiced fricatives. Admittedly, they sometimes can be said to be realised as approximants, but they do so no more than the other voiced fricatives [ð] and [ɣ]. They are, however, unlike [ð] and [ɣ] in that they occur initially, whereas [ð] and [ɣ] do not. The initial counterpart of [ð] is voiceless [θ], and no velar fricative occurs initially in most varieties of Icelandic. In initial position, voiced and voiceless labiodental fricatives, /f/ and /v/, are in opposition: *vara* [vaːra] 'last' vs *fara* [faːra] 'go', and similarly initial [j] and [ç] distinguish between minimal pairs: *Jón* [jouːn] 'John' vs *hjón* [çouːn] 'married couple'. In the latter case it is possible to analyse [ç] as underlying /hj/, so that it is not certain whether the voiced and voiceless palatal fricatives should be taken as two underlying phonemes (cf. §1.3). However that may be, the fact remains that /j/ and /v/ are the only voiced fricatives that are in opposition to other phonemes in initial position. This may perhaps be taken as evidence that /v/ and /j/ are the only underlying voiced fricatives. [ð] can be said to be a voiced allophone of the phoneme /θ/ (orthographic *þ*), since [θ] and [ð] are in complementary distribution. It is not clear how [ɣ], orthographically *g*, should be analysed phonologically. It alternates morphophonologically both with a voiceless fricative as in *dagur* [daːɣʏr] 'day' : *dags* [daxs] 'day' (gen.), and with a stop [g̊] as in *saga* [saːɣa] 'story' : *sagna* [sag̊na] 'story' (gen.pl.). It is not immediately obvious what underlying form should be chosen if one systematic phoneme is to represent all three variants, but obviously one candidate will be a voiced fricative. In that case, /v, j, ɣ/ would form a class of voiced fricatives. But /ɣ/ would behave differently from the others since it would not have a voiced fricative allophone initially. So there seems to be at least some reason to keep [ɣ] apart from /v/ and /j/.

This might open a way for a grouping of the sort we would wish for, since within, for example, the feature system proposed by Chomsky & Halle (1968:318), /r/ could be made to form a natural class with /j/ and /v/ under the feature [+continuant], although in a system like that of Ladefoged (1971:49–52, for example) the 'naturalness' of the class is not as great. Anyhow, there is a significant difference in the mode of articulation of /r/ and the other 'sonorants' /l, m, n/ which might be sufficient to justify a split; /r/ is more continuant or fricative-like than the lateral and the nasals. If one can say that /v/ and /j/ are phonemically voiced fricatives, it is quite conceivable that the same could be said of /r/. /r/ has two allophones, a voiced and a voiceless one as in *mark* [mark̥], and it is easy to analyse the voiceless variant as conditioned by voiceless surroundings. It seems, then, if we put aside the question of the phonological status of [ɣ], that a case could be made for grouping /j, v, r/ together as a class of voiced continuants; and on this basis and that of some feature or features making /p, t, k, s/ a natural class, which should not be too difficult to find, it should be relatively easy to define a qualification in the syllabification principle. I will not investigate further this alternative here, since so many questions concerning the whole phonology of Icelandic immediately arise, and an account along these lines will only become comprehensible in the context of a more complete analysis of Modern Icelandic phonology.

2.5 Stress

Apart from a very brief mention of stress (§2.1), very little attention has been paid to its relation to length and quantity. As we have seen, there are several complicated problems connected with the concept of stress. It seems sensible to approach these problems with two basic questions in mind. (A) What is the function of stress (i) as a part of linguistic structure and (ii) in linguistic use or performance? (B) How is stress realised phonetically? Although it may turn out in the end that these questions cannot be answered independently of one another, a distinction between these aspects should be kept in mind.

I mentioned (pp. 13–14) that, from the point of view of function, one could distinguish between what I called 'unmarked' or 'lexical' stress and 'marked' or 'contrastive' stress, but that (from the point of view of question (B)) there was no difference in the phonetic realisation of the two types of stress. Assuming that this is correct, and given that our point of view is phonological rather than semantic, I will largely confine the discussion to lexical stress, assuming that what will be said of the phonology of lexical stress, will also be applicable to contrastive stress. In order to illustrate more clearly the conceivable operation of stress rules, I will also discuss the stress pattern of compound words.

As briefly mentioned, the main rule of word stress is that non-compound words have primary stress on the first syllable. There was also said to be a secondary stress on the third syllable and on every second syllable after that. The following are examples showing this: $\overset{1}{taka}$ 'to take', $\overset{1}{\alpha lla}$ 'to be going to', $\overset{1}{almana}\overset{2}{k}$ 'calendar', $\overset{1}{almana}\overset{2}{kanna}$ 'calendar' (gen.pl.def.). This simple stress-pattern is disrupted in compound words. The structure of compound words in Icelandic is rather complicated, and there is no room to investigate that matter in any detail here, but a few brief remarks are needed. There are many types or degrees of compounds in Icelandic, and indeed some cases occur which should perhaps not even be considered compounds, at least not from the phonological point of view. As examples of this type we can cite forms like *vitlaus* [vɪhtlœyːs] 'foolish' (literally 'wit-less') and *torfæra* [tʰɔrfaiːra] 'obstacle' (derived from *tor–*, a prefix, signifying difficulty and *færa*, a stem related to the verb *fara* 'to go'). As a sign of the non-compound nature of these forms we can refer to the fact that they have short first vowels even though their first constituents end in single consonants: *vit-* and *tor-*. The final consonants of these first parts also undergo phonological rules that operate within simple words: the final /t/ of *vit-* is preaspirated in front of the /l/, and the /r/ of *tor-* is devoiced by the following voiceless /f/. Although the form *torfæra* shows non-compound-like behaviour in the shortness of the vowel and the voicelessness of the /r/, it is in at least one respect compound-like as far as segmental phonology is concerned: it has a voiceless [f] medially, which normally occurs only initially, its voiced counterpart, [v], usually occurring medially. Both of the forms show signs of being compounds rather than non-compounds in that the second components bear secondary stress and have long vowels. Forms, similar to the ones mentioned above, but with a looser connection between the two parts, are *litlaus* [lɪːtlœyːs] 'colourless' and *torleystur* [tʰɔːrleistʏr] 'difficult to solve'. The form *litlaus* has a long vowel in the first component and no preaspiration on the /t/, and the form *torleystur* has a long vowel in the first component. (The latter word can also be pronounced with a short first vowel, in which case it shows similar behaviour to *torfæra* except for the fact that the sequence /rl/ does not become [rdl] as it usually does in non-compound words.) The forms *litlaus* and *torleystur* are definitely phonological compounds, since there are rules that are blocked by the existence of some kind of boundary between the two parts. (See Orešnik 1971 for an enumeration of such rules.) What this boundary actually is, I will leave open for the moment, but we may call it a kind of 'weakened word boundary'. The examples given above seem to indicate that there is a scale of closeness of connection between constituents of compound words in Icelandic. The 'closest' compounds mentioned here are, then, *vitlaus* and *torfæra,* and the 'loosest' are *litlaus* and *torleystur* pronounced with a long first vowel, and in between is *torleystur* pronounced with a short vowel.

The problem of compound words is related to the problem of stress because, at least for the 'looser compounds', the rule for the distribution of secondary stress mentioned above is broken. Forms like *l$\overset{1}{i}$tl$\overset{2}{a}$us* have a stress on the second syllable, since that is the first (and in this case the only) syllable of the second part of the compound. Similarly, *v$\overset{1}{a}$rðh$\overset{2}{u}$ndur* 'guard dog' (*varð-* is a stem meaning 'guard', cf. *vörður* ' a guard' ; *hundur* means 'dog') has a secondary stress on the first syllable of *hundur* rather than on the third syllable of the word as a whole.

There is probably more than one way of accounting for these facts. One could for example say that Icelandic has one stress rule something like this:

(9) Primary stress falls on the first syllable of every word and a secondary stress falls on every second syllable, counting from there, except when the word is a compound. If the word is a compound, then a secondary stress falls on the first syllable of every new constituent of the compound.

This would be an incomplete formulation of the rule. It would for example have to be expanded in order to take care of forms like *rakarameistari* 'qualified barber'. This is a compound consisting of two trisyllabic forms, which take a secondary stress on the third syllable when standing as independent words: *r$\overset{1}{a}$kar$\overset{2}{a}$* and *m$\overset{1}{ei}$star$\overset{2}{i}$*. In *rakarameistari* the strongest stress is on the first syllable, and on the first syllable of the second part of the compound is another fairly strong stress peak, and on the third and the sixth syllable there seem to be weak stresses, which look like reflexes of the secondary stress which appears on the component forms, when they stand independently. If superscript numbers 1, 2, 3 indicate relative strength of stress, the stress pattern of the compound can be indicated like this: *r$\overset{1}{a}$kar$\overset{3}{a}$m$\overset{2}{ei}$star$\overset{3}{i}$*. Although seemingly complicated, an account along these lines seems at least conceivable.

An alternative way of accounting for the stress pattern of Icelandic is to make use of the transformational cycle as Chomsky & Halle (1968) do in dealing with stress in English; I propose that this is a better way of dealing with the phenomena. In this case, lexical stress would be assigned in two stages, at the non-compound level and at the compound level. In order for this to work a mechanism of some sort for generating compounds will have to be set up. This mechanism could be conceived of as a rule weakening the boundary between the two (or more) lexical items to be bound together as a compound word. This would mean that, in their most abstract forms, compound words are such that between their constituents they have full word-boundaries. The components are assigned stress in the regular way as if they were independent words. And if the boundary between the two words has been weakened by the compound-forming rule, the stress pattern is readjusted, making the first part of the compound the strongest and at the same time making all other stress peaks comparatively weaker. It may be that this is just the main stress rule reapplied on a later cycle, the units now being components of the compounds rather than syllables.

One might wonder whether it is the same pattern, of one prominent unit followed by a neutral one and then an alternation between rises and falls, that is responsible for the rhythm of sequences like *andskotans-djöfulsins-helvítis asni*, equivalent to something like 'bloody, fucking, blooming fool', where the sequence preceding the word *asni* 'fool', is a complex of three swearwords. In my speech, the first part, *andskotans*, carries the heaviest emphasis, whereas a secondary weight seems to fall on the third word *helvítis*. This seems to be very similar to the pattern we see in lexical stress, where we have an alternation between stressed and unstressed units. If the rule readjusting the stress of compound words is the main stress rule reapplied with constituents of compound words as units, one would expect the same type of alternation in compound words. The problem is that compound words are rarely more than two components and if they are longer, there is usually a hierarchy in the structure, as in *vegagerðarforstjóri*, 'road-construction manager' where *vega-gerðar* 'road-construction' and *for-stjóri* 'manager' are compounds that are again amalgamated into a compound, so we have a structure:

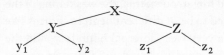

(Or perhaps a further diagram:

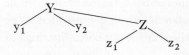

is more appropriate from the phonological point of view, since the first component is phonologically more prominent than the second one.) Thus, loose compounds like the swearword-complex mentioned above seem to be the only cases where this sort of prediction can be tested. Another type of sequence that might show the same type of alternation are sequences of the type *gamli, góði, gráhærði maðurinn* 'the good, old, grey-haired man', but I will not explore that here.

Within the framework that we are trying to form, the derivation of *rakarameistari* could be something like the following (# # here denotes a full word boundary and # a weakened word boundary; the numbers indicate relative strength of stress):

Main stress rule: $\overset{1}{\text{ra}}\text{kar}\overset{2}{\text{a}}$ # # $\overset{1}{\text{m}}\text{eistar}\overset{2}{\text{i}}$
Weakening of word boundary: $\overset{1}{\text{ra}}\text{kar}\overset{2}{\text{a}}$ # $\overset{1.}{\text{m}}\text{eistar}\overset{2}{\text{i}}$
Readjustment of stress: $\overset{1}{\text{ra}}\text{kar}\overset{3}{\text{a}}$ # $\overset{2.}{\text{m}}\text{eistar}\overset{3}{\text{i}}$

(It may be unfortunate to use the same type of notation for the secondary stress assigned by the main stress rule and the one deriving from weakening of the primary stress, since they are definitely not the same phenomenon; but in an informal presentation like this, it is of no great significance.)

I need hardly point out that there are many loose ends and unanswered questions still to be dealt with, and this may not even work in principle. It is not clear, for example, what governs the application of the rule weakening the word boundary. It seems doubtful whether all compounds can be listed in the lexicon, since the process of forming compound nouns and adjectives of the sort described above seems to be very productive; one can make them up on the spot, so to speak, when the need arises. I can easily form new compounds like *þorskastríðshetja* 'cod war hero' and *Edinborgarstúdent* 'Edinburgh student' etc. (There seem to be more restrictions on forming new verbs by such a process.) Another problem has been mentioned above, namely that different degrees of closeness of the compounds seem to be allowed for; in our terms, the weakening of the word boundary seems to be allowed to be of different degrees. Forms like *vitlaus* and *torfæra* seem to have a very weak internal boundary, and the form *torleystur*, with the alternative pronunciations of a long or a short vowel in the first component, seems to have varying degrees of closeness of connection between the two components. Evidently, the whole problem of compounds in Modern Icelandic is too complicated to be solved here, but we have seen enough to be able to start co-ordinating our ideas concerning the relation between stress and syllabification, quantity and length.

We can take as examples two compound words which show 'considerable closeness of connection' (or weakness of internal boundary) between the two constituents: *þjóðvísa* [θjouðviːsa] 'folk song' and *leikvöllur* [lɛiːkvœdlʏr] 'playground'. The former has the constituents *þjóð-* 'people' and *vísa* 'a verse, a song', and the latter has the constituents *leik-* 'game, play' and *völlur* 'a field'. On the basis of these forms we can make two observations concerning length and related matters.

Firstly we see that the first component of *þjóðvísa* has a short vowel in a stem which ends in a single consonant. This means that the following /v/ is included in the environment that determines the length of the vowel. The length rule is therefore dependent upon the rule that forms the compound by reduction of the word boundary. In a grammar operating with rules that apply in sequence, this would be taken to mean that the length rule is applied after the compound forming rule, or that the compound-forming rule feeds the length rule.

Secondly we see that the second constituents also show a distribution of length that fits the length rule: we have a relatively long vowel in *vísa*, but a relatively short one in *völlur*. It is not likely that the mean duration of 'long' vowels in second parts of compounds like *vísa* above will turn out to be the same as that of, say, *vísa* when occurring as a separate word, but we are of course not talking in absolute terms, but dealing with structure. We can see that there is a phonological difference between a short and a long vowel in the second part of compounds like *þjóðvísa* by comparing the nominative singular with the genitive plural: *þjóðvísna*, where two consonants follow. In the genitive plural the [i] is definitely shorter than in the nominative. It seems, then, that a length alternation in vowels also prevails in parts of compounds which have a secondary stress. One way of interpreting this is to assume, in line with what was suggested above concerning stress, that length is also distributed in two stages: 'first' in non-compound words and then 'again' (using the time sequence metaphor common in generative phonology) when compounds have been formed. If length were assigned only once, say 'after' the formation of compounds, the length rule would be much more complicated.

I will present here an outline of an account of the phenomena in question, based on a set of five phonological rules or principles, something like the following:

(10) (a) A stress rule assigns primary stress to the first syllable of every simple word and a secondary stress to every second syllable from there.

(b) A rule forms compounds by reducing the strength of the boundary between two or more words to be combined.

(c) A compound stress rule strengthens the stress of the first constituent of a compound and reduces the strength of other stress peaks. (This is possibly (a) applied recursively.)

(d) The syllabification principle (8) applies to all stressed syllables, wherever it can.

(e) A length rule applies to stressed syllables wherever it can, the domain being strings defined by the principle (8).

This mechanism would give the following derivation for the forms *þjóðvísa* and *leikvöllur* (there are a number of more or less unjustified assumptions made here about the underlying representations of the forms in question, but they are irrelevant to the problems discussed here):

Underlying forms:

/ # þjouð # # visa # /   / # lɛik # # vœdlʏr # /

The stress rule (a) is applied to these forms, giving:

/ # þjouð # # visa # /   / # lɛ́ik # # vœ́dlʏr # /

The length rule is applicable to both components of both forms, lengthening the vowel in the appropriate environments:

/þjou:ð # # vi:sa # /   / # lɛ́i:k # # vœ́dlʏr # /

(I assume that the syllabification principle applies automatically before the length rule to define its environments.) These forms are then made subject to the compound-forming rule. This would give:

$$/ \# \overset{1}{\text{þjou:ð}} \# \overset{1}{\text{vi:sa}} \# / \quad / \# \overset{1}{\text{lɛi:k}} \# \overset{1}{\text{vœdlʏr}} \# /$$

The compound stress rule then applies, giving:

$$/ \# \overset{1}{\text{þjou:ð}} \# \overset{2}{\text{vi:sa}} \# / \quad / \# \overset{1}{\text{lɛi:k}} \# \overset{2}{\text{vœdlʏr}} \# /$$

Since we now have a new stress pattern, the syllabification principle can apply once more, pushing the syllable boundary as far back as possible from the vowel of the syllable bearing the heaviest stress. We can represent the output like this, disregarding the weakened word boundary, which may still be there:

$$/ \# \overset{1}{\text{þjou:ð}} \text{v} \$ \overset{2}{\text{i:sa}} \# / \quad / \# \overset{1}{\text{lɛi:k}} \$ \overset{2}{\text{vœdlʏr}} \# /$$

But the form for *þjóðvísa* does not now follow the rules of length distribution, so the length rule is applied once more. In the case of *leikvöllur* we can make it apply vacuously, since the form already has the right distribution of vowel length. The output will then be:

$$/ \overset{1}{\text{þjouðvi:sa}} / \quad / \overset{1}{\text{lɛi:kvœdlʏr}} /$$

Here again, it is unnecessary to stress that this is far from being a permanent solution to the problems, but it does seem to me a plausible way of approaching them. If such a framework is adopted, it becomes necessary to define the length rule more precisely than has been done so far.

In the derivation outlined above the length rule functions as an 'everywhere rule' which is reapplied whenever its structural analysis is met. It furthermore both lengthens and shortens vowels according to the environment. This can probably be represented most clearly by formulating the length rule as a two-sided transformation. It has been suggested by Lass (1974:322–3, see also references) that historical changes may be represented as kinds of two-sided rules, stating both what *does* happen and what does *not* happen at the same time. The rules can be said to have both a 'positive' and a 'negative' part. What is needed here is something similar, except that in this case both parts can be said to be 'positive' in that they imply changes when necessary, but these changes are in opposite directions and complementary, so to speak; one making vowels long and the other making them short. The length rule would then be stated in two parts: one part says that a vowel will be long if it is followed by one (or no) consonant within the same stressed syllable, and the other says that a vowel will be short if it is followed by two or more consonants within the same stressed syllable. We can represent this rule as follows:

(11) (a) SD: V C^1 $

          1 2 3

      SC: 1 ⇒ [+long]

  (b) SD: V C_2 $

          1 2 3

      SC: 1 ⇒ [−long] Condition: the syllable is stressed

Part (a) applies to all stressed vowels that are not marked [+long] before a single or no cosyllabic consonant, and part (b) applies whenever a vowel is met that is not short before two or more cosyllabic consonants. As the rule is used in the derivation above, it applies both to vowels which have been marked with respect to the feature [±long] and vowels which are unmarked. This means that the rule in some instances adds a feature which is not in the input and in others it changes the value of a feature that already is in the input. This gives the length rule the character of an output condition; that is, whatever the input, the output conforms to the rules for distribution of length.

In the analysis just outlined, length in vowels is determined by stress and syllable structure. This implies that stress as a phonological category is primary to quantity, and furthermore, it presumes that stress is indeed an independently definable category; that is, that segmental length (or syllabic quantity) is not simply an *exponent* of the (functional) category stress, the realisation of the stress pattern (i.e. length) being determined by reference to the segmental composition of the 'underlying' string and rules of syllabification.

There is some support for the view that stress determines quantity and length, in the behaviour of marked or contrastive stress (cf. §2.1). (This is what Benediktsson (1963a:148) calls 'morphological stress' and some others (cf. Lehiste 1970:150–1) call 'emphatic stress'.) We are talking about such examples as: *Bókin er á* BORÐINU *(ekki* STÓLNUM*)* 'the book is on the *table* (not the *chair*)', or: *Ég sat* HJÁ *borðinu, ekki* Á *því* 'I sat *by* the table, not *on* it'. Here, what one might think of as the normal or unmarked stress contour is changed in order to put the focus on the forms *borðinu* and *hjá* as contrastive to *stólnum* and *á* respectively. It seems that there is very little limit to what can be singled out with the aid of contrastive stress. As Benediktsson (*ibid.*) mentions, this marked stress can fall on otherwise unstressed syllables, for example in order to contrast different inflectional forms of the same words as in *Ég sagði 'gest*INUM*', ekki 'gest*UNUM*'* 'I said "(to) the *guest* (sg.)", not "(to) the *guests* (pl.)"'. Here contrastive stress is put on the endings -*inum* and -*unum*, marking respectively dative singular and dative plural. When the endings are stressed in this way, the vowels automatically lengthen, so that *gest*INUM becomes something like [jɛ̊sti:nʏm] and *gest*UNUM something like [jɛ̊stʏ:nʏm], (the numbers once again represent relative strength of stress). Here, if there are two phonological categories, stress and quantity (length), within an orthodox generative framework, the primary (underlying) one must be the functional unit; thus stress would be said to be the conditioning factor for length.

2.6 Some problematic forms

According to the principle above, *v, j, r* following *p, t, k, s* are assigned to a following syllable: *skrök*$*va* 'to tell a lie', *set*$*ja* 'to set', *puk*$*ra* 'to be secretive'. This presupposes that there is always a following syllable to which the *v, r* or *j* can be assigned. This is indeed generally the case; sequences like *tv, tj, tr* etc. do not normally occur word-finally. There is, however, a set of exceptions to this. These are a limited number of nouns, generally derived from intransitive verbs of action. For example, corresponding to the verb *pukra*, there exists a deverbative noun *pukr* 'secrecy, the act of being secretive'. Similarly there are pairs like *sötra* 'to sip' – *sötr* 'the act of sipping', *kjökra* 'to wail' – *kjökr* 'the act of wailing', *sífra* 'to lament' – *sífr* 'the act of lamenting'. In these forms where we have a word-final *tr* or *kr*, there is no following vowel to connect the *r* with, so one would expect a syllabification like *pukr*$, and thus a short vowel according to the length rule. This is not the case, however; *pukr, sötr,* and *kjökr* all have long vowels.

It may seem that this is serious counterevidence to the analysis suggested above. I am not sure that it is, however. It seems that the forms in question are marginal in the language, and they seem to have a special status in the system; it can even be said of some of them that their well-formedness is doubtful. I am, for example, not at all sure that I can accept a form like *lötr* from *lötra* 'to walk slowly'. In a way, these forms have a similar status to derived forms in English like the verb *to comrade* in sentences such as *don't you dare comrade me* (= 'don't you dare call me comrade'). The derivational relationship is purely from one surface form to another, i.e. the noun *pukr* is derived from the verb *pukra*, just as the verb *to comrade* is derived from (the speech act of uttering) the noun *comrade*. Of course, it can be said that this peculiarity is morphological and should therefore not be related to the phonology. But the fact that these forms are morphologically (derivationally) special may act as an 'excuse' for them to go contrary to otherwise valid phonological generalisations.

Similar phenomena are mentioned by Kahn (1976:121–4) from English. There are two generalisations that can be made about the distribution of low vowels preceding /r/ and nasals in some forms of American English:

(a) Instead of [æ], orthographic *a* appears as [a] in front of a cosyllabic /r/: *car*, (with [a]) but *carriage* (with [æ]). (In the latter form, the /r/ begins the second syllable.)

(b) [æ], orthographic *a*, is raised to something similar to [ɪe] in front of a cosyllabic *n* or *m*: *can* with [ɪe] (or something similar) vs *canon* with [æ].

These generalisations could conceivably be set up as phonological rules for the dialects in question. But Kahn points out that in forms like *Lar'* derived from *Larry* and *Jan'*, derived from *Janice*, these rules do not apply. *Lar'* has [æ] instead of [a] and *Jan'* has [æ] instead of the raised variant. These phenomena seem to be of the same sort as those we have seen from Icelandic: secondary derivational processes are allowed to lead to breaches of otherwise valid phonological generalisations. I will therefore conclude, tentatively, that these facts are not to be taken as direct evidence against the rules they break, but that they have to be dealt with in some special way. It may perhaps be said that they show that phenomena like the length rule in Icelandic and the 'syllabification principle', and the stress assignment rule connected with it, as well as the rules governing the distribution of [æ], [a] and [ɪe] in American English, operate at a relatively abstract level in the phonology, since they are not absolutely exceptionless. But then: Are there any phonological regularities absolutely without exceptions?

Concerning the Icelandic examples, it can be added that the length rule (and the processes related to it) is not the only rule broken by forms of this sort. The forms *pukr, sötr, kjökr* and *sífr* (the last of which does not break the length rule) break another general rule, namely that $Cr \{^{\#}_{C}\}$ (C = any Icelandic consonant) does not occur in Icelandic. It has been proposed (Orešnik 1972) that there is active in Icelandic an epenthesis rule which inserts /ɣ/ (orthographic *u*) in the appropriate environments. This would account for my (and many other people's) tendency to pronounce the forms in question with an 'epenthetic' /ɣ/: *pukur* [pʰɣːkʰɣr], *kjökur* [cʰœːkʰɣr] etc. Still another rule is broken by forms of the same type. From the verbs *grenja* 'to cry, to howl' and *hneggja* 'to neigh', nouns like *grenj* [ģrɛnj] 'crying' and *hneggj* [n̥ɛjː] 'neighing' can be derived. The first of these forms breaks the generalisation that C*j* is generally not allowed word-finally in Icelandic, and, depending on the way the palatal in *hneggja* [n̥ɛjːa] is analysed, the form either breaks the same principle or one forbidding a palatal stop in word-final position.

It is worth noting that all these rules broken by the deverbative nouns look very much like syllable structure constraints, and this may be the character of the length rule as well. Indeed my last formulation of the rule (11) (p. 51) suggests this in a way, since it is basically an output condition, a well-formedness constraint on phonological forms. But it seems that this constraint may not hold on the most concrete of phonological levels.

2.7 The problem of 'exponence' and the nature of the analysis

The foregoing discussion has left two basic problems unsolved. Although they seem unrelated, it is sensible to discuss them together because they both relate to a point that has to be clarified concerning the theoretical status of this account of the data.

One of these questions is the one I have mentioned concerning the relation of the functional category stress to the more 'phonetic' categories of quantity and length and the possibility that other phonetic properties are exponents of stress. I shall not be able to give a satisfactory answer to this question here, if only for the reason that we have no experimental data that would tell us exactly what is going on phonetically. But a few comments are in order.

One thing might be mentioned as suggesting that 'stress' is useful in phonological analyses for purposes other than just accounting for length phenomena. In native words, the vowel system that occurs in stressed syllables is much richer than that occurring in unstressed ones. The full thirteen-vowel inventory listed above (§1.3) is made use of in initial (stressed) syllables, whereas in other positions the regular set is three: /ɪ/, /a/, and /ɣ/ (which is sometimes lowered to [ɔ] in front of /n/). This 'polysystemicity' goes back to the prehistory of Icelandic (cf. Benediktsson 1962), but there are signs that this is changing. There are loan-words and neologisms that have other vowels than the three mentioned above occurring in final (unstressed) syllables: *party* [pʰarti̥] 'party', *strætó* [straiːtou] 'bus', *Sissú* [sɪsːu] a nickname for *Sigrún*. This argument for the existence of stress as a separate phonological category seems thus to be very weak. In fact, I can think of very few phonological phenomena that could be used as independent evidence for an analysis of stress as a separate phonological category, apart from those mentioned above in connection with the discussion of syllabification. There it was mentioned that 'tenseness' or half length of consonants like the [s] in *hestur* and the [n] in *grenja* seemed to be governed by laws defined in the same environments as the length rule, i.e. by stress and syllable structure. But it was suggested that the 'tenseness' of the consonant was perhaps only one aspect of the length regularity, given the fact that the 'tenseness' co-occurs with shortness of the preceding vowel. It was also mentioned that preaspiration seemed to have a distribution governed by laws similar to those governing quantity (cf. also Liberman 1970).

We may now turn to the second unresolved problem. We saw (§2.6) that some facts seemed to suggest that the syllabification which apparently created the simplest definition of the length rule did not accord well with the behaviour of deverbative forms like *pukr* and *sötr*. These are formed by a process which could be described as a deletion of the infinitival ending of verbs like *pukra* and *sötra*. The process of forming deverbative nouns like this is probably quite new and has its origins in contexts like: *vertu ekki með þetta pukr* 'leave off this secrecy' or: *hættu þessu sötri* 'stop this sipping'. If this process is an innovation, one may wonder whether one should put the whole problem into historical perspective. (This is of course only too easy in a basically historical study like this one.) One might suggest that the analysis given in the preceding sections is not adequate as an account of the present situation in Icelandic phonology, but is perhaps valid in a more abstract perspective of the Icelandic language. The considerations that seem to support this concept of the stressed syllable are mostly related to what, from the phonetic point of view, seem to be rather abstract factors. The considerations used in justifying the analysis have either to do with morphophonemics or with what one might call, in a rather broad sense, phonotactics. These abstract factors would not necessarily have direct relevance in the actual use of language, but would perhaps belong to what is called by Linell (1974:28–9) 'higher-order knowledge' of language.

One way of looking at these generalisations and the account described above is to say that it is valid for an earlier stage in the development of Icelandic. We saw that the generalisation that the stressed vowel system was richer than the unstressed one was becoming more obsolete, as new forms with 'unstressed' vowels other than /ɪ/, /a/ or /ʏ/ ([ɔ]) were introduced. This makes the distinction between stressed and unstressed syllables that is implied by the analysis less clear than it presumably was before. Similarly, the forming of new words like *pukr, sötr, hnegg* etc., which go counter to certain formerly valid phonotactic generalisations, can be taken as a sign of a change in the system. Thus, one might say that the analysis described in §2.5 is only valid for a slightly older stage of Icelandic than the present one, and that a system of that sort had at one time prevailed.

However, a more realistic approach to these phenomena is perhaps to look upon regularities like the ones we have seen, not as absolute rules but as reflexes of speech habits of varying age (cf. Árnason 1978a), and simply admit that an analysis like the one presented above is never going to fit exactly as a description of the output of speakers, because they are constantly forming new habits, among them the generation of forms like *partý, strætó, Sissú,* and *pukr, sötr, sífr* etc. These innovations may run counter to regularities that derive from older innovations or interpretations of linguistic inheritance and thus they may spoil pre-existing patterns. I suggest that the account of morphophonemic and phonotactic regularities given above is not strictly valid as a synchronic description of any stage in the development of Icelandic, either as accounting for any sort of 'psychological reality' or as an exhaustive account of the linguistic behaviour of present-day speakers, but it is still valuable as accounting for certain facts about Icelandic. One might say that one aspect of the structure of latter-day Icelandic is that these regularities can be detected. The existence of these regularities derives from the emergence at some stages in the history of the language of certain speech habits. The ways in which individual speakers go about producing the observed output is a different matter. It is also not the aim of this analysis to account for every bit of regularity (or irregularity) observed in the behaviour of speakers of Modern Icelandic.

If we wanted to move closer to what might be called 'psychological reality' or 'behavioural reality' and to try to bring this phonological account closer to, say, actual behaviour in speech production we might suggest an account along the following lines:

A stressed syllable consists of an onset and a rhyme (cf. Fudge 1969). The rhyme consists of a vocalic nucleus followed by a coda. The quantity of the rhyme is constant as a function of stress (to put it another way: varies proportionally with the strength of stress). There are two types of rhyme, one where length falls on the consonant as in *mann* [manː] and the other where length appears on the vowel as in *man* [maːn]. The difference between the syllable types is thus based on the place of length. The place of length is predictable in two types of cases: (i) when no consonant follows the vowel, as in *spá* [spauː] 'prophecy', *te* [tʰɛː] 'tea', in which case length is on the vowel, and (ii) when more than one consonant follows the vowel as in *hestur* [hɛsˈtʏr], *grenja* [ɡ̊rɛnˈja], in which case the length falls on the postvocalic consonant and leaves the second consonant as an onset of the following syllable: [hɛsˈ$tʏr] [ɡ̊rɛnˈ$ja]. If no vowel follows, as in *hest* [hɛsˈt], the final consonant is assigned to the preceding syllable as a 'termination' (cf. Fudge 1969). This holds unless the vowel is followed by /p, t, k/ or /s/ followed by /v, j/ or /r/. In this case, length falls on the vowel, and the consonantism functions as onset to the following syllable, or, in the absence of a following vowel, as in *pukr*, is assigned to the preceding syllable as a 'termination'.

I will not follow this up, but only mention it as a conceivable way of giving a reasonably concrete account of the data from a phonological point of view. It seems not unlikely that constructs of the type just described will be more easily relatable to observable behaviour in speech production, which might be counted as an asset. The relation between morphology and phonology, however, will be more complicated, since phonological and morphological regularities as in *hús–húss* and *vor–vors* (cf. p. 20 above) cannot be explained under one heading, and the account of the distribution of long and short vowels is not as simple.[5]

Apart from the obvious effects the type of analysis we adopt will have on the question of the phonological status of stress and its relation to length and quantity in our descriptive system, there is a further connection between this and the question of exponence. This relates to the ambiguity in the use that has been made of the term 'stress'. I have used it in connection with phonotactics, in helping to define the sort of phonological structures that occur in the language, and I have used it in a discussion of the phonetic correlates of focus or emphasis. It is only in the latter context that it makes sense to ask whether something is an 'expression' or 'exponent' of stress. In the phonotactic context, the stressed syllable is an abstract unit which generates certain structures but not others, and it is not necessary to look for any special 'representatives' of stress in the phonetic signal. As already mentioned, the analysis described in the present section seems easier to relate to the more observable aspects of speech behaviour, and thus the question of exponence is more sensible in that context. We might say, in that context, that stress is realised by quantity which in turn is distributed as segmental length according to the rules loosely described. We may, because of our lack of phonetic data, leave open the question of whether some other things are exponents of stress. (If no other phonetic phenomena occur as possible exponents, one may of course wonder whether some term in the trichotomy 'stress', 'quantity', 'length' is superfluous.)

So, in the context of the 'maximalist' solution described in §§2.4 and 2.5, interpreted as an account of phonotactics, the question of exponence does not arise. But we may observe that it is also possible to look on the more concrete account just given, not as a model where the semiotic function of each phonological entity is defined by relating it to a specific underlying marker of reference, but as an analysis of the phonological patterns and structures that occur. In that case the question of exponence does not arise in the context of this latter account either. It is perfectly legitimate to investigate the phonological pattern of a language without looking in every case at the function of each and every feature as clearly defined. It seems that, more often than not, the use speakers make of their language is idiosyncratic, and that phonological structures like any other linguistic structures can be put to varying use.

NOTES

1   A similar suggestion is made, according to Pétursson (1972), by Liberman (1971a). Liberman, it seems, connects length and stress in Icelandic and considers the former simply to be (in Pétursson's translation) the 'sommet quantitatif', the 'quantitative peak' of the syllable. This type of analysis is also accepted by Steblin-Kamenskij (1960).
2   There is, actually, a rather dubious assumption behind this, namely that [ð] is different from [θ] at the level on which syllabification takes place. There are good reasons to believe that [ð] and [θ] can be looked on as allophones of the same phoneme (see §1.3). If we note this, we have to take account of the fact that [θj] and [θv] are permissible word-initial clusters: *þjóð* [θjou:ð] 'nation', *þvo* [θvɔ:] 'to wash'. This may leave [ðj] and [ðv], phonologically /θj/ and /θv/, in exactly the same place as /sj/, /tj/ etc. and /nj/, /mj/ etc.
3   It is worth pointing out, in connection with the mention of the law of finals and the law of initials, that the syllabification proposed by Vennemann (1972) and Garnes (1975a) would break the law of initials, since forms like *lausra* 'loose' (adj.gen.pl.) would have to be syllabified *lau–sra*, giving syllable-initial /sr/, which is not permitted word-initially, so this syllabification does not seem to be preferable in respect of the law of finals and the law of initials.

4   I leave out of the discussion here what to do with intervocalic sequences of more than two
consonants, mainly because they cause no problem as far as the length rule is concerned.
At first glance it seems that they might be syllabified basically in the same way; that is,
with as many consonants as possible belonging to the stressed syllable, the exception
being when the clusters end in /p, t, k, s/ + /v, j, r/. This would for example give: ösk–ra,
fölsk–vi, but ræksn–i, berkl–ar etc.

5   It is possible that still another line of approach may be worth considering: It is shown in
Orešnik & Pétursson (1977) that in Southern Icelandic speech the difference in duration
between long and short consonants in forms like man and mann is not as great as usually
implied. Orešnik & Pétursson even suggest that a length correlation no longer prevails in
consonants in Southern Icelandic. There is reason to doubt that the data can be as
unequivocally interpreted as Orešnik & Pétursson suggest, but they do seem to indicate a
shortening tendency in long consonants, which is reminiscent of the West Germanic and
Danish degemination (cf. chapter 3). In that case one might want to interpret this as a
sign of the growing centrality of the vowel in the forming of the contour of the syllable
which, it is suggested below (pp. 93–4), is characteristic of German, English and Danish.

3 Length and quantity in related languages

3.1 Faroese

Faroese can be said to be the closest to Icelandic of the Scandinavian sister tongues. Many parts of the morphology and syntax are similar although there are of course notable differences. In the phonology, which is our concern here, there are also similarities, although here again the differences are substantial. Assuming that Icelandic and Faroese derive from a common variety of Nordic, it can be said that Faroese has shown a still greater tendency to diphthongise long vowels than has Icelandic. It is also notable that there is greater phonological dialect variation here than in Icelandic.

Modern Faroese phonology shows an important (for us) similarity to Icelandic in that vowel 'length' is predictable in stressed syllables on the basis of the following consonantism (see below for the reason for inverted commas around 'length'). The main rule is the same as in Icelandic, namely that vowels are short when followed by two or more consonants, but long otherwise. This indicates that Faroese has undergone a quantity shift like the Icelandic one.

As in Icelandic, there are exceptions to this rule of length distribution in that in most dialects there are sequences of two postvocalic consonants that have long vowels preceding them. These are $p, t, k, s + j, r$ and $p, k + l$ (Lockwood 1955:8; Zachariasen 1968:46). An interesting difference, compared with Icelandic, is the fact that pl and kl are preceded by long vowels (and have no preaspiration) whereas in Icelandic these are preceded by short vowels (and have preaspiration). It is also interesting that tl behaves differently from pl and kl in Faroese. It is probably no coincidence that kl and pl are permissible word-initial clusters whereas tl is not. It will make an interesting study to attempt an analysis of the length rule in Faroese in terms of syllabification and compare the results with Icelandic.

The exception to the length rule mentioned above is, however, not

60

valid for all Faroese dialects. In the dialect spoken on the southernmost island of Suðuroy, vowels are short in front of all sequences of two or more consonants, including those that are exceptional in the other dialects (Zachariasen 1968:47). Thus, forms like *vitja* 'to visit' and *vetrar* 'winter' (nom.pl.) have short stressed vowels in the dialect of Suðuroy. There is, in this dialect as well as the others, a difference between (i) the *p*, *t, k, s* + *j, r* and *p, k* + *l* sequences and (ii) other postvocalic sequences like *tl, tn* and *kn*, in that preaspiration appears on the stop only in (ii), i.e. *vetrar* has a pronunciation something like [vɛtrar], but *vatn* 'water' something like [vahtn]. This fact, Zachariasen suggests, could perhaps be taken as an indication that the shortness of the vowels in front of *tj, kr* etc. in the Suðuroy dialect is of rather recent origin, since it may seem that preaspiration arose historically on the stops *p, t, k* when preceded by short vowels. This, as well as the other particulars concerning the length rule in Faroese, provide interesting material for study, for which there is no space here. Anyway, it can be said that roughly the same situation prevails in Faroese as in Icelandic as far as quantity and length are concerned.

To give a simple and reliable picture of the history of the Faroese vocalism is difficult, partly because of the lack of evidence and partly because the development seems to have been so complicated. To make things still more difficult, there are considerable dialectal differences, and I know of no comprehensive study of Faroese dialects (see, though, Jakob Jakobsen's overview in Hammershaimb 1891:LVII–LIX). Attempts at synchronic analyses are to be found, for example, in Bjerrum (1964), O'Neil (1964), S. Anderson (1972b), Taylor (1973) and Árnason (1976); and phonetic studies are to be found in Hammershaimb (1891 :LVII–LXIV) and Rischel (1964). What I have to say about Modern Faroese is largely based on data from Tórshavn-speech; cf. Lockwood (1955) and Árnason (1976).

The most striking feature of Faroese, compared with Icelandic, is that the difference between 'long' and 'short' vowels as distributed by the length rule is much more qualitative. In particular there are five vowels, the reflexes of Old West Scandinavian /uː/, /au/, /oː/, /aː/ and /a/, /eː/ and /æː/ (cf. §4.2.1), which show alternations between diphthongs in the long environments and monophthongs in the short environments. There are morphophonemic alternations between [ʉuː] and [ʏ] (historical /uː/), [ɛiː] and [ɛ] (historical /au/), [ɔuː] and [œ] (historical /oː/), [ɛaː] and [a] (historical /a/, /eː/ and /æː/) and [ɔaː] and [ɔ] (historical /aː/). It seems that these alternations reflect three historical changes. (For work on the history of the Faroese vowel system, see e.g. Chapman 1962:131–4; Amundsen 1964; Rischel 1968.) Firstly, this shows that the old long monophthongs /uː/, /oː/ and /aː/ have become diphthongs (in long environments at least). Secondly, it shows that the diphthong /au/ (Modern Icelandic [œy]) has become front and unround and lost its second component when short. Thirdly, it shows that the old short /a/ has become a diphthong in long environments. I suggest that these changes reflect, along with the quantity shift, three basic processes that have affected Faroese stressed vowels: (i) a widespread diphthongisation of old long monophthongs, (ii) a monophthongisation (loss of the second component) of diphthongs in the short environment of the length rule created by the quantity shift, and (iii) a diphthongisation of old short /a/ in the long environments of the length rule. In addition to these, which I would call the major changes in Faroese vocalism, a number of mergers occurred, for example old short /ǫ/ merged with /o/ in front of nasals, and /ø/ elsewhere, and old long /eː/ merged with /æː/, which in turn merged with old /a/, giving [ɛaː]–[a] in the northern and central dialects, but [ɛː]–[ɛ] in the southern dialect area. There are also some qualitative changes (apart from those already mentioned) which do not concern us here. To give a rough idea of the changes involved, I present here a correspondence table between (reconstructed) Old Faroese (basically the same as Old Icelandic) and Modern Faroese vowels (cf. Rischel 1968:109; Árnason 1976:59). As can be seen from table 2, diphthongisation has taken place in the following old long vowels: /iː/ and /yː/, /oː/, /aː/ and /ǫː/, and /uː/. That is, these vowels have diphthongal variants in long position in most dialects: [ɷyː], [ɔuː], [ɔaː] and [ʉuː] respectively. The old /eː/ and /æː/ have a diphthongal long reflex in the central dialect, which might mean that they have undergone the same type of process (eː, æː ⟶ æː ⟶ [ɛa], or something similar), but having merged with an old short vowel (/a/), their status is somewhat special (I will come to this later). There are two possible ways of accounting for the short reflexes of these vowels. One is to assume that /uː/, /oː/ and /aː/ ~ /ǫː/ (and perhaps /æː/) did not diphthongise in the shortening environments, but there were direct changes aː, ǫː ⟶ [ɔ] (or whatever), oː ⟶ [œ] and uː ⟶ [ʏ] in the appropriate surroundings. Another possibility is that these vowels diphthongised both in the shortening and lengthening environments, but ɔu, ɔa and ʉu were later monophthongised in the shortening environments. In that case, it would be most natural to assume that the

TABLE 2. *Correspondence table for Old–Modern Faroese*

Old	Modern Long	Short	Dialect
/iː/ /yː/ /i/ /y/	ǫyː	ǫy	
	iː	ɪ	
/eː/	ɛaː	a	Central
/æː/	aː	a	North
/a/	ɛː	ɛ	South
/e/	ɛː	ɛ	
/ø/ /ǫ/ /øː/	œː	œ	
/u/	uː	ɷ	
/uː/	ʉuː	ʏ	
/oː/	ɔuː	œ	Central
	øuː	œ	North
	ɔuː	ɔu	South
/o/	oː	ɔ	
/aː/ /ǫ/	ɔaː	ɔ	
	ɒː	ɒ	North
/ei/	aiː	ai	
/ey/	ɔiː	ɔi	
/au/	ɛiː	ɛ	

long vowels in question were diphthongised before the shortening part of the quantity shift (the one making vowels short in front of two or more consonants, cf. chapter 4) became operative. In that case, the first vowel of *húsfólk* [hʏsːfœlk̥] 'people of the house', which derives from old /uː/, will have developed something like this: *uː* ⟶ *ʉu* by diphthongisation, and then by shortening/monophthongisation *ʉu* ⟶ [ʏ]. Similarly the long /aː/ would have developed along the following lines in shortening environments: *aː* ⟶ *ɔa* ⟶ [ɔ]. For the old /iː/ and /yː/, however, the shortening did not lead to a monophthongisation, since the modern short reflex is diphthongal ([ǫy]). In this case there is a further complication in that there is a merger of an originally rounded and an unrounded vowel. It has been suggested that the roundness of the Modern Faroese diphthong stems from the /yː/, that is that the result of the merger of /iː/ and /yː/ was a rounded vowel, which later diphthongised (cf. Amundsen 1964:57–8; Rischel 1968:101–2). It is worth noting, incidentally, that, whatever else may have happened, the merger and common diphthongisation seems to have preceded the quantity shift, since otherwise it would be difficult to account for the fact that both show the same (diphthongal) quality in shortening and lengthening environments. If the merger of /iː/ and /yː/ can be dated on the grounds of manuscript spellings, we thus have a possible *terminus post quem* for the quantity changes.

The hypothesis that the old long vowels that show diph-thong–monophthong alternation first diphthongised in all environ-ments and were later monophthongised in shortening environments is made more plausible by the fact that the original diphthong /au/, which has the modern long reflex [ɛiː], has lost its second component in the shortening environments. It is, therefore, essential to assume that a (post-quantity-shift) monophthongisation took place, and in consequence it would be natural to assume that it affected the new diphthongs *ʉu, ɔu* and *ɔa* (and perhaps *ɛa*) as well as *ɛi*. The exceptionality of [ɔyː] – [ɔy] in having a diphthongal short allophone would be explained in a way similar to [aiː] – [ai] (old /ei/) and [ɔiː] – [ɔi] (old /ey/).

The case of old short /a/, which along with old /eː/ and /æː/ shows a diphthongal long reflex, is special. Here we have an old short vowel that has diphthongised and merged with old long vowels. This is unusual within the Faroese system, both because the general tendency is to keep old long and short vowels apart, and because the other old short vowels have remained basically monophthongs (although some movement can often be detected in the long variants). A conceivable background for this situation is that old /eː/ and /æː/, having merged, diphthongised to something like *ɛa* which came later to appear as a monophthong in the short environments and, after the quantity shift, old /a/ diphthongised when long and merged with the reflex of old /eː/ and /æː/. This is very hypothetical and will need further justification before being accepted as a valid explanation. One fact that may be interpreted as an indication that the modern pair [ɛaː] – [a] has a special historical background, is that (in certain dialects at least) it appears to be the second part of the diphthong that 'remains' in the short environment, whereas in the the other diphthongs, it seems to be the first component that remains ([ʉuː] – [ʏ], [ɔaː] – [ɔ], [ɛiː] – [ɛ]).

Rischel (1968:96) suggests that the 'quantity shift' took place in two steps in Faroese, by (i) a lengthening of short vowels before single consonants and (ii) a shortening of long vowels in front of two or more consonants, and that the shortening took place somewhat later than the lengthening. He does not, however, present any positive arguments for this relative chronology of the quantity changes. As will be suggested below for Icelandic (and Norwegian and Swedish), it seems natural to assume that the lengthening and shortening did not take place simultaneously, but I know of no evidence that can be put forward in support of one or the other of the relative chronologies. The fact that the short alternants of many diphthongal vowels appear as monophthongs cannot be used as an argument in this case, for example maintaining that the shortening manifests itself as a monophthongisation in some cases, and is therefore likely to have occurred later than the lengthening of old short vowels. There is no reason, even if the 'shortening' was really a monophthongisation, to assume that it took place later than the lengthening, and anyway, there is always the possibility that the monophthongisation was secondary, as is suggested above.

The relative or absolute timing of the Faroese quantity changes remains, therefore, an open question, but it is clear that what happened must have been very similar to what took place in Icelandic.

3.2 Norwegian

As is well known, Modern Norwegian shows a great deal of dialect variation with respect to phonology. The dialect differences suggest that the phonological development from Old Norwegian, which is usually assumed to have been close to Old Icelandic and relatively uniform, has varied considerably. Quantity seems to have been no exception; as opposed to a uniform situation in Modern Icelandic, there is a considerable difference between Norwegian dialects as far as the quantity situation is concerned. The situation in the modern dialects can give us extremely valuable indirect evidence of how quantity developed in Norwegian, and it is therefore useful to make the present state of affairs the starting point.

In most Norwegian dialects the distribution of length is basically the same as in Icelandic, Faroese and most Swedish dialects. We have long vowels occurring in stressed syllables in front of single consonants, in front of hiatus and in word-final position. Short vowels occur under stress in front of two or more consonants and also in front of geminates (long consonants). The types of stressed syllables that occur are then: $V{:}C$, $V{:}\$$, $V{:}\#$ and VC_2, where C_2 stands for two or more consonants or a long (geminate) consonant. This general situation shows that a quantity shift has taken place, given that stressed syllables of the type VC, and

V:C₂ occurred in Old Norwegian, as in Old Icelandic.

If we start by looking at the Old Norse short syllables of the type VC, we see that the Modern Norwegian dialects show differing reflexes of these. Some dialects have (in some cases) eliminated this syllable type by lengthening the consonant, whereas in other cases the vowel has been lengthened. As we have seen, Faroese (and Icelandic) eliminated this syllable type by lengthening the vowel (there are minor exceptions to this, cf. e.g. Faroese *summar*, Common Nordic *sumar* 'summer' and Modern Icelandic *fram* [fram:], OI *fram* 'forward') so already in this respect Norwegian distinguishes itself from the other West Scandinavian dialects. The general rule for Norwegian is that the northern dialects and to some extent the eastern ones show a tendency to lengthen the consonant, whereas the southern and western dialects favour a lengthening of the vowel (see Indrebø 1951:221). Thus we have, for example, in the dialect of Trøndelag (near Trondheim) *vætta* (ON *vita* 'know'), and in Tromsø in the far north we have *vette*, as opposed to *vi·ta* in Sogn (near Bergen) (these forms are taken from Christiansen 1946–8:130). The distribution of consonant lengthening vs vowel lengthening corresponds well geographically with the distribution in Swedish, where consonant lengthening is mainly a characteristic of the northern dialects (*Sveamål*), but vowel lengthening a characteristic of the southern dialects (*Götamål*). This alone shows that the quantity shift was not as uniform in Norwegian (and Swedish) as it seems to have been in Icelandic and Faroese, judging from the situation in the modern languages. The Modern Norwegian situation shows that at least two changes could affect the ON short syllables of the type VC, one lengthening the vowel and the other lengthening the consonant. These changes are in a sense mutually exclusive; that is, where one occurs the other does not, but it can be said that they aim at the same results, since they both lengthen previously light syllables. There are dialects which lengthen vowels in some environments but consonants in others (cf. Christiansen 1946–8:132), but one can generally say that consonant lengthening is a northern (and eastern) feature and vowel lengthening a southern one.

Even though the general situation in Modern Norwegian is that the Old Norse light syllables have been lengthened, there are exceptions to this. In the dialect of Tinn in Telemark (in the south, west of Oslofjorden) disyllabic forms like *vikú* 'week', *vytå'* 'know' and *smakå'* 'taste' with a short first vowel and even a 'quantitative and expiratory overweight on the second syllable'[1] (*kvantitativ og ekspiratorisk overvekt på etterstavingen*) are reported to occur (Christiansen 1946–8:132). The monosyllables, however, seem to have lengthened in this dialect. The fact that a lengthening in monosyllables and a lengthening in polysyllables do not necessarily co-occur shows us that the lengthening of stressed vowels that has affected Norwegian can be split up into two changes, which we can state informally like this:

(1) $V \longrightarrow \bar{V} /\_C$

(2) $V \longrightarrow \bar{V} /\_CV$

In most dialects (which lengthen vowels) both of these changes have been completed, but in the Tinn dialect, only the first has occurred. The Tinn dialect seems then to be a conservative variety of Norwegian with respect to the development of quantity. But there is a still more conservative dialect. This is the one spoken in Northern Gudbrandsdalen. Here, both monosyllables and disyllabics retain ON short vowels in stressed syllables: *lăs* (ON *las*) 'read' (past) *lĕsa* 'read' (pres.) (Indrebø 1951:221). In this dialect, neither of the two vowel lengthenings has taken place.

A phenomenon worth mentioning in connection with the development of the ON short syllables is the so-called 'vowel balance'. This is a feature that is often used as an isogloss distinguishing between the two major dialect areas in Norway, these being the west on one hand and the east on the other. The eastern dialects show reflexes of the vowel balance, whereas the western ones do not. A distinction is made between ON disyllabic words which were 'balanced' and those which were 'overbalanced'. The balanced words were the ones with a light first syllable, for example *vita* 'know', and *dagar* 'days'. Here a 'balance' is said to have prevailed between the two syllables, since their quantity was similar. The overbalanced words were those with a heavy first syllable: *høyra* (OI *heyra*) 'hear', *kasta* 'throw' and *blása* 'blow'. In the vowel balance areas the vowels of the second syllables developed differently according to whether the first syllable was light or heavy, i.e. whether they were balanced or not. The result varies according to dialects, but in all vowel balance areas the second vowels of balanced words showed more resistance to weakening or deletion than in the overbalanced words. For example, in the southern part of the eastern region we get *ve·ta* (ON *vita*) with a final -*a* retained as opposed to *kastə* (ON *kasta*) with a final -*a* 'weakened' to -*ə*. Similarly, in Trøndelag, further north in the eastern region, we have *vætta* (ON *vita*) with a retained vowel as opposed to *kast* (ON *kasta*) with apocope. Western (and also northern) dialects on the

other hand show the same treatment of the second vowel irrespective of
the historical quantity of the first syllable. This we can see, for example,
in the Sogn dialect. Here we have *vi·ta* and *kasta* both with a final *-a*
retained; and in the dialect of Salta in Northern Norway we get *vet·*, *kast*
with apocope in both forms. (The data are again taken from Christiansen
1946–8:130–1.) Christiansen (119) considers the retention (or resistance
to weakening) of the second vowel in the balanced words to be caused by
the fact that both syllables of those words carried equal stress, or weight.
As support for this hypothesis Christiansen cites the above-mentioned
forms *viku'*, *vytå'* and *smakå'*, with a heavier stress and a longer vowel in
the second syllable. The argument is presumably that it is easier to
explain the fact that stress is on the second syllable, if it previously was
not inferior to the first syllable as far as stress or 'weight' is concerned.

Another possibility is that the balanced words had 'disyllabic accent',
similar to what Allen (1973:170–8) suggests existed in Latin, i.e. that the
stress stretched over two syllables when the first one was light. Allen says
(176): 'In the disyllabic matrix the peak of stress falls on the short (lax)
vowel of its first syllable, which is the nucleus of the matrix; the vowel of
the second syllable then functions as an accompaniment of (thoracic)
arrest.' This could, Allen suggests, explain metrical equivalence of two
light syllables with one heavy one, but, more importantly, it explains
certain 'peculiarities' in the phonology and morphophonemics of Latin
verbs (164–5) and can be used in accounting for regularities in the
'placement' of stress in Latin (1969:198). One might, then, suggest that
in dialects like that of Tinn, where there are words with original light first
syllables and vowel balance, disyllabic stress contributed to the relative
equality of the two syllables. But this would not work as well for those
dialects that have both vowel balance and lengthening in the first syllable,
i.e. forms like *ve:ta* with a lengthened first syllable but a full [a]-vowel in
the ending as opposed to *kastə* with an originally long first syllable and a
reduced vowel. If, as is suggested below, monosyllabic stress is
responsible for the lengthening in the first syllable and vowel balance is
conditioned by disyllabic stress, we seem to have a contradiction. A
conceivable solution would be to assume that we have here two historical
layers of ways of coping with the 'weakness' of the first syllable of a matrix
consisting of a short vowel with only one consonant following in a
dynamic stress pattern. One could say that at some (perhaps earlier) point
in time the dialects that have both vowel balance and lengthening in the
first syllable had a tendency to disyllabic stress but at some other (perhaps

later) point they favoured the other solution, i.e. lengthening the first syllable. If the chronological order is the one implied, one might suggest that the lengthening in the first syllable was due to influence from dialects that from the beginning adopted that solution.

One might thus say that vowel balance viewed as a reflex of disyllabic stress and the lengthening of originally light first syllables are two means that were used in the Norwegian (and Swedish) dialect area to adapt forms like Old Norse *vita* to a (perhaps new) expiratory stress that demanded considerable 'material' to expand on. Sometimes the second vowel was incorporated as a part of the stress matrix and sometimes the first syllable was 'fortified' by lengthening either the consonant or the vowel.

Another relevant consideration is that of word tones. These word tones, usually called Accent 1 and Accent 2, are different prosodic contours of words, based mainly on pitch variation (cf. Gårding 1973:30–46, 1977:29–45). Different words may have different tones or accents in most Swedish and Norwegian dialects, and minimal pairs have been cited to show that they are distinctive, even though their function is clearly marginal (cf. Haugen 1967). The historical origin of these tones is probably that Common Nordic disyllabic (and polysyllabic) words had different pitch contours from the monosyllables. At the oldest stage this difference in contours was probably predictable from the number of syllables in the words: polysyllables had the contour that later became Accent 2, but monosyllables had the contour that was to become Accent 1 (cf. Oftedal 1952:219, 221–2). Later, when some monosyllables became disyllabics by, for example, the affixation of the definite article (*dag + inn > daginn* 'the day') and the development of epenthetic vowels before final liquids or nasals (*akr > aker* 'a cornfield'), these new disyllabics still retained the same Accent 1 contour. Now some disyllabics had Accent 2 and others (the new ones) had Accent 1, and the distribution of accents was no longer predictable from the number of syllables.

It is interesting to see whether there can have been some connection between the development of quantity and the accents. The data from the Tinn dialect, as mentioned above, seem to indicate that the lengthening of short monosyllables preceded the lengthening in polysyllabics, and, as was the case with vowel balance, it is conceivable that Accent 2 had something to do with this. The majority of disyllabic words had Accent 2 at the time when the lengthening started taking place, and the conservation of disyllabics could then perhaps be ascribed to the fact that they had Accent 2. This could be made more plausible by observing that it is a general characteristic of the modern Accent 2 that it has a relatively late pitch peak, which could give the second vowel of a disyllabic form more prominence than it would otherwise have (cf. Gårding 1973:44). It is also possible that the vowel balance and Accent 2 were interrelated and that they both combined to make polysyllabics resistant to the quantity shift.

There is one type of word which could help to decide whether Accent 2 had any effect on the development of quantity, namely the disyllabic forms with Accent 1. If Accent 2 tended to prevent first syllable lengthening, the Accent 1 words should have followed the monosyllables. A thorough investigation of the dialect material is needed in order to decide this, and I have found no allusion to this in any of the reference books I have seen on Norwegian. There is, however, some evidence to the contrary in that in some Swedish dialects in which the quantity shift has not been completed, the Accent 2 disyllabics show a greater tendency to lengthen the first vowel than those with Accent 1. Söderström (1972:91–2) cites examples from Luleå dialects in Sweden, which show this. There are pairs like *be`ka*, (verb) with Accent 2 (grave) and a long vowel vs *be'ke* (def.sg.) with Accent 1 (acute) and a short vowel. This seems, if anything, to indicate that Accent 2 makes a favourable rather than unfavourable environment for the lengthening of the first vowel. I will return to this briefly in §3.3.

If we turn now to the Old Norse 'overlong' syllables, i.e. the type $V:C_2$, we see that this type has generally been excluded in Modern Norwegian. This shows that a historical change something like

(3) $V: \longrightarrow \check{V} \ / \text{—} C_2$

has taken place. But here again, there are exceptions. In the dialect of Setesdal (in the south), forms with a long vowel or a diphthong followed by a long consonant are reported to occur (Indrebø 1951:222): *no^{u}tt, lē^{i}ttə* (ON *nótt* 'night', *léttr* 'light'). This shows that the change (3) has not been completed in all dialects, just as (1) and (2) have not yet been completed in all dialects either.

To summarise, then, we see that in Norwegian the following four historical rules affecting stressed (or first) syllables have operated:

(4) (a) $V \longrightarrow \bar{V} \ / \ \text{—} C$

(b) $C \longrightarrow \bar{V} \ / \ \text{—} CV$

(c) $C \longrightarrow CC \ / \ V\text{—}$ (Consonant lengthening)

(d) $\bar{V} \longrightarrow \check{V} \ / \ \text{—} C_2$

From the sketchy picture presented above we see that the 'quantity shift' in Norwegian cannot have been a single, sudden turnover (*omvæltning*), but rather a set of changes, which affected different dialects at different times and in different ways. Sometimes consonants are lengthened and sometimes vowels, and some dialects have to a certain extent retained the old prosodic structure. In view of this, one must ask whether the term 'quantity shift' is appropriate. Why would we want to group these rules together under a common term? The reason is, of course, that the overall effect of these changes is to change the rhythmic structure of the language so that all stressed (first) syllables have the same quantity, i.e. either a short vowel + two or more consonants (assuming that long consonants can be analysed phonologically as geminates), or a long vowel + no more than one consonant.

When two or more apparently separate rules behave in this way, that is, giving a unified and simply statable result, the term 'conspiracy' has been used in synchronic phonology (cf. Kisseberth 1970).

Roger Lass (1974) has suggested that similar things appear in historical development. He sees in the development of quantity in English and Scots a gradual tendency to make vowel length predictable rather than phonemic. This tendency manifests itself in a number of apparently unrelated changes, which take place at different times in the history of the English dialects in question. Lass calls this 'linguistic orthogenesis'.

If the terms 'conspiracy' or 'orthogenesis' are to be applied in historical linguistics, the development of quantity in Norwegian seems to fit the terms extremely well. We have changes taking place at different times, which aim at a simply statable result. It would then seem to be proper to use these terms to denote the quantity changes in Norwegian, rather than using the term 'quantity shift', which seems to imply that a sudden revolution took place. But even if the terms 'conspiracy' or 'orthogenesis' are adopted, it does not necessarily mean that we have given a satisfactory account or an *explanation* of the facts. Inventing a name for things is, of course, not the same thing as stating what they are. In the case of Norwegian (and the other Scandinavian languages) the quantity conspiracy can perhaps be explained in very down-to-earth terms in the following way. It is not unnatural that stressed parts of utterances tend to become phonetically longer than their underlying structure may imply. In the case of the old light stressed syllables, this may have resulted in two more or less accidentally distributed phonetic changes: a lengthening of the vowel, or a lengthening of the consonant. Between generations these phonetic data get reinterpreted time and again, and the 'underlying grammars' of younger generations may be slightly different from the grammars of older generations, until at some stage the (once perhaps irregular) phonetic alternations reach a firmer status in the language system. These systematisations may occur gradually. For example, rule (4a) may become a part of the grammar of some dialect at an earlier stage than rule (4b). When the stage is reached where both (4a) and (4b) are incorporated into the system, a language learner may make the generalisation that stressed syllables are all long or heavy. This could be a very simplistic explanation for the disappearance of old light stressed syllables.

Another historical accident may have eliminated the old overlong syllables. The phonetic reason for this change may have been that long vowels tended to be shorter than predicted by their underlying forms, when followed by more than one consonant. A phonetic alternation like this may have been reinterpreted by younger generations, incompletely at first, until a generalisation that phonemically long vowels are shortened before two or more consonants reaches the status of some kind of a phonological rule in the language. When these two more or less accidental changes in the language – the lengthening of short vowels and the shortening of long ones – are completed, one can imagine a reinterpretation of the facts by a new generation of speakers who make the generalisations that all stressed syllables have the same quantity, and the length of vowels is predicted by the following consonantism.

3.3 Swedish

The quantity system of Modern Standard Swedish is the same as those of Standard Norwegian, Faroese and Icelandic, as far as length in stressed syllables is concerned; that is, stressed vowels are long when followed by no more than one consonant, and short when followed by two or more consonants (including geminates). As is the case with Icelandic, it has been a matter of dispute how to analyse this synchronic situation phonologically, that is, whether the phonemic length belongs to the consonants (Eliasson & La Pelle 1973) or to the vowels (Elert 1964:12–46). I will not be directly concerned with that problem here, but will look briefly at the phenomena from the historical point of view.

Given that Swedish derives from a common Nordic ancestor with free vowel length and stressed syllables of varying quantity, i.e. light (VC), heavy (V:C or VCC/VC:) and 'overlong' or hypercharacterised (V:CC/V:C:), we see that a quantity shift has taken place, since no light and no 'overlong' stressed syllables are to be found in Standard Swedish. As we have seen, the quantity shift in Norwegian was not nearly as regular as the one in Icelandic seems to have been. Whereas the Icelandic quantity shift, generally speaking, only affected vowels, i.e. short vowels are lengthened and long ones shortened according to the environment, some Norwegian dialects sometimes lengthen consonants in old light syllables. The same is true of Swedish. In many northern dialects the consonant is often lengthened if the vowel is non-low and the consonant is /p, t, k/ or /s/. The more general rule for Swedish, however, is to lengthen the vowels. The different development of old short syllables as far as lengthening of vowels or consonants is concerned often shows up in Standard Swedish. Thus, in Standard Swedish, we get *gata* [gɒ:tʰa] 'street' with a lengthened vowel (cf. Old Icelandic *gata* 'road') as opposed to *vecka* [vɛk:a] 'week' with a lengthened consonant (cf. OI *vika* 'week'). Geographically the main rule for Swedish, as for Norwegian, is that the southern dialects tend to lengthen the vowel, whereas the northern ones have a tendency to lengthen the consonant according to the rules mentioned above (Wessén 1945:60–2). Apart from this variation concerning the lengthening of consonants vs the lengthening of vowels, there is in Swedish dialects a further irregularity with respect to the development of quantity in that, as in Norwegian dialects, the quantity shift has not everywhere reached its final stage.

Söderström (1972) describes Swedish dialects which have, to a varying extent, retained old light syllables. A striking feature concerning the retention of old light syllables is that a considerable difference shows up, according to whether the old short syllable is in a monosyllable or a disyllable. Monosyllables show a greater tendency to lengthen their only syllable than do the disyllables their first syllable (Söderström 1972:88). The areas that Söderström's study covers are the following: (i) Överkalix and Nederkalix in the far north-eastern part of Sweden; (ii) the area around Piteå, further south on the east coast (both of these are in the Norrbotten region); (iii) Nordmaling, still further south on the coast, a little to the south of Umeå in the northern part of Ångermanland; and (iv) Ragunda in Jämtland. All of these dialects are within the larger area of Norrland. The first three have still largely retained old light first syllables in disyllabics, while mostly having lengthened monosyllables. This can give inflectional paradigms where there is a morphophonemic alternation in the same word between short vowels and long vowels or diphthongs according to whether a syllable (an inflection ending) follows or not. Thus, the nominative singular of Standard Swedish *väv* 'a cloth' has in Överkalix, Nederkalix, Piteå and Nordmaling a long vowel or a diphthong /veːɪv/, /veːv/, /vɛːv/, whereas the plural, with the ending /-a/, has a short first syllable: /veva/, /vɛva/ (Söderström 1972:129). The Ragunda dialect (iv) seems to be not as conservative as the other dialects mentioned, since only disyllabic words with Old Swedish /i/ and /u/ are reported from that dialect with light first syllables. It seems that the Old Swedish low vowel /a/ shows the greatest tendency to lengthen, whereas the high vowels show more resistance, for example the Old Swedish word *bit* 'bite' shows up in Överkalix as *bĕd* with a short vowel (Söderström 1972:58), whereas Standard Swedish *mat* (OI *matr*) 'food' shows up as *mẹd* with a long vowel (Söderström 1972:57).

These synchronic facts offer strong evidence that the lengthening of old light syllables took place first in monosyllabic forms and later in disyllabics. This agrees well with the statement made by Noreen (1904:123) that signs of the lengthening in monosyllables have become general in Swedish manuscripts after 1350, whereas clear signs of the lengthening in disyllabics are no older than c. 1500. This, furthermore, supports what has already been said about Norwegian dialects, the Tinn dialect retaining short vowels only in polysyllabics, but the apparently more conservative dialect of North Gudbrandsdalen retaining a short vowel both in monosyllables and disyllables. One can hypothesise from this that it is a common feature of all Norwegian and Swedish dialects that they lengthened short monosyllables before they lengthened the first syllables of di- and polysyllabics. If this is correct, the Northern Scandinavian dialects, Norwegian and Swedish show different behaviour from Danish in the south, since, as we shall see (§3.4), old light monosyllables were never lengthened in Danish, only the first syllables of polysyllables.

I do not claim to be able to explain here why these subsets of Scandinavian dialects, i.e. Danish on the one hand and Norwegian and Swedish on the other, developed differently in this respect; I can only make a few suggestions. In §§3.4 and 3.6 it is suggested that the consonant shortening (degemination) that occurs in Danish and disrupts the development of vowel length may be the same as that which affected German and English, and it seems not unlikely that a contact with Southern or Western Germanic people may be responsible for this other piece of peculiar behaviour on the part of Danish. To draw any conclusions about this, one must of course make a careful study of the chronology and geographical distribution of the phenomena involved.

If we (tentatively) ascribe the peculiar development in Danish to West/South Germanic influence, a natural corollary of that would be to say that the genuinely 'Nordic' way of lengthening old light syllables is to start with monosyllables, i.e. having the chronological order:

(a) $V \longrightarrow \bar{V} / \_ (C)$

(b) $V \longrightarrow \bar{V} / \_ (C) V$

This seems to be supported by the facts in Swedish and Norwegian dialects. As to why the quantity shift took this form in Norwegian and Swedish, a number of relatively plausible explanations can be proposed, but they may turn out to be difficult to choose between, let alone prove.

As mentioned in connection with Norwegian, two Continental Scandinavian (as opposed to Danish) features look as though they may have had some relation to the development of quantity and stress, the so-called vowel balance and the word tones. A third phenomenon that may be (and probably is) relevant is the so-called *jamning* (Norwegian) or *tilljämning* (Swedish). This is a vowel assimilation between the first and the second vowels of disyllabic words. It can be both progressive and regressive, that is, we can either get, for example in Norrlandic Swedish, *lovo* from Old Nordic *lofa* 'to praise' with the second vowel assimilating to the first, or *vuku* from Old Nordic *viku* 'week' (acc.sg.) with the first vowel assimilating to the second (Bergman 1973:106). This assimilation only takes place in words with old light first syllables, and is most prominent in northern and western Norrlandic dialects in Sweden. All of these phenomena can be said to indicate a certain balance between the first and the second syllables of disyllabic words with short first syllables.

Perhaps the least likely of these phenomena to be connected with the development of quantity is the tones. Firstly, there does not seem to be any difference in the tonality of disyllabic words according to whether they have old heavy or light first syllables. This in itself does not, of course, prove that it could not have had some special effect on the old light-syllable words, but there is no compelling reason to assume that it should have either. Secondly, the above-mentioned data from the Nederluleå dialect (§3.2; cf. Söderström 1972:91), namely the pair *be`ka* with Accent 2 and a long vowel vs *be´ke* with Accent 1 and a short vowel, seem to suggest, if anything, that length goes with Accent 2 (which is original on disyllabic forms) and that shortness goes with Accent 1 (which is original on monosyllables). In view of this, it seems unlikely that Accent 2 by itself caused the disyllabics to retain their original light syllables longer than the monosyllables. A third factor that may be mentioned as indicating that the length phenomenon and the word tones were relatively unrelated is that, as far as is known, there seems to be no difference between the pitch variation in Accent 2 words with light first syllables and in those with heavy first syllables in dialects which have retained the length difference (see Gårding 1973:34, 1977: 32 and references).

Both the vowel balance and the *tilljämning* are characteristic of Northern Swedish dialects (Wessén 1960:50–2, Bergman 1973:104–5), and we have seen that within the Swedish dialect area, it is in the northern dialects that we find retained old light syllables, with the disyllabics more conservative. In §3.2 I mentioned that the vowel balance could be connected with stress, one suggestion being that some sort of secondary stress was placed on the second vowel in the 'balance words', and another that these words formed a disyllabic stress matrix in such a way that the stress was distributed over both the first and the second syllable. One could take *tilljämning* as representing the same general phenomenon. The first and the second syllable tend to assimilate and there is no clear sign of one of them 'dominating over' the other in any way. If both of these phenomena, the *tilljämning* and the vowel balance, are relatable either to relative balance of stress between the first and the second syllable or to disyllabic stress, one might wonder whether the relative lateness of the lengthening of old light first syllables could be related to this.

3.4 Danish

As mentioned above, Danish shows some un-Scandinavian features with respect to quantity. It can, for example, be maintained that vowel length is free or distinctive in Danish, whereas this is not the case in the other Scandinavian languages. I shall try to give a brief survey of the development in Danish by way of comparison.

Compared to the Common Nordic system of two (or three) degrees of syllabic quantity (light, heavy and perhaps hypercharacterised), the situation in Modern Standard Danish can be described roughly as follows (cf. Rasmussen 1972:57):

(5) *Monosyllables*
    VC   *hat* [hætʰ] 'hat'

VCC *hest* [hɛstʰ] 'horse'
V´C *pæn* [pʰɛ´n] 'nice'
VC´ *pen* [pʰɛn´] 'pen'

The acute accent here represents the *stød*, which can fall either on the consonant (*pen*) or the vowel (*pæn*) in monosyllables. (On the phonetic nature of the *stød* see e.g. Jespersen 1922:118–9; P. Andersen 1954:320.) The *stød* could be seen as a surface realisation of underlying length in the vowels, and perhaps in the consonants too. (Of course this only applies to the voiced consonants, since the unvoiced ones, for example /s/, 'cannot' take *stød*; cf. e.g. Jespersen 1922:156.) As support for the analysis of *stød* as a surface marker of underlying length in the vowels we can cite the fact that '*stød*-less' dialects show long vowels, where the '*stød*-dialects' have *stød* on vowels. In the South Sjælland dialect the difference between *pæn* and *pen* is in vowel length, the former having a long vowel, the latter a short one. Another fact, perhaps more important, is that there occur morphophonemic alternations between a *stød*-vowel and a long one: *man* [mæ´n] 'conjure' (imp.), *mane* [mæ:nə] 'to conjure'. The reason for this is that the *stød* does not (generally) appear in disyllabic words, cf. the following:

(6) VCV *falde* [falə] 'fall'
VCCV *hente* [hɛntʰə] 'fetch'
V:CV *male* [mæ:lə] 'paint'
V:CCV *hoste* [hɔ:stə] 'cough'

These data would fit a descriptive system where vowel length is an underlying feature which is in some dialects realised as *stød* in monosyllables. The following minimal pairs fit that analysis very well:

(7) *hale* [hæ:lə] 'tail' vs *halve* [hælə] '(the) half'
hvile [vi:lə] 'rest' vs *vilde* [vilə] '(the) wild'
hvil [vi´l] 'rest' (imp.) vs *vild* [vil´] 'wild'

But there are examples which show an alternation between long and short vowels in the same morpheme, and in some environments a phonemic distinction between long and short vowels is impossible. Examples showing morphophonemic alternation between long and short vowels are:

(a) *tabe* [tʰæ:bə] 'lose' – *tabte* [tʰabtə] 'lost'.
(This represents the fact that long vowels do not normally occur in front of consonant clusters, except /st, sk, bl, bn/.)

(b) *mad* [mæð] 'food, feed' (imp.) – *made* [mæ:ðə] 'to feed'.
This second example reflects the fact that in the environment -CV, short

vowels sometimes become long (or take the *stød*). This is not a general rule, however, since we have examples like *vind* [vin´] 'win' (imp.) and *vinde* [vinə] 'to win' with no length alternation. It is perhaps possible to make the rule more general by analysing the postvocalic consonant in *vinde* as underlyingly long, but this is a problem in the synchronic phonology of Modern Danish, with which I am not directly concerned (see e.g. Hjelmslev 1951/73; Basbøll 1970–1 on this matter).

The examples given above show that there are observable regularities and alternations that can be traced back to two length changes of the sort that affected the other Scandinavian languages: a shortening of vowels before two consonants and a lengthening before one consonant. And indeed, if we look into the history of Danish, we find traces of these changes taking place. Rasmussen (1972:63) describes the two following quantity shift rules:

(8) $V \longrightarrow V\colon / \_\_ CV$ (c. 1300)

 $V\colon \longrightarrow V \ / \_\_ CCV$ (fifteenth century)

The Modern Danish alternations, whatever their status is in the synchronic system, are quite clearly reflexes of these historical changes.

The fact remains that Modern Danish shows striking dissimilarities from the other Scandinavian languages in that vowel length/*stød* seems quite clearly to distinguish between minimal pairs, whereas in the other Scandinavian languages this is generally not the case. True, arguments have been put forward for vowel quantity being phonemic in the other Scandinavian languages, but there are no phonetic minimal pairs, where the vowel quantity seems to be the only distinctive factor, since short vowels are always followed by clusters or long consonants in a stressed syllable, and therefore arguments can be held in favour of the vowel length being redundant. This is much more difficult, if not impossible, in Danish.

The reason for this difference between Modern Danish and the other Modern Scandinavian languages is perhaps that Danish underwent a general shortening of long (geminated) consonants. The dating of this change seems to be disputed, mainly because there is little or no orthographical evidence for it. Skautrup (1944:254) dates it as early as 1300, but Rasmussen (1972:167) seems to date it later, as late as the beginning of the sixteenth century. On grounds of simplicity we must assume it to have taken place later than the lengthening in (8), since otherwise the form *vilde* should have a long vowel. Whatever the dates of these changes, the consonant shortening must have neutralised a large part of the environment, which in the other Scandinavian languages determines the length of the preceding vowel. This can be illustrated by the word pair *vild* 'wild' (OI *villr*) in the definite form *vilde* (OI *villi*, OD *villæ*) and *hvile* 'rest' (OI *hvila*, OD *hvilæ*). The respective Old Danish forms must have been approximately [vilːə] and [(h)viːlə]. These forms were unaffected by the two changes in (8), but then a change took place which can be stated informally like this:

(9) C: ⟶ C / V __

This change seems to have been general and affected all long consonants in postvocalic position. After this we can hypothesise a situation where the forms are (I use the Modern Danish orthographic forms as references): *vilde* [vilə] and *hvile* [(h)viːlə]. In this situation the only thing keeping the forms apart is the difference in the vowels, which must have been mostly durational. One might then say that length had become phonemic. A similar thing, but slightly more complicated, happened to the monosyllables. We can take *vild* (the indefinite form of the same adjective) and *hvil* (imperative of *hvile*) as examples. According to (9) these forms would develop in the following way: [vilː] → [vil], [(h)viːl] → [viːl]. This is actually the situation in the *stød*-less dialects of Modern Danish. But other dialects use the placement of the *stød*, which is considered to be the historical reflex of Accent 1 (which was restricted to monosyllables and is still in existence in Norwegian and Swedish), to distinguish between these forms: *vild* [vil'], *hvil* [vi'l]. An explanation of this could be that the *stød*-dialects have also undergone phonetic shortening of the vowels in monosyllables, in which case there is nothing left to distinguish the two forms by except, perhaps, the peak of the old Accent 1, which may have been in a different place in words of different syllable structure, for example on the consonant in VC:-types, but on the vowel in V:C-types. (The phonetic character of the *stød*, based on glottal movement, forming a sort of creak or half-closure of the vocal cords, could well be interpreted as evidence that it is a reflex of the pitch peak of the old Accent 1. Because of the 'sonorous' origin of the *stød*, it 'cannot fall' on voiceless consonants; cf. Jespersen 1922/49:156.) The shortening of the vowel in monosyllables would be the historical origin of the synchronic phonological rule set up by, for example, Hjelmslev (1951/73) and Basbøll (1970–1), making *stød* a surface marker of underlying length.

If Danish has developed in the way suggested above, a quantity shift started to affect it, perhaps in a slightly different way from the other

Scandinavian dialects. But before the quantity shift could be brought to its end, Danish was affected by a change of an un-Scandinavian type, which blocked the way for further development along the same lines. Why this happened in Danish in particular and not the other Scandinavian dialects is not certain, but it is perhaps not a coincidence that German and English have no long consonants either. It seems quite likely that there is a connection.

3.5 Gothic

It has been a matter of lengthy dispute whether Wulfilian Gothic had distinctive vowel length or not. Some scholars of the structuralist school have argued that the Gothic vowel system did not have length as a distinctive feature. The main argument is that the synchronic evidence, mainly the graphemic system used in extant manuscripts of Wulfila's Bible translation, does not show directly that the length distinction prevailed. There is, for example, no distinction made in the spelling between PGmc. (Proto-Germanic) /u/ and /ū/ in forms like *sunus* 'son' and *bruþs* 'bride' which on comparative grounds can be reconstructed with historically short and long vowels respectively (cf. OI *sonr/sunr* vs *brúðr*). There is, however, one historical long vs short distinction which is consistently made in Gothic spelling, namely that between PGmc. /i/ and /ī/, spelled *i* and *ei* respectively: *greipan* 'to catch' (OI *grípa*) vs *gripum* 'catch' (past, 1p.pl.) (OI *gripum*). This spelling difference has been interpreted by those who maintain that the length distinction was lost in Gothic as representing a difference in quality rather than quantity, i.e. that the length opposition had been replaced by a qualitative opposition in these vowels. As a representative of those who maintain that vowel

TABLE 3. *Gothic vowel system (after Marchand 1973 :95)*

		Front	Central	Back
High	Close	i		u
	Open	ɪ		
Mid	Close	e		
	Open	ɛ		o
Low			a	

length was non-phonemic in Gothic I may cite Marchand (1973). He sets up the vowel system shown in table 3, where /i/ is represented in the orthography by *ei*, /ɪ/ by *i*, /e/ by *e*, /ɛ/ by *ai*, /a/ by *a*, /u/ by *u* and /o/ by *au*. In addition to this, Gothic had the diphthong /iu/, written *iu*. As can be seen, Marchand assumes that the PGmc. diphthongs /au/ and /ai/ had been monophthongised into /o/ and /e/ respectively.

If we assume that pre-Gothic Germanic had the vowel system shown in table 4 (cf. e.g. Prokosch 1939:99–105), the Gothic situation claimed by

TABLE 4. *Pre-Gothic Germanic vowel system*

Short	Long	Diphthongs
i u	ī ū	
		ai au iu
e	ē ō	
a		

Marchand presupposes the following changes:
(a) Merger of i, e > i
(b) Monophthongisation: ai > ε̄, au > ō
(c) 'Breaking': i > ε, u > o / __ h, h̨, r
(d) Quantity shift

The order in which these changes are listed above would probably not necessarily reflect their chronological order, but basically these should be the effects, when Gothic is compared with PGmc. The quantity shift would be a (perhaps context-free) loss of length as a distinctive feature in the vowels resulting in a merger of all long–short vowel pairs (some of which reflected partly PGmc. monophthong–diphthong opposition, for example, PGmc. /ō/, /au/–/o/), except PGmc. /i/–/ī/, which are kept apart in Gothic by a difference in height.

If Marchand, and others who claim that vowel length was non-phonemic in Gothic, are right, then Gothic must have undergone a quantity shift similar to the Scandinavian one, only approximately a thousand years earlier. The results were, however, much more drastic for the vowel inventory of Gothic than for the Nordic languages, in that only in the case of /i/–/ī/ was the distinction taken over by a qualitative difference. We have, as far as I can see, no means of deciding for Gothic just how this change came about, for example whether long vowels were shortened in front of consonant clusters and short ones lengthened in front of a single consonant and a hiatus, in which case the change was originally context-determined, or whether it was context-free, simply a loss of a feature, which, incidentally, must have had a considerable functional load in the language.

When these considerations are borne in mind, it seems reasonable to consider whether the synchronic evidence can be taken to be as conclusive as Marchand assumes.

Recently, Vennemann (1971) has made a case for length as being distinctive in Gothic. He points out that synchronic processes indicate that a distinction was made between the historically long and short /i/–/ī/ and /u/–/ū/. He points out that the breaking before *h*, *ḥ*, *r*, which seems to have been an active allophonic rule in Gothic, only affects the reflexes of short PGmc. /i/ and /u/. That the breaking only affected reflexes of historically short /i/, but not reflexes of historically long /ī/, is shown, for example, by alternations in the strong verb *gateihan* (1st inflectional class), with the past 1p.pl. *gataihum* as compared to *greipan*, which belongs to the same inflectional class and shows the past 1p.pl. *gripum*. The breaking only occurs in the past 1p.pl. of *gateihan*, where a historically short /i/ precedes /h/, but *ei*, representing a historical long /ī/, is left unchanged. That the historically short and long *u* were also kept apart with respect to the breaking is shown by examples like *brukjan* 'to use' (with a historically long vowel), *bruhta* (past) without breaking, as opposed to *bugjan* 'to buy' (with a historically short vowel), *bauhta* (past) with breaking in the past before an *h*. The last example furthermore suggests that the alternation was synchronically active in Gothic, since *u* and *au* alternate in morphonologically determined environments. Whenever the *h* appears after a historically short *u*, the latter turned into what is represented in the spelling by *au*, probably phonetically something like [ɔ]. This, as Vennemann points out, indicates that the reflexes of short and long PGmc. *u*, as well as *i*, were phonologically different in Gothic, but it does not show that the distinctive feature in either case was length.

That the feature that kept the vowels apart was indeed length is, according to Vennemann, shown by the different behaviour of these phonemes with respect to Sievers' Law (Vennemann 1971:106–9). The so-called Sievers' Law is a peculiar behaviour of the inflectional endings in the so-called *ja*-stem nouns and verbs. When a *ja*-noun has a heavy or a polysyllabic stem the nominative ending is *-eis*, but when the stem is light, the ending is *-jis*: *hairdeis* 'shepherd' vs *harjis* 'army'. A similar distribution prevails in the *ja*-verbs: *waurkeis* 'you work' vs *nasjis* 'you save'; the ending after a heavy root is -*eis*, but after a light one it is -*jis*. (Vennemann proposes that the explanation of the consonantal character of the beginning of the ending in the case of light stems is to be found in the fact that the originally (semi-)vocalic beginning of the ending forms a consonantal onset for the final syllable in this case but not in the case of the heavy stems. Thus, one could suggest that there is a difference in syllabification: *hair$deis* vs *har$jis*.)

Vennemann points out that the term heavy as it will have to be applied in this context comprises roots of the form VCC ... and also roots of the form V̄C ..., where V̄ represents a historically long vowel: *sokeis* 'you look for' and *veneis* 'you hope' have -*eis*. The comparative evidence points in both cases to a historically long vowel, cf. OI *søkir* (with *i*-umlaut /ō/ > *œ*) 'you fetch, go after' and *ván* 'hope' (with PGmc. /ē/ > *á*). The roots *sok*- and *ven*- can only be heavy if they have a long vowel, and if the long vowels are analysed as bimoric, the stems *sok*- and *ven*- will have the same number of morae (i.e. three) as the VCC stems. The high vowels behave in the same way as *e* and *o* in this respect: when *ei* precedes a single consonant, the ending is -*eis*, and when *i* precedes, it is -*jis*: *gasleipeis* 'you damage' vs *bidjis* 'you ask'; and we get *brukeis* 'you use' (with a historically long vowel) as opposed to *hugjis* 'you think' (with a historically short vowel) which shows a parallel distinction between two types of *u*.

The facts do not, however, provide such conclusive evidence for a length distinction in vowels as Vennemann maintains. The argument hinges on the assumption that Sievers' Law was a synchronically active phonological process in Gothic, but this cannot be taken for granted. The other Germanic dialects, as well as Gothic, show reflexes of Sievers' Law. Old Icelandic can be considered to have developed two different inflectional classes, the so-called *ia*-stems (old heavy *ja*-stems) like *hirðir* (gen. *hirðis*) 'shepherd' and *ja*-stems (old light *ja*-stems) like *herr* (gen. *hers*) 'army'. It is quite impossible to incorporate Sievers' Law into Old Icelandic phonology as an active phonological process. The same applies to Old High German and Old English, which show reflexes of Sievers' Law in their inflectional system, but can hardly be taken to contain it in their synchronic phonology. The fact that Sievers' Law has left marks in all the other Germanic dialects must be taken by the comparative method as evidence that it operated in Common Germanic or Proto-Germanic. If this is so, one cannot exclude the possibility that it was fossilised in

Gothic as it is in the other dialects. So the fact that the ending -*eis* appears after historically heavy roots but -*jis* after historically short ones in Gothic proves nothing for the synchronic phonology of Gothic. Indeed, Vennemann himself mentions examples from the morphology of Gothic which he calls exceptions to a synchronically active Sievers' Law in Gothic. These are neuter *ja*-stem, and masculine *jan*-stem nouns. These have the same ending in the genitive, regardless of whether the stem is long or short, whereas, as we saw, the masculine *ja*-stems and the *ja*-verbs show distribution according to Sievers' Law. Both *kuni* 'kind, kin' with a light stem and *arbi* 'heritage' with a heavy stem, which are *ja*-stem neuter nouns, have genitives in -*jis*: *kunjis, arbjis*. Similarly *wilja* 'will' and *bandja* 'captive', which are *jan*-stem nouns with a light and a heavy stem respectively, both have genitives in -*jins*. There seems to be no way of accounting for this exception unless we refer to morphological features as Venneman (1971:110) does. But this seems to indicate that the Sievers' Law alternations in Gothic were morphologically rather than phonologically motivated, and in that case the length distinction in vowels had nothing to do with the synchronic reflexes in Gothic of Sievers' Law, which probably was phonological only in Proto-Germanic or Proto-Indo-European.

The fact that Sievers' Law cannot prove that length was still free in Gothic vowels does not mean that it was not so. I find it just as likely that length distinguished between *ei* and *i* and 'long' and 'short' *u*. The different behaviour of historically long and short *u* with respect to breaking shows that they were different, whether in quantity or quality (or perhaps both). It seems, then, that the spelling did not make a distinction prevalent in the phonology of Gothic, namely that between historically long and short *u*. It is of course hard to say what this distinction was, but it seems at least probable that it was based on length. It is a well known fact that length, especially in vowels, was irregularly represented in Germanic writing (cf. e.g. W. Keller 1908; Benediktsson 1968), and this could well have been the case in Gothic. If we know for a fact that Proto-Germanic /u/ and /ū/ were distinct in Gothic and that the orthography did not reflect that distinction, we can put the question like this: Is it more likely that quantity distinctions were left unmarked in the orthography than quality distinctions? This is probably not a very easy question to answer, but given the fact that length was not marked consistently in Germanic manuscripts and that it was not generally marked in Latin orthography (cf. Allen 1965:64–5), even though such a distinction did prevail in Latin, it seems to be very likely that this was the case in Gothic too, and that the difference between the two *u*'s was that of length. It seems, then, more probable that the difference in *ei–i* and the two *u*'s was one of length, and that *e* and *o* were also phonologically *long* even though their only short counterparts were conditional allophones of *i* and *u* respectively. The length opposition is also likely to have distinguished between *a* as in *dags* 'day' and *a* (*an*) as in *fahan* 'get', even though nasality cannot be excluded.

To conclude this section on Gothic, let me say this : It seems likely that length was distinctive in Gothic (i) on historical and comparative grounds, (ii) because breaking seems to be sensitive to a distinction between two *u*'s, not marked in the orthography, and (iii) because the distinction most likely to be left out in the spelling is length. However, this is far from being proven, and can perhaps never be.

The main problem with Gothic is of course that it left no descendants (except Crimean Gothic) among the modern Germanic languages, so we are missing an important piece of evidence, namely comparative evidence from younger stages of the language, that can be used in the case of the other dialects. This means also that we do not have a history of Gothic to compare with the developments in the other Germanic languages, which might have given important clues.

3.6 German

It would go beyond the limits of this thesis to account for the development of quantity in German in any detail, but a brief survey, by way of comparison with the Scandinavian phenomena, is in order.

Old High German and Old Saxon had free vowel length and, for Old High German at least, there were no distributional limits on combinations of long and short vowels with following long (geminated) and short (single) consonants or consonant clusters. Old High German could thus have stressed syllables of the three types we have set up for Old Norse, namely light (short vowel + one consonant), heavy (long vowel + one consonant or short vowel + long consonant or consonant cluster) and 'overlong' or hypercharacterised (long vowel + long consonant or consonant cluster). But if we look at the situation in the modern dialects we see that there is a marked difference between the Scandinavian languages (except Danish) and Modern German, in that in most German dialects vowel length is undoubtedly phonemic. However, the old, we may call it Germanic, quantity system has not been left intact in German dialects. All German dialects reported on in R. E. Keller (1961) show some traces of changes which are reminiscent of the Scandinavian quantity shift. Two historical rules of a quantity shift type are particularly widespread, applying with most regularity in the north. These are a lengthening of vowels in open syllables:

$$V \longrightarrow \bar{V} \mid \_\_ CV$$

and a shortening of long vowels in front of two or more consonants:

$$\bar{V} \rightarrow \breve{V} \mid \_\_ C_2$$

(Cf. e.g. von Kienle 1960:37–42; Paul/Mitzka 1963:77–9.)

The open-syllable lengthening shows traces in all German dialects except the southernmost ones (Schwyzertütsch (High Allemannic), cf. von Kienle 1960:37; R. E. Keller 1961:44, 93–4). It seems to be most original in the northern part of the German dialect area and is reported (von Kienle 1960:37) to have already been active in West Low Franconian in Old High German times, i.e. before 1050. The shortening of vowels before consonant clusters seems to have been more irregular, in that different clusters shorten the preceding vowels at different times (von Kienle 1960:40–1), but in most modern dialects vowels are short before two or more consonants.

The North Saxon Dialect around the Lower Elbe (near Hamburg) described by R. E. Keller (1961:339–81) shows reflexes of these changes very clearly. Both the open-syllable lengthening and the shortening before consonant clusters have taken place regularly in this dialect, but (as in Danish and many other German dialects) old short vowels remain short in monosyllables (closed syllables). This means that vowel length does not become completely predictable by the following consonantism, but there are still regular morphophonemic alternations between long and short vowels within inflectional paradigms, for example where there was formerly an alternation between mono- and disyllabic forms. Thus, the singular of *Dag* 'day' and *Slag* 'blow' have short vowels, being historically monosyllabic, whereas the plurals, which are originally (underlyingly?) disyllabic, have long vowels: *Daag′ Slääg′*. Also the verbs *greipen* 'to seize' and *legen* 'to tell a lie' have long vowels in their infinitives, but in the pres.3p.sg., where the ending -*t* is added, forming a cluster following the vowels, the vowels are short (R. E. Keller 1961:349). It is striking how similar these phenomena are to the Danish situation described above, and it comes as no surprise, given the geographical proximity and the cultural relations between the areas in question.

As mentioned above, the open-syllable lengthening and the shortening of vowels before consonants have not reached all German dialects, especially the southern ones. In these there are, however, traces of other quantity-shift-like changes. Among these is the so-called 'Leichtschlussdehnung', according to which vowels are lengthened in monosyllables ending in 'lenis' consonants (cf. R. E. Keller 1961:45–8). In Upper Austrian (R. E. Keller 1961:203–18) the combination of this and the lengthening of vowels in open syllables, here called 'Leichtinnendehnung', has led to a system where length is predictable according to the nature of the following consonantism: 'Every vowel before a lenis or a nasal plus lenis is long, every vowel before a fortis or nasal plus fortis is short' (R. E. Keller 1961:204).

Bannert (1976) treats similar phenomena in the dialect of Central Bavaria. Here vowels are short before long or 'fortis' obstruents, but long before short or 'lenis' ones. According to Bannert, the basic difference between fortis and lenis consonants is one of duration. Other phonetic differences, such as in voicing and sometimes in occlusion vs friction, can then be derived from the basic durational feature (1976:36–8). In Bannert's phonological analysis the difference between the forms *Feda* [feːtr] 'feather' and *Feta* [fetːr] 'cousin' lies in the place of the feature [+long]. In the former case it appears on the vowel, but in the latter it appears on the consonant. Redundancy rules then account for the length and quality of other segments as need be. In this analysis quantity is a prosodic '*Merkmal der komplementären Länge von Vokal und Konsonant*' (Bannert 1976:38–42; italics his).

Although there are similarities between the quantity situation in these High German dialects and the Scandinavian situation, there is, from the historical point of view, a significant difference in that the distribution of length cannot be directly predicted on the basis of a historical distinction between heavy and light postvocalic consonant sequences, and the length alternation is a result of a different set of changes from those that affected the Nordic dialects. Also, it seems that syllabic quantity cannot be said to be constant here, since there exist syllables with length neither in the consonant nor in the vowel: [lãŋ] 'long'. This is not permitted in Icelandic or Faroese, nor in most dialects of Swedish and Norwegian.

Before leaving German, I would like to comment briefly on the development of the consonants. As mentioned above (§3.4), Danish does not have any geminated consonants, having undergone a consonant degemination. It was also mentioned that German (the northernmost dialects at least) has undergone a similar change, there being no opposition between long and short consonants. I suggested that this degemination affected the development of quantity in Danish and could (partly at least) account for the 'un-Scandinavianness' of Danish with respect to quantity. There is very scanty mention of the German degemination in the handbooks I have consulted, but a look at Keller's (1961) description of the dialects shows it clearly. In Danish, this degemination has been connected with the weakening of medial stop consonants (*klusilsvækkelse*) and other phenomena, which have minimised the functional load of the long/short distinction (cf. Rasmussen 1972:67). In many central German dialects a weakening of medial consonants, similar to the Danish one, has taken place (cf. Mitzka 1954). We see, then, that Danish is 'un-Scandinavian' in more respects than in having what might be called distinctive vowel length. The relation of these factors raises interesting questions as to whether the degemination can have had some influence on the development of vowel quantity, and whether the degemination (which seems to have taken place in English too) is a Danish innovation or whether it spread from the West Germanic dialects. But in order to be able to answer these questions, one would have to take a close look at the chronology and geographical distribution of these phenomena, and there is no room for such an investigation in this context.

3.7 English

The development of length and quantity in English has been treated as a whole in Lass (1974), and most of what follows will be a recapitulation of that. Other works dealing with length and quantity in English from the historical point of view include Vachek (1959), Dobson (1962) and Grundt (1973).

In Old English, length was free or phonemic in vowels (as well as consonants), and the general rule was, as in the other oldest Germanic dialects, that long and short vowels could occur in any stressed environment. It is maintained by Vachek (1959:446) that the length was basically gemination, or 'bimoricness' (cf. §6.1 below). The only exception to the principle that long and short vowels had a free distribution is that in final open stressed syllables only long vowels occurred. This was caused (Lass 1974:326) by a lengthening of stressed word-final vowels, which goes back to Common West Germanic (if not Common Germanic) times.

As was the case with all the other (surviving) Germanic dialects, this system suffered a series of blows, which led to, or aimed at (cf. Lass), the disruption of the 'Germanic' quantity structure. These changes are listed by Lass (1974:327–33) as the following:

(a) Shortening of long vowels in front of sequences of three consonants (sixth–seventh century).

(b) A shortening of long antepenultimate vowels before two consonants (sixth–seventh century).

(c) A lengthening of vowels before clusters of liquid or nasal plus homorganic voiced stop (around the end of the ninth century).

In the eleventh century, generalisations were made of the two sixth–seventh century shortenings mentioned above:

(d) A shortening of long vowels before sequences of two (instead of the earlier three) consonants.

(e) A shortening of long vowels in antepenultimate position in front of only one consonant (instead of two as before).

(f) The last common English change to occur was the so-called 'open-syllable lengthening', according to which vowels (particularly non-high ones) lengthened in the first syllable of disyllabic words with one consonant following. Along with or before (as a prerequisite for?) the lengthening, the high and mid vowels lowered. These changes took place in the twelfth to thirteenth centuries.

These changes all contributed to making vowel length predictable in an increasing number of environments. In fact, the only places where it was free after these changes was in monosyllables ending in single consonants. But this was enough to maintain a dichotomy in the system between phonologically different vowels, which derived from the old long (diphthongal) and short vowels respectively. This dichotomy was reinforced by a later neutralisation in some of the environments that had come to determine the length of vowels. These were a shortening (degemination) of long consonants (Jespersen 1909/61:146) and the loss of the final 'weak *e*' (*ibid.*:186–9). These changes, which probably took place in the fourteenth and fifteenth centuries, removed two sets of environments on the basis of which vowel length was predictable. The degemination removed shortening environments (long consonants), and the loss of the final *e* removed lengthening environments by turning disyllabics into monosyllables and thus closing formerly open syllables.

One need hardly emphasise the similarity of these English changes to the development in Danish and German. As a consequence of these changes the quantity situation is similar in all these three languages, and different from that of the Scandinavian ones (apart from Danish). There are certain environments where the length (or 'tenseness') of vowels is predictable, but others where it is not, and thus must be seen as an inherent property of the vowels themselves and not derived from the syntagms in which they appear.

Although in most English dialects vowel length (or 'tenseness') is thus 'phonemic', or free, there is an important exception in that Scots has developed a system where vowel length is predictable to a great extent. This was brought about by changes that took place in the seventeenth century, according to which all long vowels and diphthongs shortened everywhere except in front of voiced continuants /r, v, z, ð/ and a boundary, and the non-high short vowels *e, a, o* lengthened in the same environment (i.e. where long vowels stayed long) (cf. Lass 1974:320). This change, which has come to be called Aitken's Law since its exposition by Aitken (1962), led to a situation in most Modern Scots dialects where vowels (except the reflexes of Middle English *i* and *u*) have long and short allophones according to the environment: long before /r, v, z, ð/ and a boundary and short elsewhere. The exceptionality of the ME high /i, u/ seems to be that they were not affected by the lengthening that occurred in front of /r, v, z, ð/ and a boundary. Thus the vowels [ɛ̈] and [ʌ] that are the reflexes of ME *i* and *u* in the Fife dialect of Modern Scots (cf. Lass 1974:316) only appear as short, whereas other vowels, as a general rule, have both long and short variants.

Lass points out that Aitken's Law can be seen as the '(nearly) last step in a series of directed changes . . .' that seem to aim at making vowel length predictable on the basis of the environment (326). He mentions that the Scottish situation is reminiscent of the Scandinavian one since in most Scandinavian dialects vowel length can be predicted in stressed syllables. Here also there are exceptions, as we have seen, and one might then want to say that Scots is on a par with those Scandinavian dialects that have almost 'made it' to predictable vowel length.

I think, however, that the similarity should not be overemphasised. We have seen that in some High German dialects, vowel length has become predictable on the basis of the nature of the following consonantism. But I mentioned that both the environment of the rule governing length and the historical changes that brought about the situation in the German dialects were different from the corresponding Scandinavian phenomena. Similarly, it is important, I think, that Aitken's Law, viewed both as a historical change and as a synchronic rule of length distribution, is quite different from the things we have seen from the Scandinavian languages. Perhaps the most important difference between Aitken's Law and the Scandinavian changes is that the central change in Scots is, according to Aitken (1962), a general *shortening* of long vowels (with the above mentioned exceptions), whereas the Scandinavian quantity shift seems to have 'aimed at' what we may call uniformisation of syllabic quantity, by making all previously light syllables heavy and by eliminating previously 'overlong' or hypercharacterised syllables by shortening long stressed vowels before two or more consonants. Thus, whereas Scandinavian (apart from Danish) has now as a rule only syllables of heavy quantity, Scots sides with German and English in having both light and heavy stressed syllables, cf. for example [di:v] 'deafen' vs [dif] 'deaf' (Aitken 1962:2), the quantity of which is determined by the inherent length of the vowel. Of course, the importance one assigns to this difference will depend on the criteria one uses. A typology based on the existence or not of free phonological length in vowels would put Scots (and some forms of High German) in a category with the Nordic languages, whereas a typology based on the uniformity or not of syllabic quantity would put Scots in a category with English and German. The analysis of quantity and length in Icelandic described in chapter 2 emphasises the central status of the stressed syllable with an 'axiomatically' set quantity, and in chapter 4 this centrality of the stressed syllable will be related to the development of these phenomena from Old to Modern Icelandic, and rules of stress and syllable shape are suggested as the forces that basically determined the development of length and quantity in Icelandic. If these ideas are justifiable (and it seems that they can also be applied to Faroese, Norwegian and Swedish), it follows that there is a basic difference between the development in Icelandic, Faroese, Norwegian and Swedish on the one hand and the rest of the surviving Germanic languages on the other. The elimination of free vocalic length and the striving for uniform syllabic quantity was much weaker in the West Germanic dialects and Danish than in the northern dialects.

Although it thus seems that there is an important split in the Germanic dialect area concerning the development of quantity, it must of course not be forgotten that all the surviving Germanic dialects show reflexes of a tendency to eliminate free length in vowels, so that in a larger context one can say that the differences between the development in the north and in the south and west are merely variations on a common theme.

3.8 Western European (dis)unity in quantity and stress

Sommerfelt (1951/62) points out that there seems to be a common core in the development of quantity and stress in the languages of Western Europe. In Latin, for example, a change took place which is strikingly similar to the Icelandic quantity shift (cf. Spence 1965). Classical Latin is assumed to have had free vowel length with a distinction between two sets of vowels, long and short, and a corresponding distinction between four combinations of vowels and consonants: VC, V:C, VCC and V:CC. Three basic changes later modified this original order of things. Quality changes took place which formed a discrepancy in the relation between the long and the short subsystems. For example old short $\bar{\imath}$ and $\bar{u}$ were lowered to obtain quality similar to that of old long $\bar{e}$ and $\bar{o}$. In addition to this, a simplification took place in the old quantity pattern and its relation to stress. Long unaccented vowels were shortened and short vowels under stress lengthened (Spence 1965:14), and also long vowels in formerly hypercharacterised syllables (V:CC) were shortened (cf. Allen 1973:66). All these changes resulted in a system where stressed syllables had a system of seven vowels /i, ẹ, ę, a, u, ǫ, ọ/ which were assigned length on the basis of the shape of the consonantism following, by a rule similar to the Icelandic length rule described in chapter 2. As we have seen and will see in more detail below, these phenomena bear a close resemblance to what must have taken place in Scandinavian, and in Icelandic in particular.

According to Sommerfelt (1951/62:83), it is a common Western European characteristic that 'the function of energy takes the form of stress, and that the quantitative differences, where they subsist, are entirely subordinate to stress'. This Sommerfelt sees as a result of a development that started in Greek, where there can be seen in the third century BC[2] signs of the development of stress accent and the loss of 'significant' vowel length. During the next 1,300 years, changes take place in late Latin and the Germanic languages that to a varying extent bring length and quantity under the subordination of stress. Sommerfelt sees this as a spread from one language to another of the same type of speech rhythm which started to develop in Greek and subsequently moulded the prosody of more or less all Western European speech.

From a relatively distant point of view such as that adopted by Sommerfelt (1951/62), the pattern may seem clear enough, but a closer look at the more down-to-earth worlds of the individual dialects indicates that certain things fit less well into the picture than one might wish. It is, for example, a major complication in the pattern that, in spite of changes in English, German and Danish that can be looked on as aiming at a uniformisation of the quantity of stressed syllables, these three languages (or at least most of their dialects) still dichotomise between long and short (tense and lax) vowels and heavy and light stressed syllables; partly, one might say, as a matter of conservatism, and partly as a result of what appear as innovatory changes like the 'degemination' of consonants (cf. the English distinction *beat–bit*, *seat–sit*).

This split in the Germanic dialect area demands an explanation which does not seem easily available. True, one can say that quantity and length are 'subordinate' to stress in Danish, German and English, since a distinction in quantity or length is only possible under stress. But the difference is that in the Nordic languages (Danish apart) syllabic quantity is uniquely determined by stress, which is not the case in the other Germanic languages.

I will not attempt to give any sort of satisfactory explanation of this difference, but only mention a few points that seem to be worth bearing in mind in any attempt at accounting for the phenomena. It seems that the concept of disyllabic stress (Allen 1973:170–9) may turn out to be useful in accounting for disyllabic forms like English *sitting* or *sunny* with two light syllables, while it would not help in accounting for monosyllables like *sit* and *sun*. An important element here is the degemination or shortening of old long consonants. This change, like the shortening of vowels in Scots, seems to go counter to a general trend, since the 'canonical form' (cf. Anderson & Jones 1977:159–79) that otherwise seems to be 'aimed at' for stressed syllables is a maximal one. The stressed syllable in Germanic can be said to have a tendency to absorb the maximum of phonological 'material', typical changes being lengthenings and epentheses or absorption of quality from unstressed syllables into stressed ones by umlaut and related phenomena.

It may well be that the basic difference between the typical Scandinavian structure of the stressed syllable and the West Germanic one lies in the role played by the vocalic nucleus in determining the prosodic contour of the syllable. In Scandinavian it seems that, at a certain stage in the development at least, the vowel tended to adapt itself to the consonantal frame surrounding it, whereas in the south (and west), although a similar tendency (for example in Middle English lengthenings and shortenings) had been shown earlier, the vowel is more independent of the following consonantism. Where, as in English, we can refer to a difference in *Silbenschnitt* or contact between the vowel and the following consonant, according to whether the vowel is short or long, lax or tense, that must be seen as dependent on the choice of vowel. One could say that in the south the choice of vowel determines the shape of the syllable, whereas in the north the prosodic shape of the vowel is determined by the structure of the syllable.

The problem from the historical point of view is of course in deciding how this split in the Germanic dialect area came about. It would appear that to think in terms of 'prosodic independence' of vowels may be heuristically useful.

NOTES

[1] This 'overweight' on the second syllable is perhaps related to Accent 2, which in this area has a pitch peak on the second syllable as well as the first syllable (cf. Oftedal 1952:223).
[2] Actually, the evidence is not clear until the third century AD.

4 The development in Icelandic

4.1 Introductory

4.1.1 The prosodic (or syntagmatic) aspect and the segmental (or paradigmatic) aspect. Before the main discussion of the development of quantity and length in Icelandic, I would like to emphasise a distinction between two aspects of the changes in question. One can look at the problem, firstly, from the point of view of the inventory of phonological units and the paradigmatic relations between phonological segments and features. For Old Icelandic, for example, a vowel system can be set up with a 'distinctive feature' of length playing a central role in creating a paradigmatic dichotomy between a long and a short subsystem of vowels (see e.g. Benediktsson 1959:286–95, 1972:137–8, 146), whereas in Modern Icelandic the distinctive function carried by this feature has been taken over by quality features, and vowel length has become subordinate to stress and is no longer free. We can then say that the quantity shift in Icelandic resulted in the substitution of quality features for the length feature. This was brought about by a series of changes in length according to the environment and prior changes or quality shifts in the vowels. We can call this the paradigmatic or distinctive feature/segmental aspect of the change insofar as we are looking at the effect of the change on the inventory of distinctive features and segmental phonemes and their relations.

There is, however, a second, equally important aspect of the problem, which may even prove to be more important when we start trying to form explanations as to how the changes in question came about. We may call this the prosodic or syntagmatic point of view. From this angle, we may say that the quantity shift was a change in the rules governing the quantity of stressed syllables. As we have seen, Old Icelandic allowed, theoretically at least, for four types of rhymes in stressed syllables:
(a) A short vowel plus one consonant: *fat* 'a piece of clothing'.
(b) A short vowel plus two or more consonants: *fatt* 'erect' (neuter).

(c) A long vowel plus one consonant: *fát* 'confusion'.

(d) A long vowel plus two or more consonants: *fátt* 'few' (neuter).

Two mathematically possible alternatives are missing from this list, namely those of a long or a short vowel without a following consonant. When a vowel appears in this environment, i.e. in front of another (syllabic) vowel or a silence, as in *snúa* 'to turn', *fé* 'money', it has been suggested (Benediktsson 1968:40) that the length distinction was (from the paradigmatic point of view) neutralised, since no opposition between long and short vowels occurs. An older theory is that vowels were long in this environment, and in that case one might say that a phonotactic constraint demands a long vowel there.

There is evidence to show that in Old Icelandic there was, from the prosodic point of view, a difference in the status of at least two types of stressed syllable. In our terms we may say that there were two degrees of syllabic quantity or weight. The combination (a) formed what I will call a short or light syllable, and those under (b) and (c) formed long or heavy ones. The type of combination exemplified in (d) is sometimes said to have formed 'overlong' or hypercharacterised syllables, but it is not certain that there was any significant prosodic difference between them and the other two heavy types that would justify a category of a third degree of syllabic quantity in thirteenth-century Icelandic. In Modern Icelandic, however, there is, as we have seen, only one quantity in stressed syllables; they are all heavy. This means that types (a) and (d), if the latter had a special status from this point of view, have disappeared. One can then describe the difference between Old Icelandic and Modern Icelandic from the 'prosodic' point of view by saying that in Old Icelandic stressed syllables varied in quantity, whereas in Modern Icelandic they all have the same quantity.

4.1.2 Sources of evidence. The sources of evidence concerning the phonology of older stages of Icelandic have been described by Benediktsson (1972:116–17):

(a) The orthography of written texts can give valuable information about the phonological structure and sometimes even phonetic properties of the language it represents.

(b) Valuable evidence can be obtained from the metrics of poetry from different times in the history of Icelandic. In the case of length and quantity, our attention inevitably centres on the rhythmic structure of the metres, because the rhythmic rules of metres can give us valuable clues about the prosodic nature of the language on which the metre is constructed. Of particular interest here is the *dróttkvætt-*metre, which it is reasonable to believe based its rhythm, in part at least, on quantity.

(c) Comparative evidence can be useful; that is, evidence based on what we know about stages of Icelandic, other than any particular one under investigation, and also evidence based on what we know about related languages. In our case it is, for example, important to know that all the other Germanic dialects seem to have had, at their earliest stages at least, free length in vowels, from which it can be inferred by the comparative method that length as a vocalic feature is a Germanic inheritance and that, at some stage, Old or Prehistoric Icelandic had this feature. Indeed, comparison with other Indo-European languages shows that a length distinction in vowels can be traced back to Proto-Indo-European times.

(d) For Old Icelandic of the twelfth century, there is a very important source of evidence in addition to the three mentioned above. This is the so-called *First Grammatical Treatise*, which was written in the twelfth century and is mainly intended to suggest a solution to the problem of adapting the Latin alphabet to Old Icelandic. This, of course, gives invaluable evidence about phonology of twelfth-century Icelandic, and all the more so because it is a remarkable piece of linguistics. (For editions see Benediktsson 1972, which has a thorough commentary, and Haugen 1950.)

4.2 The phonology of Icelandic about 1200

4.2.1 The vowel system. I will start this investigation into the history of length and quantity in Icelandic by summarising what is known with relative certainty about the phonological system of Icelandic around the end of the twelfth century and the beginning of the thirteenth century.

According to Benediktsson (1959, 1965, 1972), the vowel system shortly after the time of writing of the *First Grammatical Treatise* (sometime between 1125 and 1175) was dichotomous, divided in two by the feature 'length'. Following Benediktsson we can set up the vowel system in table 5 for Old Icelandic around or shortly after 1200. The symbols can be interpreted roughly as the IPA symbols (ǫ, historically deriving from *a* by *u*-umlaut, was probably a low, back or central vowel, distinguished from /a/ by rounding).

TABLE 5. *Old Icelandic vowel system, c. 1200*

Short			Long			Diphthongs		
i	y	u	iː	yː	uː	ei	ey	au
e	ø	o	eː	øː	oː			
	a	ǫ		æː	ɑː			

As can be seen from table 5, it is assumed that there was no one-to-one correspondence between the long and the short subsystems. It is only the non-low vowels which can be said to have a regular correspondence between long and short: /i/–/iː/; /e/–/eː/; /y/–/yː/; /ø/–/øː/; /u/–/uː/; and /o/–/oː/. In the low vowels, we have probably an opposition of roundness in the short vowels, /a/ vs /ǫ/, whereas in the long subsystem the opposition between the two low vowels was probably that of frontness: /æː/ vs /ɑː/. The main reason for assuming this difference in the hierarchy and function of the features in the two subsystems is the subsequent development. In the short vowels /ǫ/ shortly after this merged with /ø/, the result being a front rounded vowel, usually represented by the symbol /ö/ (in Modern Icelandic: [œ]). The argument is that if /ǫ/ were a primarily back vowel, it would have been less likely to merge, as it did, with a front rounded vowel rather than a back one like /o/. In the long system, on the other hand, a merger took place between /æː/ (*i*-umlaut of /ɑː/) and /øː/ (*i*-umlaut of /oː/), two front vowels, differing in roundness, the result probably being a front unrounded vowel. In this case, it can be argued that it shows a relative stability of the backness–frontness feature that /æː/ merged with /øː/, retaining its frontness, rather than merging with /ɑː/, which presumably was kept apart from it by the back–front feature. These arguments may not be conclusive, but in the absence of any arguments invalidating or contradicting those presented above we may assume that the relation of the features of backness–frontness and roundness in the low vowels were not the same in the long and the short subsystems (cf. Benediktsson 1959:287–95).

Excursus.
It is worth pointing out that the analysis of the vowel system described above and worked out by Benediktsson is purely surface phonemic. There is, for example, no attention paid to morphophonemic alternations between vowels, which are, at this stage, quite regular, for example between /u/ and /y/, /o/ and /ø/ and /a/ and /e/ as a result of the historical *i*- (or *iʀ*)-umlaut, as in *flytia* – *flutti* 'move' (pres. vs

past), *kømr* – *koma* 'come' (1p.sg. vs infin.), *telja* – *talða* 'count' (pres. vs past). Also, reflexes of the historical *u*-umlaut show up as regular morphophonemic alternations between /a/ and /ǫ/ as in *kalla* – *kǫllum* 'call' (infin. vs 1p.pl.), *barn* – *bǫrn* 'child' (nom.sg. vs nom.pl.). Similarly, in the long vowels, regular alternations resulting from the *i*-umlaut show up between /uː/ and /yː/, /oː/ and /øː/, and /ɑː/ and /æː/, as in *súpa* – *sýpr* 'drink' (infin. vs 2p.sg.), *fór* – *fœri* 'go' (past indicative vs past subjunctive) and *hár* – *hæri* 'high' (positive vs comparative). This might lead generative phonologists to suggest that *i*-umlaut and *u*-umlaut are active phonological processes in the Icelandic of around 1200 and that the underlying phonemic system can be simplified accordingly, assigning, for example, [y] and [u] to the same underlying 'systematic phoneme' /u/, and [o] and [ø] to the same underlying systematic phoneme /o/, and the [e] of *telja* to an underlying phoneme /a/ etc. for the *i*-umlaut, and similarly for the *u*-umlaut, deriving [ǫ] from underlying /a/ by a *u*-umlaut rule. This is, of course, a question that deserves careful attention and, without embarking on a full discussion of the matter, I would like to make a few points which seem to me to speak against such an analysis (see S. Anderson 1974:141–6; Cathey & Demers 1976 for proposed generative analyses of this sort).

Firstly, in many cases, the *i*'s and *u*'s which would cause the umlauts do not appear on the surface, as for example in *koma* – *kømr* or *brók* – *brœkr* for *i*-umlaut, and in *barn* – *bǫrn* for *u*-umlaut. This would mean that in order for the umlaut-rules to be statable in a simple way, the generative phonologist would have to set up abstract systematic phonemes which do not appear on the surface in the relevant positions and would have to be suppressed by special rules. Furthermore, this would not work for all the umlaut-causing segments, since some of them seem to appear on the surface, as for example the *u* in *kǫllum*. The fact that there is not an if-and-only-if relation between for example *ǫ* and a following *u* seems to me to indicate that the process is not phonological, since the environment for *ǫ* is not definable in phonological terms except by setting up abstract entities which have no justification on the surface apart from the umlauted sound itself. This is still more evident in the case of the *i*-umlaut, since here there are forms which have un-umlauted sounds in front of *i* as in *tali* 'talk, speech' (dat.sg.). This, I think, shows clearly that the *i*-umlaut is not a phonological process, definable in terms of phonetically motivated phonological features, but rather a morphophonemic one, conditioned by inflectional categories. It may turn out that the morphology should contain some statements about the morphological function of the alternations /u/ – /y/ etc., but that, I think, should be called morphophonemics, not phonology; and in what follows it will be assumed that the surface phonemic system described above should be preferred to a more abstract one like:

i	u	iː	uː
e	o	eː	oː
	a		ɑː

It may be added that we would have to make some special arrangements to account for the different results of *i*-umlaut in the long and the short subsystems. The *i*-umlaut of long /ɑː/ would have to give a front *low* vowel [æː], whereas the *i*-umlaut of short /a/ would have to give a front *mid* vowel [e]. Either there will have to be two *i*-umlaut rules, one for the long vowels and another for the short ones, or a special mechanism of some sort to raise the outcome of the *i*-umlaut rule, when applied to /a/, from *[æ] to [e]. An attempt could be made to justify an automatic raising of *[æ] to [e] to eliminate a low front vowel in the short subsystem, on the grounds that there is no low back vowel either, and therefore the feature [±back] has no place in the short low vowels. I have already suggested that the short /a/ was probably a central vowel; however, the long surface phoneme /aː/ seems to have been a back vowel. If some justification of this sort could be found for the raising of *[æ], this latter objection to an abstract analysis is perhaps not so strong, but we notice that the motivation for a raising of *[æ] to [e] is sought in the symmetry of the system and, furthermore, that symmetry is the symmetry of the surface phonemic system. The raising rule would have the task of eliminating *[æ], which could spoil the surface phonemic symmetry. There is a circularity in this, as I hope is obvious. A justification for a complexity in the rule mechanism of a generative analysis is sought in the regularity of a surface phonemic system ('systematic phonetic' representation, in terms of generative phonology), which, according to the generative theory as put forward by Chomsky & Halle (1968), has no significant status, either in the linguistic system or in the descriptive mechanism.

In the system described above, the feature of length seems to have played a central role, but it is important to note that it can not have had equal functional status in all the vowels. In the non-low vowels it seems reasonable to assume that the main difference between the corresponding long and short vowels was indeed length, that is /e/ and /eː/, for example, had approximately the same phonetic qualities apart from length. The same can be said with reasonable certainty about the pairs /i/ – /iː/, /y/ – /yː/, /u/ – /uː/, and /o/ – /oː/. In the low vowels, however, we have no such one-to-one correspondence. There was no long counterpart to short /ǫ/, and there was no short counterpart to long /æː/. It is furthermore likely, as we saw above, that in addition to differing in length, /a/ and /aː/ also differed phonetically with respect to frontness–backness. It is difficult to say anything about the exact phonetic relation between long /øː/ and short /ø/, but in view of their subsequent development, it is quite likely that their phonetic properties, apart from length, were different, since the long /øː/ lost its roundness but the short one retained it in most environments. In the cases of /ǫ/, /ø/, /øː/, /a/, /aː/ and /æː/, then, it is quite possible that by about 1200 the function of length as a distinctive factor had already become less important than in the other vowels.

Garnes (1975b) has suggested that length had already been replaced in the twelfth century as a distinctive feature by differences in quality, the long vowels having diphthongised. This gives us a good reason to evaluate the arguments that can be put forward for or against vocalic length being distinctive around 1200.

As for the orthographic evidence, there are three old manuscripts which show a regular marking of what has usually been assumed to be length in the vowels. These are Stock. Perg. 4° No. 15, the *Book of Homilies* from about 1200, NRA 52, fragments of the oldest saga of Ólafur Haraldsson, from the first half óf the thirteenth century, and GkS 2087 4°, the *Annales Regii*. These manuscripts use an acute accent to distinguish historically-long vowels from historically-short ones. A thorough investigation of the evidence of the *Book of Homilies* was made by Benediktsson (1968), and his conclusion is that the accent was used mainly to mark length, and that irregularity in the notation of forms where the vowel preceded an internal or an external word boundary was caused by the fact that quantity was neutralised in this position at the time of writing of the manuscript. Benediktsson's investigation also shows that the accent was quite frequently used over digraphs denoting the diphthongs /ei/, /ey/ and /au/, its occurrence on these digraphs ranging (according to the different hands) from 24.8 per cent to 75.3 per cent in front of consonants and from 0.0 per cent to 30.0 per cent in front of hiatus or a boundary. These data lead Garnes to propose that the accent was used in the *Book of Homilies*, and also in the later manuscripts, NRA 52 and GkS 2087 4°, not to denote difference in length, but rather diphthongal quality. There are a number of queries one can make concerning this hypothesis.

It is true that the old long vowels /aː/, /oː/, /eː/ and /æː/ (< /øː/, /æː/) became diphthongs in the history of Icelandic. Evidence for this is to be found for /eː/ as early as the thirteenth century in sporadic spellings like *ei* or *ie* in place of the older *e* or *é* spellings. Around 1400 the regular notation for the old /eː/ was either *e* or *ie* (Þórólfsson 1925:xiv–xv, 1929b:233–4). This was interpreted by Benediktsson (1959:298) as showing that /eː/ probably tended quite early to diphthongise to [ei], but in order to avoid a merger with the old diphthong /ei/, it subsequently turned towards [ie] and later became [je]. The Modern Icelandic reflex of this vowel is [jɛ] which is best analysed as a sequence of two phonemes, /j/ + /ɛ/. Evidence for the diphthongisation of /æː/ to its Modern Icelandic reflex [ai] is not to be found until about 1400, according to Þórólfsson (1925:xviii), or even later, around the middle of the fifteenth century (cf. Benediktsson 1977:42). It is important to note that this is only indirect evidence and nothing but a *terminus ante quem* for the diphthongisation.

The evidence is spellings like *dæginn* for older *daginn*. This form has the Modern Icelandic reflex [daijɪn], the main change that took place being a palatalisation of the velar fricative represented in the spelling by *g*. The fact that the symbol *æ* is used in denoting a sequence, phonetically something like [aj], shows that by the middle of the fifteenth century, when the first examples of this type of spelling occur, it must have come to represent diphthongal quality in forms like *sækja*. This could have been going on for quite some time before the sequence [aɣ] beame [aj], which accidentally caused the diphthongisation to show signs in the spelling.

Indirect evidence of a different sort can be put forward to indicate that old /aː/ had started to diphthongise quite early. Old short non-high vowels in front of nasal + a velar (*ng*/*nk* in the spelling) show diphthongal reflexes in most Modern Icelandic dialects, OI *langur*, MI [lauŋɡ̊ʏr], 'long' (masc.). The old high short vowels /i/ and /u/ show here the MI reflexes [i] and [u]: OI *ungur*, MI [uŋɡ̊ʏr] (instead of [ʏŋɡ̊ʏr]), 'young', OI *þing*, MI [θiŋɡ̊] 'parliament' (instead of [θɪŋg]). This has often been taken to indicate that a lengthening took place in these environments before the quantity shift. It is just as likely, however, that the change before *ng*/*nk* was a diphthongisation, the vowels developing a high glide in front of the velar nasal. This is suggested by the fact that the reflex of short /ö/ (< /ǫ/, /ø/) is usually represented in manuscripts that show signs of the change in front of *ng*/*nk* by *au* in these environments, which is the regular symbol for the old diphthong /au/, MI [œy]. Signs of this change before *ng*/*nk* appear as early as around 1300, in that the old short vowel /a/, for example, is represented in the manuscripts by symbols which otherwise denote the old long /aː/. If the change in the old short /a/ before *ng*/*nk* was a diphthongisation, then the employment of the symbols previously only used for the old long /aː/ would seem to indicate that it had begun to diphthongise as early as about 1300. (This was suggested to me by Stefán Karlsson of the Arnamagnæan Institute in Reykjavík.) The high vowels pose no problem for the hypothesis that the change before *ng*/*nk* was a diphthongisation, since the glide that was added was a high one agreeing in roundness with the original vowel; and if the change was indeed a raising of the last part of the vowel, it is only natural that the MI outcome should be fully high vowels /i/, /u/, rather than /ɪ/ and /ʏ/.

It may be added that it is usually assumed that the diphthongisation of the old long vowels must have preceded the quantity shift, both because the diphthongal quality had to be there when length became predictable, to take over its function in the system, and because the essential environment for diphthongisation is usually assumed to be long duration; and the phonetic diphthongisation, it is assumed, must have been completed before the old long vowels started developing shortened allophones.

It is, then, consistent with Garnes' proposal that there must have been a period before the quantity shift was completed when the old long vowels /eː/, /æː/, /oː/ and /ɑː/ were diphthongised, and in that respect it is conceivable that the accents over these vowels denoted diphthongal quality in the early manuscripts. But there is another fact that does not fit her proposal, namely that the high vowels /iː/, /yː/ and /uː/ are still monophthongs in Modern Icelandic, and it is highly unlikely that they were ever anything else. Thus, if Garnes were right in assuming that the accent denoted diphthongal quality, it should have been omitted over the high vowels. This is, however, not the case. It is impossible to interpret the statistics adduced by Benediktsson (1968) as showing any significant difference between the occurrence of the accent over the high and the non-high vowels.

Another fact which speaks against Garnes' proposal is that the author of the *First Grammatical Treatise* (referred to as the First Grammarian) explicitly states that there is a length correlation in the vowels. The passage is translated by Benediktsson as follows:

But even though I do not write more vowel symbols than the vowels that have been found in our language – eighteen made out of the five Latin vowels – it is well to know that there is yet another distinction [*grein*; *KÁ*] in the vowels – both in those that were in the alphabet before, and in those that have now been put in – a distinction which changes the discourse, (according to) whether a letter is long or short, just as the Greeks write a long letter with one shape, and a short one with another. Short *e* they write this way: ε, but the long one like this letter is: η; short *o* in this way: o, but the long one in this way: ω. This distinction, too, I wish to show, because it changes the discourse just like the previous ones, and I shall mark the long ones with a stroke to distinguish them from the short: *far*: *fár*, *rǎmr*: *rǎmr*, *ǫl*: *ǫ́l* . . . [*ǎ* is the symbol used by the First Grammarian to denote a nasalised *a*].

(Benediktsson 1972:218–21)

The most natural interpretation of this is that the First Grammarian is talking about a durational correlation between otherwise similar vowels, and we would need very good grounds for any other interpretation. Garnes tries to cast doubt on the validity of this evidence by arguing that the First Grammarian was 'hard-pressed to come up with minimal pairs' to show opposition between long and short vowels (Garnes 1975b:4). She

mentions that a number of the examples given by the First Grammarian
are not minimal in the strictest, twentieth-century sense. It is
noteworthy, however, that most of these 'suspicious' examples are not
solely concerned with vowel length. Three examples pertain to a length
distinction in consonants, namely *u be*, the names of the letter *u* and *b* as
opposed to *Ubbe*, a man's name; *hǫ dǫ* 'a tall (woman) died' (two words) as
opposed to *hǫddo/*, gen.sg. of *hadda* 'handle' (one word); and *afarar* as
opposed to *affarar*. (It is difficult to say exactly what the words in the last
pair are, since the sentence which presumably followed, illustrating the
meaning, is left out in the only extant manuscript of the treatise;
Benediktsson 1972:244–5.) These three pairs are, as I said before,
intended by the First Grammarian to illustrate the difference between
long and short consonants and have nothing to do with the question
whether length was distinctive in the vowels. Two other examples which
Garnes cites are intended to illustrate opposition between nasality and
non-nasality, namely *í sá* 'one could see through' (literally 'in saw') with a
nasalised long *í* as opposed to *ísa*, acc.pl. of *ís* 'ice', and *þu at* 'you (were)
at' as opposed to *þuat* 'pressed down' with a nasalised *ú* (Benediktsson
1972:218–19). The examples concerned with vowel length are: *seþo* vs
séþo, framer vs *fra mér* and *Goþrøþi* vs *góþ røþi*. The first member of the
first pair is probably the imperative of the verb *séa* 'to see' + the 2p.sg.
pronoun *þú* 'thou'. The second member is assumed to be past 3p.pl. of the
(irregular) verb *sýia* 'nail together'. In this case the vowel of *sé*, which is
historically long, is opposed to another historically long one. This is the
only example which can be said to cause problems, since identical vowels
seem to be used to illustrate a difference in length. The next pair, *framer*
vs *fra mér*, is intended to illustrate the opposition between a short and a
long nasalised *e*. True, the *-mer* in *framer* 'forward, brazen' (masc.pl.) is a
second syllable of a disyllabic word, and therefore presumably
unstressed, whereas *mér* is an independent word, 'me' (dative), but there
is no doubt that the two *e*-vowels were distinct. What probably forced the
First Grammarian to use such a far-fetched minimal pair was the
difficulty of finding a long and a short nasalised vowel in minimal opposition. The third pair, *góþ røþi* vs. *Goþrøþi*, is even less problematic.
This pair is intended to illustrate the distinction between a long /øː/ and a
short /ø/. The first member of the pair is two words, *góþ*, neuter pl. of the
adjective *góþr* 'good' +*røþi*, 'oars', whereas the second is a compound
man's name. Here again, there is no real problem; *-røþi* and *røþi* were
undoubtedly kept apart by short vs long vowels. There may also have

been some differences in stress, one being a second part of a compound and the other an independent word, but there is no doubt that the vowels were distinct. It will be noticed that there is also a distinction in length in the first parts of the examples, that is, between *góþ*, and *Goþ-* of *Goþrøþi*. In this sense, the pair is not minimal, but we notice that it is non-minimal in a special way, since in both vowels it is length that distinguishes, and it may well have seemed appropriate to the First Grammarian to throw in this extra example of the length distinction as a decoration. We can perhaps call *Goþrøþi* vs *góþ rǿþi* a double minimal pair.

To return briefly to the only problematic example, namely *sé þú* vs *séþu*, Benediktsson (1972:138–9, cf. 1968:42–4) has proposed an explanation, according to which the opposition long vs short was neutralised before a hiatus and a boundary. Benediktsson also proposes that the representative of the 'archiphoneme' occurring in the neutralising environment was 'identified with' the short vowels at the time of writing of the *First Grammatical Treatise*, and therefore the First Grammarian could use *sé* with an *e*-sound in neutralised position to illustrate a short vowel opposing a long one. If this explanation is valid, there is no problem. There seems, however, to be something not quite right about assuming that a non-distinctive occurrence of a feature (that is, the feature occurring in environments in which it is redundant) can be used to illustrate the distinctive function of that feature. There may be a solution to this problem. We may very well say that the length distinction was neutralised in front of a hiatus or silence, since no minimal pairs with a short vowel opposing a long one in this environment are found, but it is interesting to see what happens when there is a morphological alternation between forms ending in a vowel and forms with a consonant following. There are many examples of this to be found, for example in nouns with a stem ending in a vowel taking consonantal endings: *tré* 'tree', genitive *trés*. A similar alternation is to be found in weak verbs like *fá* 'paint' when they take the preterite ending *-þa* or the past participle ending *-þ*, as in *fáþa*, *fáþ* 'painted'. Phonologically, we seem to have a forced choice between a distinctively long or a short vowel, unless the morphological boundary played a major role in phonology, which seems rather unlikely, especially in the monosyllabic forms *trés* and *fáþ*. In cases like these, then, we seem to have a morphophonemic alternation between a neither-long-nor-short 'archiphoneme' and a long or a short vowel. The choice between a long or a short correlate of the archiphoneme could go either way; that is, we could either have an alternation: 'archiphoneme'–short vowel or an alternation: 'archiphoneme'–long vowel. In *seþo*, written in one word in the manuscript, we could easily be dealing with such a case. As we saw before, the form consists of the stem of the verb 'to see' + enclitic pronoun -*þo* (or *þú*). In Modern Icelandic the corresponding form is *sjáðu*, where the -*ðu* can be analysed as an ending (cf. Árnason 1974:19) even though it is historically an enclitic pronoun. The same has probably been true of the form *seþo* (cf. Benediktsson 1963b); the -*þo* may have behaved like a regular inflectional ending from the phonological point of view, forcing a choice between a long or a short vowel, and in this particular paradigm the alternation could have become 'archiphoneme' –short vowel. If this were so, then the *e*-sound in *seþo* was a perfectly legitimate short vowel and could be used to demonstrate the distinctive function of length in the *e*-vowels.

Finally, it should be mentioned in conjunction with the evidence from the First Grammarian that Garnes does not maintain that the *distinction* between historically long and short vowels had disappeared, rather that length had been replaced by features of quality as distinguishing marks between the old long–short vowel pairs. In that case, the First Grammarian's 'difficulty' in finding minimal pairs would be just as difficult for Garnes to explain as it would be for those who maintain that length was the distinctive feature. Even if the function previously held by the length feature had been taken over by some qualitative differences at the time the *First Grammatical Treatise* was written, the vowels were still kept apart and the First Grammarian should have had no trouble in finding pairs that showed the distinction. The paradox is that Garnes agrees that the vowels were distinct, but claims that the First Grammarian had difficulty in finding minimal pairs because the distinctive feature(s) was (were) qualitative instead of quantitative as before.

To summarise, then, the testimony both of the *Book of Homilies* and of the *First Grammatical Treatise* seem to agree on a dichotomy which corresponds to that between historically long and short vowels. Furthermore, the First Grammarian explicitly calls this distinction one of length. From this review of the evidence, we have so far found no reason to disbelieve him.

There is still one fact which must not be overlooked, even though it often is, perhaps because it is so obvious. This is that the Icelandic orthography, which was formed in the twelfth century, uses the same symbols to denote long and short corresponding vowels. How can that be explained? The most likely explanation is that they must have been phonologically related. As in Latin writing the main function of the symbols was probably to denote vowel quality, and it seems to be hard to explain why the same symbols were used for /i/ and /iː/, /e/ and /eː/, /o/ and /oː/, and /a/ and /aː/ unless we assume that they had approximately the same quality but were distinguished by a variation in duration.

4.2.2 The prosodic system. 4.2.2.1 *The evidence of metrics.* As mentioned at the beginning of this chapter, there are two aspects to the length problem in Icelandic (and of course the other Scandinavian, and indeed Germanic, languages): the paradigmatic one concerning the vowel system and its distinctive features and phonemes, and the prosodic one concerning the rhythmic structure of the language and syllabic quantity.

As has been said many times, there were four types of combinations of vowels plus consonants theoretically possible at the stages of Icelandic which still had distinctive vowel length. These were: VC, VːC, VC$_2$, VːC$_2$ (C$_2$ denotes two or more consonants, including geminates, analysed as two identical consonants).

From the prosodic point of view it is customary to classify these four types of syllables according to quantity, and then a syllable having a rhyme consisting of long vowel + consonant is grouped together with a syllable consisting of short vowel + long (geminated) consonant or two or more consonants, these being called long or heavy. The syllables consisting of long vowel + long consonant or two or more consonants are sometimes called overlong (hypercharacterised). The syllables of the type VC are called short or light. From the prosodic point of view, the diphthongs are seen to have the same function as long vowels. In terms of morae, the vowels and diphthongs can be said to have had two morae, whereas a short vowel had only one. We thus get the following classification of syllables:[1]

  light (or short): VC *fat* 'a piece of clothing'

  heavy (or long): $\begin{cases} \text{VːC} & \textit{fát} \text{ 'confusion'} \\ \text{VC}_2 & \textit{fatt} \text{ 'erect' (neuter)} \end{cases}$

  hypercharacterised
    (or overlong): VːC$_2$ *fátt* 'few' (neuter)

As a source of evidence for features of the sort just mentioned a prime candidate must of course be metrical rhythm, and naturally metrics of the poetry of different times is commonly cited as evidence in the literature on quantity in Icelandic (see e.g. Þórólfsson 1929a; Karlsson 1964; Benediktsson 1968). It is, however, important to bear in mind (see Benediktsson 1968:46–7) that metrics cannot be taken without comment as direct evidence about linguistic facts, since the metres have rules of their own, and there is not necessarily always a one-to-one correspondence between linguistic elements, such as (for example) stress or quantity, and the rules of metrics, even though they are evidently related.

In discussion of metre and poetic language a distinction is usually made between four 'poetic levels' (cf. Allen 1973:104ff and references), those of 'form', 'structure', 'composition' and 'performance'. 'Form' is said to define the general type of metre, say sonnet or *dróttkvætt*, whereas the term 'structure' is used to refer to the particular patterns (allowed for within the realm of a particular form) that can be seen as characterising particular poems. In a way one could say that the structures are variant representatives of the more abstract and general forms. The level of 'composition' is 'the implementation of the structure in terms of its linguistic realization' (Allen 1973:104), and finally there is the 'performance' of the poem by particular persons at particular times and places. Of prime importance for the present discussion is the relation between linguistic structure and poetic structure; in particular, we will want to understand as well as we can how the poetic system derives its forms and structures from the structures of the everyday language, and conversely how the everyday language is used in the composition of poems, for, as is pointed out by Kuryłowicz (1970:5), one can sometimes speak in terms of 'Regeln der *metrischen Umbildung* von gewissen phonologischen und prosodischen Zügen der Umgangssprache' (emphasis his). All these considerations will complicate our interpretation of metrics as a source of evidence of linguistic phenomena (although they do not necessarily diminish the value of this evidence).

Early modern writers on Old Icelandic metrics, such as Sievers (1893), note a correlation between quantity and stress on the linguistic side and the scansion of poetic text into more-or-less regular feet (*pedes, Füsse*) on the metric side. But Sievers and others noted discrepancies between, for example, linguistic quantity on the one side and its value in the metre on the other. It seems, for instance, that monosyllabic forms of the type VC (short vowel + one consonant) could function both as 'Hebungen' (ictuses) and 'Senkungen' (drops) (Sievers 1893:58) in the Eddic metres.

If we are right in assuming that Old Icelandic had stressed syllables of varying quantity, that means that this variation could be used to create a rhythm based on regular alternations between heavy and light syllables, as was done in classical poetry. We must remember, however, that in all likelihood length was not the only rhythmic or prosodic feature in the language which could be utilised to create poetic rhythm. There is no doubt that stress was also very important. We can then say that Old Icelandic provided two means for poets to create rhythm in their verse: length and stress. They could alternate both long and short syllables, and stressed and unstressed ones. When we study the rhythmic laws of Old Icelandic poetry, we must, then, consider both possibilities. It is possible that one metre based its rhythm on stress alternations, and another on length alternations, and we cannot exclude the possibility that some or all metres used a mixture of both. Or that the two linguistic prosodic features created a basis for 'two metrical schemes in a kind of counterpoint', which Eliot suggested (1942; referred to in Allen 1973:111) created part of the charm in the hexameter poetry of Virgil. Allen describes this as deriving from the presence of both quantity and stress as semi-independent variables in the prosodic system of Latin. We must of course remember, though, that in Icelandic, heavy quantity and stress always coincided temporally within the word whereas this was not the case in Latin; but it seems that the important thing is that both linguistic categories existed and could be used in poetry, perhaps to create a sort of 'tension' (cf. Allen 1973:110–12) in the rhythm.

Old Icelandic poetry is usually divided into two different types, the so-called 'Eddic poetry' and the so-called 'skaldic poetry'. The former is generally considered to be of older origin than the latter, the metres and much of the subject matter being of common Germanic origin. The skaldic poetry, though, is considered to be purely Nordic in origin, although it is often thought to be partly due to Celtic influence. It is the poetry of the (mostly Icelandic) skalds (*skáld* 'poet') who were often employed at the courts of Norwegian kings and made poems about these kings' heroic ventures. These were often recited at the courts for the entertainment of the kings and their warriors. The metres of these poems were much more rigid than the Eddic metres, both rhythmically and as far as rhyme and various other poetic devices are concerned.

The most important mediaeval authority on skaldic poetry is Snorri Sturluson whose 'Háttatal' ('Inventory of Metres'), which forms one part of his *Edda*, most probably was intended as a handbook for poets who wanted to keep up the old tradition of skaldic poetry. 'Háttatal' is considered to have been completed during the winter of 1222–3. It is a

poem about the Norwegian King Hákon Hákonarson and his protector,
Earl Skúli. The poem is so composed as to show the various metres that
could be used in skaldic poetry and had been used, according to Snorri,
since the start of the skaldic tradition in the ninth century. Snorri also
wrote a commentary on the metrics, explaining the peculiarities of each
variant, and these commentaries are interspersed between the stanzas
illustrating the metres. As a rule, one stanza illustrates each metrical
variant.

The basic form for most of skaldic poetry was the so-called *dróttkvæðr
háttr* or *dróttkvætt* (meaning originally 'the court metre') which
consisted of eight lines (*vísuorð*) to each verse. Each line consisted,
according to Snorri, of six syllables. The verses were further decorated
and bound together by internal (to the line) rhyme and alliteration. As an
illustration of the metre Snorri gives the following stanza:

> Lætr, sá's Hákon heitir,
> hann rekkir lið, bannat
> jǫrð kann frelsa, fyrðum
> friðrofs, konungr, ofsa;
> sjalfr ræðr allt ok Elfar,
> ungr stillir sá, milli,
> gramr á gipt at fremri,
> Gandvíkr, jǫfurr, landi.
>
> (cf. Jónsson 1912–15 AII:52 and BII:61)

We are particularly interested in the rhythm; as we see, Snorri is
consistent in having six syllables to a line in this verse, but later he says:[2]

The metres have a licence (*leyfi*) to have syllables *slow* (*seinar*) or *quick* (*skjótar*) so
that there is an increase or a decrease from the correct number of [i.e. of syllables
according to] the rules, and [syallables] may be found so slow that five syllables are
in the second and the fourth line [of each half verse], as is here:

> 7. Hjalms fylli spekr hilmir
> hvatr Vindhlés skatna,
> hann kná hjǫrvi þunnum
> hræs þjóðár ræsa;
> ýgr hilmir lætr eiga
> ǫld dreyrfá skjǫldu,
> styrs rýðr stillir hersum
> sterkr járngrá serki
>
> ('Snorra Edda', p. 218; my translation and italics)

It is evident that Snorri's basic metrical unit is the syllable (*samstǫfun*),
but he makes an interesting distinction between types of syllables, slow

and quick, and it seems likely that he is speaking of our distinction between long and short ('heavy' and 'light') syllables. If we look at lines 2, 4, 6 and 8 of the seventh stanza of 'Háttatal', which Snorri refers to as being exceptional as they only have five syllables, we see that all syllables except the final (unstressed) ones are either of the type VC_2, V:C or V: #. If we, for example, scan the second line with the symbols $-$, denoting a heavy syllable and $\smile$, denoting a light one, we get:

> hvātr Vīndhlēs skatña

We see that all the syllables, except the very last one, are heavy according to the classification above. Similarly, we can scan the fourth line in the following way:

> hræs þjōðār ræsä

and the sixth and eighth lines:

> ǫld dreyrfā skjǫldū
>
> sterkr jārngrā serki

The last two lines call for a minor footnote. They both have second parts of compounds -fá and -grá, ending in a vowel, which we have here scanned as heavy. But, as will be remembered, Benediktsson considers vowels in final position to be phonemically neither long nor short, and about 1200 largely 'identified' with short vowels. If the vowels were phonetically short, the syllables -fá and -grá should perhaps not be metrically heavy. But in the first place, we are not sure that they were phonetically short in every occurrence, and in the second place, in these two forms we have special cases of word-final á. The forms are both plural accusatives of adjectives having stems ending in long /ɑː/, their nominative singular forms being, respectively, fár 'coloured' and grár 'grey' (the -r is a nominative ending). The accusative plural masculine ending for adjectives is -a, and the underlying forms of fá and grá, as they appear in the context above, could then be analysed as /fɑː +a/ and /grɑː +a/; the final vowels of the surface forms could in these cases well have been phonetically long and identified with long vowels, even though otherwise word-final vowels were identified with the short phonemes. In any case, it is quite common for syllables of this type to carry the ictus in skaldic poetry (cf. Benediktsson 1968:42–3).

If we look at the other lines of the seventh stanza, namely 1, 3, 5 and 7, which Snorri seems to consider more regular, we see that they all have two light syllables: the final one of the line and one other, appearing somewhere in the middle of the line. In the first line, we have *fylli*, in the third *hjǫrvi*, in the fifth *hilmir*, and in the seventh *stillir*, all supplying a light syllable, making the total number of syllables Snorri's regular six. This seems to indicate that Snorri had some notion of a rule as to how many heavy and light syllables could occur in one line. If the number was below six, all but the last syllable had to be heavy.

A look at the next stanza of 'Háttatal' supports the hypothesis that quantity of syllables played a role in the *dróttkvætt*-metre. To this stanza Snorri gives the following introduction (again in my translation):[3]

Now, there shall be shown syllables, so quick and put so close to each other, that the length of the line is increased because of it:

    8. Klofinn spyr ek hjalm fyrir hilmis
        hjarar egg, duga seggir;
        því eru heldr, þar er skekr skjǫldu,
        skafin sverð lituð ferðar;
        bila muna gramr, þó at gumna
        gular rítr nái líta,
        draga þorir hann yfir hreinna
        hvatan brand þrǫmu randa

('Snorra Edda', p. 218)

I would like to start the analysis of this stanza by looking at lines 2, 4, 6 and 8, because they have a remarkably regular pattern. They all have seven syllables, and if we scan them in the way described above we get:

    2 hjarar egg duga seggir
    4 skafin sverð lituð ferðar
    6 gular rítr nái líta
    8 hvatan brand þrǫmu randa

If we define each light syllable as having metrically one mora and each heavy syllable as having two, we get the same number of morae in these lines as in the corresponding lines of stanza 8, that is nine. This clearly shows that light and heavy syllables, as I defined them above, had different functions in the *dróttkvætt*-metre; two light syllables could metrically equal one heavy syllable. (This looks like a parallel of the 'resolution' known in Greek, Latin, Old English and other Germanic verse.) This, of course, does not amount to saying that every long (heavy) syllable was twice as long as a short one; we must remember to keep the linguistic system and the metrical one apart. But this gives considerable support to our hypothesis that in Old Icelandic around 1200 there was, prosodically, a difference between heavy and light syllables. This evidence can then be added to what we have established about the paradigmatic distinction between long and short vowels.

The odd-numbered lines of the eighth stanza seem to be more irregular than the even-numbered ones, and it can be said that they are not very typical *dróttkvætt*-lines, far less so than the even-numbered ones. As Snorri says, they contain nine syllables, if everything is counted, but it is very likely that in lines 1, 3 and 5 at least there are examples of fusion of two syllables into one (*bragarmál* in Snorri's terminology). *Spyr ek* of line 1, for example, is probably to be scanned as one syllable, *spyr'k*; *þar er* (or *es*) of line 3 is to be scanned *þar's*; and *þó at* of line 5 to be scanned *þó't*. Thus, in these lines, the number of syllables (and morae) is cut down by one. But there are still more morae than the nine of the even-numbered lines. It is possible that Snorri's comment about syllables being put 'close to each other' applies especially to these lines, but then of course we would have to decide what he means. We may ask whether he is talking about constructions that are allowed for by the rules of the metre, or whether he is showing the sort of 'tension' or licence that is possible without moving out of the *dróttkvætt* form. In fact, as we saw, Snorri uses the term *leyfi* 'licence' to refer to these quantity based variations, and in that case he may have in mind a tension similar to what is often heard in singing when the words do not quite fit the rhythm they are sung to. Anyway, what interests us here is the fact that, apart from the syllables carrying the internal rhyme (rhyming with the penultimate syllable, which is always heavy according to the rules of the *dróttkvætt*-metre), the syllables are light. There are two syllables other than the ones mentioned above which could perhaps be taken as heavy, namely *skekr* and *þó't* (*þó at*). However, these forms probably functioned metrically as light for reasons we need not go into here.

The conclusion to be drawn from this brief look at Snorri's account of the rhythm of the *dróttkvætt*-metre and his practice in using it, is that there is a clear distinction between two types of syllables that had different functions in the metre. This must have been based on some distinction in the prosodic structure of the language, and we may take this as evidence that Old Icelandic had, at the time when Snorri composed 'Háttatal', at least two types of syllable : heavy and light. Another fact which has long been noted in writings on the *dróttkvætt*-metre confirms this. This is that it seems to be an exceptionless rule that the last foot (the last two syllables) of every line must consist of a heavy syllable followed by a light (unstressed). Thus, a line of a *dróttkvætt*-verse could only end in forms like *skatna* (VCC), *þunnum* (VCC), *ræsa* (V:C), *eiga* (V:C or VVC), *réttum* (V:CC) etc. As far as I know, there are no examples of *dróttkvætt*-lines from this period ending in forms like *daga, tala, sonar* etc. (all VC). This rule could hardly be upheld unless there was linguistically a clear distinction between heavy and light syllables.

When this metrical testimony is added to the evidence given by the orthography and the *First Grammatical Treatise* there can hardly be any doubt that a length difference prevailed in the vowels, since a historically-long vowel + one consonant was treated prosodically as heavy, whereas a short vowel + one consonant was treated prosodically as light.

4.2.2.2 *Hypercharacterised syllables*. Before leaving the prosodic aspect of length in Old Icelandic, I will look at the hypothetical distinction made above between heavy and hypercharacterised syllables. We have seen that the evidence of the metrics of skaldic poetry, more specifically that of *dróttkvætt* as described by Snorri Sturluson in the first quarter of the thirteenth century, confirms the distinction between heavy and light syllables. When it comes to the third category of 'overlong' syllables, however, there is no evidence in the poetry that they had a function different from the regular heavy syllables. They could carry the last ictus in the line – we get *réttum, traustar, hárri* etc. (all with V:CC or VVCC) alongside *sennu, leita, gáti* etc. – and I have been unable to find any other signs of their special metrical status in a survey of 1,438 *dróttkvætt*-lines from the tenth to the fourteenth centuries. We cannot automatically say that this shows that there was no prosodic difference in the language between regular heavy and hypercharacterised stressed syllables. Even though there was such a difference in the language, it would not necessarily mean that it had to show up in the rules of the metres used in poetry. But on the other hand it is quite conceivable that these syllables, having underlying long vowels and original diphthongs followed by two or more consonants were in fact phonetically no longer or not significantly longer than the other heavy syllables. It is, for example, quite possible that the underlying long vowels had shorter allophones when followed by two or more consonants than when they were followed by one or none. Whether or not such an allophonic rule existed around 1200, it is certain that at some stage it must have arisen. Something of this sort is needed to account for the shortness of the vowels in the Modern Icelandic forms *ást, stóll* etc.

It is important to note, however, that if such a rule was operative at an early stage, it did not lead to a large-scale restructuring in lexical items, for example so that the shortened long vowels merged with the phonemically short ones. There are only scattered examples of this in words like *gott* (with a Modern Icelandic monophthong /ɔ/: [g̊ɔhtʰ], which is the regular reflex of Old Icelandic short /o/), the neuter of *góður* 'good' with an originally long root-vowel. Similarly, Modern Icelandic *drottning* 'queen' and *drottinn* 'king, lord', both with an [ɔ]-vowel, presuppose a pre-vowel-shift shortening of the /oː/ in *dróttning* and *dróttinn* (both derived from *drótt* 'court, army'). Further, the Modern Icelandic nominative *minn* of the first person possessive pronoun 'mine' (with [ɪ], the MI reflex of OI short /i/) as opposed to the dative *mínum* (with MI [i], the regular reflex of OI /iː/) shows that OI /iː/ must at some stage have become identified with the old short /i/ before the two consonants in the nominative. The main rule, however, is that the old long vowels show the same reflexes in Modern Icelandic as far as quality is concerned, regardless of whether they precede one or two or more consonants: *hvítur* [kfiːtʰʏr] and *hvítt* [kfihtʰ] 'white' (masc. vs neuter) both have vowels with [i]-quality as descendants of old long /iː/.

Even though it does not seem that a shortening of long vowels in front of two or more consonants, making them merge with old short ones, was a regular phonological change that took place before the quantity shift proper, it is still conceivable that such a low-level phonological rule existed quite early. It could have operated without leading to a merger of shortened long vowels with the original short ones, just as soon as there appeared qualitative differences between the corresponding members of the long and short subsystems. As soon as, for example, the short vowels began to lower, as they must have done at some stage (giving e.g. the modern [ɔ] as a reflex of the old short /o/) and the non-high long phonemes began to diphthongise (giving e.g. modern [ou] as the reflex of the long /oː/), it was possible to shorten old long /oː/ before two or more consonants without a general merger with old short /o/. It is perhaps not even necessary to assume a great qualitative difference between the two subsystems for this to be possible. As long as a speaker could unambiguously identify the (underlying) phonological (or lexical) identity of each allophone, a relatively minor phonetic difference would be needed to keep allophones of different phonemes apart (cf. Grundt

1973:139 and *passim*), or they could even have been completely neutralised. Clues of different sorts, other than surface phonetic ones, may have helped the speaker to establish the underlying phonological 'origin' of a surface sound: syntagmatic phonological surroundings of the phone in question or, perhaps even more important, the morphological identity of the form that the sound appears in. It is conceivable that a speaker identified the [o]-sound of, for example, the form *skjótt* 'quickly' (relatively similar to the [o]-sound of *skot* 'a shot') with underlying /oː/ because of the evident morphological relationship with *skjótur* 'quick' (masc.) and *skjót* 'quick' (fem.), which had both underlying and superficial long [o]-sounds. (In terms of features, one can picture this by setting up a special phonetic feature [shortened]. The surface [o]-sound of *skjótt* could then be characterised as [+ long, + shortened] with the feature [+ shortened] added by a phonological rule, whereas the similar [o]-sound of *skot* can be characterised as merely [− long]; [+ long, + shortened] and [− long] may turn out to represent more or less the same phonetic 'reality', but the underlying origin of the two phones may be easily recoverable by phonological or morphological means.) A phonological clue could have been that the [o]-sound of *skjótt* appears in shortening environments for a long vowel, and a morphological clue could have been that *skjótt* is related to *skjót* and *skjótur*.

It seems, then, conceivable that the old long vowels were allophonically shortened in certain environments before the quantity shift proper had taken place, that is, before length was replaced by qualitative features as distinctive between the old short and long vowels. There is, however, one thing which could make it difficult in our case to assume this. As we have seen, the Modern Icelandic reflexes of the old long non-high vowels are diphthongs, and these diphthongs appear both in lengthening and shortening environments. OI *ljótr* and *ljótt* 'ugly' (masc. vs neuter) give MI [ljouːtʰʏr] and [ljouhtʰ], OI *kátr* and *kátt* 'happy' (masc. vs neuter) give MI [kʰauːtʰʏr] and [kʰauhtʰ], OI *kæta* and *kætti* 'make happy' (infin. vs past) give MI [cʰaiːtʰa] and [cʰaihtɪ], and OI *él* and *éls* 'snow shower' (nom. vs gen.) give MI [jɛːl] and [jɛls]. It has long been attested that there seems to be a connection between length and diphthongisation. Long vowels show a greater tendency to diphthongise than short ones. This is true of, for example, Faroese (cf. Rischel 1968; Árnason 1976), many modern Norwegian and Swedish dialects, and indeed of Modern Icelandic, which shows a tendency to diphthongise the long allophones of the mid vowels /ɛ/, /œ/, and /ɔ/ (Garnes 1974b). Similar tendencies show up in German and English. If we try, then, to find a reason or an explanation for the diphthongisation of the Old Icelandic non-high long vowels /æ:/ (</æ:/, /ø:/), /ɑ:/, /e:/ and /o:/, the most obvious feature to connect it with is the long duration of the vowels in question. We can say that the long duration created a favourable environment for diphthong-isation. (We cannot say that length was, or is in general, a sufficient condition for diphthongisation, for example, for the obvious reason that the OI high vowels /i:/, /y:/ and /u:/ did not diphthongise.) Presumably we would explain the diphthongisation by assuming that the longer the duration of a vowel, the greater the chances that an internal variation in the quality might occur, for example by the features of the sound, instead of being in a 'simultaneous syntagm', becoming to some extent temporally ordered (cf. H. Andersen 1972).

If we carry this over to the question of allophonic shortening of underlying long vowels, we see that, as soon as the reflexes of the old diphthongs were shortened to any significant degree, the length as a favourable environment for diphthongisation had disappeared for the (conceivably) short allophones, and there seems to be no reason why the [o]-sound of *skjótt* should diphthongise. But the fact is that it did. We may seem to be forced to conclude that phonetic diphthongisation of the old long vowels had occurred before the shortening of long vowels in front of two or more consonants took place.

This would seem to mean that if a shortening of long vowels had taken place around 1200, then the diphthongisation had taken place earlier; and in the synchronic grammar shortening was 'ordered after' diphthong-isation, if both were active phonological processes. But it may not be necessary to assume this. It was seen above that the phonetic environment for diphthongisation must have been one of length, and in the discussion that followed it was tacitly assumed this meant that all and only the phonetically long vowels should diphthongise. But this only follows if we assume that all phonological change has to be explained in phonetic terms and that phonological change is purely additive. It may well be that this is too narrow a view of linguistic change. Under this interpretation, the change is 'Markovian' in the sense that it is assumed that only phonetic surface forms can be referred to in accounting for changes and no sort of underlying systematic relations are taken into account. But it is conceivable that we have changes that behave like 'transformations' in that they affect and operate on parts of the phonology other than the mere surface forms. Within generative phonology the question of whether phonological change is purely additive, in the sense that only surface forms can change, has often been formulated as the question whether changes only occur in the 'last rules' of the phonology. It is theoretically possible for rules to be 'added in the middle of grammars' as the question has been put by King (1974). It is, then, theoretically possible that diphthongisation took place in other places than the ones where the phonetic surface conditions, which probably triggered it off in the first place, were present. This could have happened in the following way: Assume that the Icelandic vowel system had two subsystems, kept apart by a feature which we can call length. There were quality differences between the long and short vowels in addition to the difference in duration. The long vowels had shortened allophones in front of two or more consonants. Some of the phonetically long vowels (the non-high ones) started to diphthongise. We assume that a phonetic condition for the diphthongisation was the long duration of the vowels. Phonetically speaking, this environment did not exist in shortened long vowels, but these vowels were qualitatively different from the phonemically short ones, and when the diphthongisation was phonemicised, the phonetically shortened long vowels /aː/, /eː/, /oː/ and /æː/ became underlying diphthongs, because they belonged to the same phonemes as the corresponding long (unshortened) variants.

The account given above of the possible way in which phonological diphthongisation historically followed allophonic shortening of long vowels in front of two or more consonants hinges on the phrase 'belonged to the same phoneme'. It must be assumed that if diphthongisation did not take place until after the old long vowels had developed shortened allophones, then, when the underlying forms of the still long allophones became diphthongs, the underlying forms of the shortened allophones became diphthongs too. This could only take place if the shortened long vowels still belonged to the same phonemes as the long vowels. 'Belonging to the same phoneme' may be taken to mean 'having the same underlying features', and that brings us back to the feature that divided the old short and long subsystems. I have hitherto called this feature 'length', but since I have alluded to the possibility that the 'long' vowels had both long and short allophones, one may well ask whether a different term is not suitable. Are we perhaps forced to assume that as soon as long and short allophones of the old long vowels started to appear, the feature length must have been replaced in the old long vowels by some other feature or features distinguishing, for example, old /a/ from old /aː/?

This is basically only a terminological question as to what we name the 'feature' that distinguishes between the old long and short vowels after duration had become predictable in some environments. It has been suggested by Sigmundsson (1970:321) that the label 'tense' should be used to distinguish between the old long and short systems at this stage. This may at first glance seem a sensible thing to do, but the trouble is that inventing a new term does not in this case bring us much closer to any truth. We have already seen that it must be assumed that there was, prosodically, a difference between heavy and light syllables at the beginning of the thirteenth century. Syllables like *fát* were heavier than syllables like *fat*. The heavy quantity of the former syllable must stem from the length of the vowel, so, whatever name we use for the feature, among its phonetic correlates must be long duration, at least when not followed by two or more consonants. We have also seen that most probably there were differences other than length between the old long vowels and the corresponding short ones. Whether we distinguish between these categories with the term 'length' or 'tenseness' probably does not make much difference, since in any case there will have to be secondary features derivable from the underlying abstract one. If we call the vowels 'tense', we will have to set up a mechanism to account for vocalic length and quality, sometimes diphthongal, sometimes monoph-thongal etc., and perhaps also for variation in syllabic quantity. If we call the vowels 'long', the diphthongal quality will also have to be predicted by some low level phonetic rules.

Rather than choose one or the other term for this mysterious feature right away (see §6.5.1 for further discussion), I would like to summarise what we can already say about the state of the vowel system and the prosodic structure of Old Icelandic about 1200. The evidence reviewed above strongly speaks against the quantity shift being completed. The First Grammarian explicitly speaks of long and short vowels, and the rules for the rhythm of the *dróttkvætt*-metre seem to have been defined, to some extent at least, on the basis of a distinction between heavy and light syllables. This must mean that, for example, syllables like *dag(a)* and *vit(a)* still remained light at this stage and that a lengthening of the vowel had not yet taken place. There is, however, a possibility that, when followed by two or more consonants, the old long vowels had shortened allophones. Yet these shortened allophones, if they existed, did not generally merge with the corresponding short vowels, but remained allophones of the long vowels. For this to have been possible we must assume that there was not a one-to-one correspondence in terms of quality between the two systems, and that there were qualitative differences, though not necessarily significant ones, between the corresponding members of the long and short subsystems. It is likely that by about 1200, or shortly afterwards, there was already a slight difference in quality between, for example, /i/ and /iː/, the short vowel probably being lower than the long one. Similarly, a difference in quality must have prevailed between /o/ and /oː/. The short /o/ was probably somewhat lower than the long /oː/, and it is further quite probable that the long vowel was somewhat diphthongised. The relationship between the two subsystems, after the merger of /ø/ and /ǫ/ into /ö/ (around 1200) and of /æː/ and /øː/ into /æː/ (around 1250), is illustrated in table 6. In this

TABLE 6. *Relationship between the long and short subsystems, c. 1250*

Front				Back		
Unround		Round				
Long	Short	Long	Short	Long	Short	
/iː/ [iː]	/i/ [ɪ]	/yː/ [yː]	/y/ [ʏ]	/uː/ [uː]	/u/ [ʊ]	*High*
/eː/ [eʲː]	/e/ [ɛ]		/ö/ [ǫ]	/oː/ [oᵘː]	/o/ [ǫ]	
or [ⁱeː]						
/æː/ [æʲː]						
		Low central unround: /a/ [a]		/ɑː/ [ɑºː]		*Low*

system, an allophonic shortening did not have to lead to a restructuring in the lexical phonology. But if we assume that such an allophonic rule existed, we have to think of the (phonological) diphthongisation as a rather complicated process. If the diphthongisation of the low vowels was not well established and incorporated into the phonological system, but just a minor phonetic feature conditioned by the length of the vowels, we would expect the shortened long vowels not to diphthongise, since there the conditioning factor, namely long duration, was not present. But if we can assume that the phonological diphthongisation consisted in replacing underlying long (but sometimes phonetically shortened) non-high vowels in some cases by underlying diphthongs, it is theoretically possible that an allophonic shortening was an active phonological process before the diphthongisation became phonologised.

In a final note to this section we may observe that there are other factors, apart from the conceivable allophonic shortening of long vowels before heavy consonant clusters, that suggest a tendency for eliminating hypercharacterisation or overlength in stressed syllables. Manuscript spellings show that a distinction was not made between a long (or geminate) and a short consonant in front of another consonant. In early thirteenth-century manuscripts, inverse spellings like *bliɴdom* (majuscules were often used to denote long consonants) for *blindom* 'blind' (dat.pl.) are quite common. This must mean that the difference between long and short /n/ was neutralised in front of a consonant, that is, the forms *renndr* past participle of *renna* 'run' and *rendr* 'rimmed' (derived from the noun *rönd* 'rim') were homophonous. The most plausible explanation of this is that the long postvocalic /n/ was shortened in front of another consonant. In this way, instead of a sequence VCCC, we have VCC which is consistent with canonical heavy quantity in the same way as a form with an underlying long vowel shortened before two consonants.

4.3 From Old to Modern Icelandic

As we have seen, one part of the quantity shift was that the old short stressed vowels lengthened when followed by one consonant. (It is unlikely that vowels were ever phonemically short in forms like *bú* 'a household', *búa* 'to live' where no consonant followed.) We thus have in Modern Icelandic *fat* [faːtʰ] and *fata* [faːtʰa] with long [a]-vowels as reflexes of the old short /a/. In this section I will turn to the question of how or when the short vowels lengthened and how this lengthening was related to the shortening of long vowels discussed in the previous section. The questions which will be dealt with can be summarised as follows:

(a) Did the lengthening occur at the same time in monosyllables and in polysyllabics; that is, did the root vowel of *fat* lengthen at the same time as that of *fata*?

(b) When did the change (or changes) take place?

A third question which I will have occasion to consider in this section is:

(c) Why and how did the change(s) take place?

This last question is obviously related to the other two, and it will have to be borne in mind when dealing with the questions of (relative) chronology, although I will leave the main discussion of it for chapter 5.

4.3.1 The term 'quantity shift'. In works on the history of Icelandic phonology the quantity shift is usually referred to without comment as if it were one historical change which took place at some (known or unknown) definite point in time (cf. Þórólfsson 1929a; Benediktsson 1959, 1963a, 1968; Karlsson 1964). The term has been used to refer to the 'disappearance of the quantity correlation' in vowels (Benediktsson 1959:300), and the reduction of the number of syllable types from four to two (of the four types of stressed syllable: VC, V:C, VCC and V:CC ..., only two remain: V:C and VCC...) or from three to one (the hypercharacterised (or overlong) and the light (or short) syllables were eliminated, and now all stressed syllables are heavy). I have nowhere seen a comment suggesting that the quantity shift was a complex of changes, which should each be dealt with separately. This of course does not mean that everyone believes that it was a single change; in fact there have been very few detailed comments made about the nature of the change.

Regardless of what has been done before, we will obviously have to concern ourselves with this question: Was the quantity shift really a shift that took place in one step? Our superficial survey of the development in the other Scandinavian languages and our brief look at German and English have shown that changes like the components of the quantity shift do not necessarily have to occur in a block. The Norwegian dialect of Setesdal has retained long vowels and diphthongs in front of two or more consonants, the one spoken in Gudbrandsdal has had no lengthening of short vowels, and the Tinn dialect has had lengthening only in monosyllables. This shows that each component can occur without the others occurring at the same time; one could say that each part is a perfectly 'legitimate' sound change. Old long vowels could shorten in front of two consonants without a lengthening of short vowels taking place, and short vowels could lengthen in monosyllables without a lengthening in disyllabics taking place at the same time. The development in Danish shows that it was also possible for short vowels to lengthen in disyllabics by an 'open syllable lengthening', without a lengthening in monosyllables taking place. (See Weinstock 1975 for a survey of the development of quantity in the Scandinavian languages.) All this will obviously have to be borne in mind when the Icelandic quantity shift is studied.

It is also fruitful to abstract questions of a more general nature from the sort of comparative or direct empirical evidence we may have at our disposal, and ask not only how such a change as the quantity shift could have taken place, but also, from the point of view of some sort of 'theory of linguistic change', what kind of a change it is likely to have been. Apart from considerations of similarity with the development in the other Scandinavian languages and the direct evidence we can produce, we can ask, for example, whether it is likely that the loss of the length correlation in vowels and the prosodic change from three quantities of stressed syllables to one took place 'overnight', that is more or less at the same time. Or is it more likely that a number of changes 'conspired' to give the results mentioned above (cf. Lass 1974)? Such a question cannot be answered simply, since it will depend on what sort of model of linguistic change we believe in; and we are far from being able to say that we have at our disposal a well-motivated and explicit theory. If we had an adequate theory of linguistic change, one way of answering the general question posed above would be to feed the two alternatives, the one assuming that everything happened at the same time and the other assuming that we are dealing with a historical conspiracy, into an 'evaluation measure' incorporated into our theory. Given the relevant data and the two alternative hypotheses, the evaluation measure should tell us which alternative is 'more highly valued' and therefore more likely to be the correct one. Even though we are not lucky enough to have at our disposal such an explicit theory of linguistic change, there is nothing to prevent us from guessing which of the alternative models for the quantity shift, the 'overnight alternative' or the 'conspiracy alternative', is likely to be more highly valued on such an evaluation measure (or whether they would perhaps get the same marks, that is be equally likely or unlikely; or simply whether the question is undecidable).

At least three kinds of consideration bear on the problem of forming an adequate theory of linguistic change, and more specifically of forming an evaluation measure for the naturalness of linguistic changes. Firstly, we must consider the extralinguistic context in which language operates; in connection with sound change, we must, for example, consider which model for a particular change is most easily relatable to phonetic reality. In other words, we should form our general theory in such a way as to be able to evaluate the phonetic plausibility of individual models of changes. Secondly, we must bear in mind considerations of formalism. We may prefer one model of a particular change to others on the grounds that the one we shoose is, say, simpler to state within the general framework in which we are working. It may, for example, require fewer rules or fewer symbols than others. Criteria of this sort are of course useless unless we can be certain that our formal framework has some empirical content, and that simplicity in the description reflects linguistic naturalness or simplicity. This brings us to the third type of consideration, which is our knowledge of the *structure of language*. Obviously, our ideas about language structure will have to be kept as clear as possible of bias from particular descriptive models and formalisms, since in synchronic linguistics the models are only attempts to describe language structure; they are merely put forward hypothetically. But if we can be reasonably certain that we have established some facts about the synchronic structure of language in general (linguistic universals) or about a particular language at some synchronically defined stage, we will want statements which we make about language change to be compatible with these facts, and we can also hope that these facts may help us to make discoveries about linguistic change. In this way we can say that knowledge about linguistic structure will have an effect on the way we evaluate hypotheses about linguistic change. In using this sort of evidence in evaluating hypotheses about language changes, we must, of course, make sure that the things we claim to know about the structure of lanaguage in general, universal grammar, or the grammars of particular languages, are relevant to the historical changes with which we are dealing.

I have set up a choice between two models for the quantity shift, the 'overnight alternative' and the 'conspiracy alternative'.[4] We can start by trying to imagine how we can relate the two alternatives to phonetic reality. We can, for example, ask what phonetic conditions could have triggered the change, or changes (depending on which alternative we eventually choose). I have already suggested that the shortening part of the length rule in Modern Icelandic probably stems originally from an allophonic shortening of long vowels in front of two or more consonants. In phonetic terms, I have tried to make such a hypothesis plausible by assuming that a phonetic segment tends to adapt to its surroundings as much as its distinctive function and underlying features allow. If we assume that a stressed vowel and the consonantism following it formed some sort of unit, perhaps defined by stress (a 'phonetic syllable'), it seems, in some way at least, to make sense to expect the duration of the vowel to alternate according to the number of consonantal segments following it; that is, if an underlyingly long vowel were followed by two or more consonants, one could expect it to be relatively shorter than when followed by only one consonant, and shorter than implied by its underlying features. If we look at the beginning of the shortening of the long vowels in this way, we do not have to assume that it had any connection with a lengthening of vowels in other environments.

Looking at the lengthening of short stressed vowels in front of one consonant and trying to relate it to phonetic reality, we can suggest that when the vowels bore stress, they tended to become longer than would be directly predicted by their underlying features. This assumption derives considerable plausibility from the fact that experiments have shown a close connection between stress and duration of vowels in a great number of languages (cf. Lehiste 1970:125–42 and references). This lengthening of vowels could well take place without the shortening of long vowels in front of two or more consonants taking place at the same time.

From the phonetic point of view, then, there is no need to assume that these two phonetic changes occurred at the same time, and it seems quite likely that they came up at different times.

From the formal point of view there is an important difference between the strength of the claims made by our two alternative hypotheses. The 'overnight' hypothesis makes a stronger claim, in that it assumes that the two changes occurred together. The 'conspiracy' alternative makes a weaker claim; it is neutral with respect to time, and makes no claims as to whether the changes took place at different times or at the same time. The discussion of the possible phonetic conditions for the lengthening of short vowels and the shortening of long ones does not seem to offer any support for the stronger claim made by the 'overnight' hypothesis. It can thus be said that the 'conspiracy' hypothesis is a better theory of the relation in time between the lengthening of short vowels and the shortening of long ones, since it does not make assumptions that cannot be justified. In the absence of any evidence to the contrary, it seems, then, from this point of view, that it is preferable to assume that there was no connection in time between the lengthening of short vowels and the shortening of long ones. The dating of these two changes is therefore purely a matter of investigation using any external evidence we may find. I am not, of course, saying categorically that the two changes did not occur at the same time, but that there is no more reason for us to expect that they did so than to expect them to have taken place, say, six decades apart.

Considerations of rule writing have little value here, since the significance occasionally assigned to notational formalism has clearly shown itself to be unjustified at this stage (cf. e.g. Chen 1976:211ff for clear examples where considerations of notational simplicity lead to either clearly wrong or to unsatisfactory conclusions in historical linguistics).

We seem to have the means of formalising, at least partly, both the 'overnight' and the 'conspiracy' hypotheses about the relation between lengthening and shortening of stressed vowels. The 'overnight' hypothesis could be formalised along the same lines as a two-sided transformation (with a lengthening and a shortening part) of the kind set up in chapter 2 (p. 51) for the synchronic length-rule in Modern Icelandic. The 'conspiracy' hypothesis could be formalised simply as a set of rules with their chronological order either left unmarked (if we do not know when the changes took place) or marked by the dates we can put on them using external evidence. I shall not embark on the, to me, hopeless task of trying to decide which of the alternative hypotheses is formally simpler. A simplicity or naturalness measure for a formalism will have value only in as far as we can show that it fits a certain amount of well-established linguistic data. And the sort of data we should be looking for are facts about events like the quantity shift. We shall, therefore, find justification for one or the other formalism in facts that can be established about the quantity shift, but not vice versa.

It seems, then, that the most sensible thing to do is to choose the 'conspiracy' alternative, that is to make no *a priori* assumptions about the relative chronology of the shortening of old long vowels and the lengthening of old short ones. It may well be true, as I have suggested, that the old short vowels had already shortened by about 1200. If we now examine the lengthening of short vowels, we will recall that in related languages a lengthening could take place in monosyllables without a lengthening occurring at the same time in polysyllables, and vice versa. It seems, then, plausible that this was the way things happened in Icelandic. It is theoretically possible that the lengthening took place in two steps. Like the question of the chronological order of the shortening of long vowels with respect to the lengthening of short ones as a whole, this is of course an empirical question. It may be interesting, however, to consider whether there is something in the nature of the lengthening change (or changes) which would lead us to expect one order rather than the other; that is, whether it is likely that the short vowels lengthened simultaneously in monosyllables and polysyllabics, or whether one lengthening preceded the other in time. It has already been suggested that stress had something to do with the lengthening. We have no evidence as to whether the stress pattern of monosyllables and polysyllabics was in any way different at those periods when the lengthening must have taken place. It is perhaps permissible to speculate, though, that the monosyllables would have had more stress on their only syllable than, for example, the disyllabics had on the first of their two syllables. It was seen (§3.2) that an explanation along these lines was adduced for vowel balance and other phenomena in Norwegian dialects. We have absolutely no indication that this was the case in Icelandic, but, should there have been a difference in the time at which the two lengthenings occurred, it would not be surprising if the lengthening started earlier in monosyllables. If this were indeed the case, the lengthening in Icelandic would show more similarity to that in Norwegian and Swedish than to the lengthening in Danish, German and English. This would conform with the general fact that Modern Icelandic, Faroese, Norwegian and Swedish have all developed the same quantity system.

Although we have more or less discounted the significance of formal considerations of rule writing, we may mention that it seems, in some sense at least, to be simpler from that point of view to assume that all stressed syllables lengthened at the same time. This is so because it takes up less space on paper and fewer symbols to write down a single rule like:

$$V \longrightarrow V : / \_\_ C^1$$
$$[+\text{stress}]$$

which describes a lengthening of all non-long stressed vowels in front of a single consonant, than to write the two rules:

$$V \longrightarrow V : / \_\_ C \#$$
$$[+\text{stress}]$$

and

$$V \longrightarrow V : / \_\_ CV$$
$$[+\text{stress}]$$

with different datings. But it is highly unlikely that this has any significance in this context.

It remains, then, purely a matter of empirical investigation to find out whether lengthening of vowels was a single historical change (whatever that means) or whether it took place in two steps, separated by some time interval. Both alternatives are conceivable, and it is difficult to say which one is 'more natural' and should be 'more highly valued' in a general theory of linguistic change, and therefore more to be expected.

4.3.2 Dating the changes. In the foregoing, I have touched on some 'internal arguments' that could be used in dealing with the quantity shift, its nature and chronology. In other words, I have tried to imagine what sort of assumptions we would make about it in the absence of any external, philological evidence. In particular I have tried to relate possible hypotheses about the change to phonetic reality. In the present section I will examine the external evidence that can be found. This evidence will come in the main from poetry of different periods or, more specifically, metrics. This is virtually the only evidence we can use, since the orthography of texts, which often can give information about phonological development and can help to date changes, was not affected in any drastic way by the quantity shift, as there was no change in the phonemic inventory in the sense that phonemes merged or split, and the same graphemic system could be used before and after the change; only the phonetic value of the symbols was changed.[5]

We have seen that, judging from the situation in the Norwegian and Swedish dialects which still have not completed the quantity shift, the short vowels seem to have lengthened earlier in monosyllables than in polysyllabics in continental Scandinavian. On the other hand, we saw that in Danish the short vowels only lengthened in polysyllabics, old short monosyllables still being light.

In relation to our knowledge of the other Scandinavian languages, it will now be interesting to see whether we can discover how the Icelandic short vowel lengthening proceeded, that is whether it proceeded in the continental Scandinavian way or in the Danish and West Germanic way, or whether Icelandic took a third alternative, for example lengthening all short stressed vowels at more or less the same time.

4.3.2.1 *The evidence of 'dróttkvætt'.* We have already seen that the *dróttkvætt*-metre seems to have had a rhythm which, in part at least, could be defined in terms of rules for alternations of heavy and light syllables. This can be taken to confirm that around 1200 there was a linguistic difference between these, with the light syllables consisting of an old short vowel followed by no more than one consonant. Of equal importance to us now is the fact that as soon as there was a change in the prosodic structure of the language, this was liable to show up in the poetry. For instance, if a lengthening took place in old light syllables, they could take on the function previously only performed by heavy ones. We saw, for instance, that in the *dróttkvætt*-metre the penultimate syllable of each line always had to be heavy. This is a virtually exceptionless rule in the oldest poetry. The last foot of the line is always a 'long-stemmed' disyllabic word, i.e. forms like *manni, hestum, æsir, nóttu* etc.; 'short-stemmed' words like *tala, bera, kona* etc. could not stand in this position.

Consequently, if at some later time exceptions to this rule are found – for example, *tala* occurs as the last foot of a line – this must mean either that there has been a change in the rules of the metre, or that the first syllable of *tala* has become heavy so that it can carry the last ictus of the line.

Quantity played a further role in the *dróttkvætt*-metre, as we have seen, in that there was at least a tendency to keep the number of morae (cf. above, p. 112) in each line constant, granted that two light syllables could have the same value as one heavy syllable (two morae). A very common type of *dróttkvætt*-line is one that has a regular alternation between heavy stressed and light and/or unstressed syllables, thus:

> undrask ǫglis landa ('Þormóðr Kolbrúnarskáld', a *lausavísa*; cf. Jónsson 1912–15 A1 :288)

Using the moraic measure, we can scan this line as having nine morae. It can also be analysed as consisting of three feet, each a trochee. It is perhaps worth noting that if we assume that the rhythm was based on quantity alternations, it can be represented in musical notation, assuming that it is a 3/4 rhythm:

| ♩ ♪ | ♩ ♪ | ♩ ♪ |
| undrask | ǫglis | landa |

The number of this type of *dróttkvætt*-lines is endless. I will cite here only a few:

> olli Ólafr falli ('Erfidrápa Ólafs helga' 1.3)
> mildings máls, en guldu (*ibid.* 2.7)
> Rauð í rekka blóði (*ibid.* 14.1)
> Meinalaust í mínu (*ibid.* 25.3)
> Hǫrða valdr of faldinn ('Hákonarflokkur' 2.2)
> Ríkr gaf hlenna hneykir (*ibid.* 5.1)
> Heim kom hilmir Rauma (*ibid.* 9.5)

(For reference to the texts see below p. 131.)

Another very common type of *dróttkvætt*-line is the following:

> alvaldr skipum haldit ('Hákonarflokkur' 1.2)

In this line, instead of having a regular alternation between heavy and light syllables we have two consecutive heavy syllables followed by two consecutive light ones. This can also be represented in the following way:

| ♩ ♪♪ | ♪♪ | ♩ ♪ |
| alval | dr skipum | haldit |

If we count the morae of this line, we see that we still have nine, only now they are distributed differently over the words in the line. Further examples of this type of scansion are:

> tāllaūst vīðŭ bālă ('Erfidrápa Ólafs helga' 1.2)
> sŏkn strīðs fy̆rŭm rīðă (*ibid.* 1.6)
> ūthlaūpŭm grăm kaūpăst (*ibid.* 4.2)
> hănn sy̆fðĭ svá þy̆fðĭr (*ibid.* 5.4)
> raūð brūnăn hjǫr tūnŭm (*ibid.* 14.8)
> aūðmīldr săkăr gīldĭ ('Hákonarflokkur' 2.4)
> Upplǫnd fărĭt brǫndŭm (*ibid.* 3.6)
> vīkeīds gĭafĭr rīkŭm (*ibid.* 9.2)

A third type of line, which is also very common, is exemplified in the eighth stanza of Snorri's 'Háttatal':

> hjărăr egg dŭgă seggĭr (etc., cf. p. 112)

Here, instead of the line starting with a heavy syllable, it starts with two light ones, but the number of morae is still the same. Further examples are:

> snărĭr fŭndŭst þăr þrændă ('Erfidrápa Ólafs helga' 11.3)
> jǫfŭr măgnăr gŭð făgnă (*ibid.* 25.2)
> sŭmĭr skŭndŭðŭ ŭndăn ('Hákonarflokkur' 2.8)
> hvătĭr fŭndŭ þat skătnăr (*ibid.* 9.6)

If *dróttkvætt*-lines do in fact follow this rule as to the overall length of the line, counted in morae, they provide good evidence for the prosodic structure of the language. In the same way that, when forms like *tala* are found to be regularly functioning as the last foot of a line, we suspect a change has already taken place either in the rules of the metre or in the underlying language, so, when a line occurs with too few morae according to our principle, we suspect that it was composed after the lengthening of the vowel in old light syllables has taken place. For example a line like:

> hvatir fundu skatnar

which is exactly like the preceding line except that one light monosyllable is removed so that the line only has eight morae, would arouse suspicion: only if the first syllable of *hvatir* is taken as heavy does the line fit our principle.

In search of evidence for the lengthening of old short vowels I will, therefore, examine some *dróttkvætt*-poetry from different periods for signs of changes in the pattern described above.

To do this I have investigated the following material:

(a) 'Glymdrápa' by Þorbjörn hornklofi from about 900 (Jónsson 1912–15 AI:22–4) (64 lines).

(b) *Lausavísur* (occasional stanzas) composed in the *dróttkvætt*-metre and ascribed to Egill Skallagrímsson in 'Egils saga' (Jónsson 1912–15 AI:48–59). These allegedly date from the tenth century, but the authenticity of some of them has been questioned (340 lines).

(c) 'Erfidrápa Ólafs helga' by Sigvatr Þórðarson, from about 1040 (Jónsson 1912–15 AI:257–65) (206 lines).

(d) 'Hákonarflokkur' by Sturla Þórðarson, probably composed in the years 1263–4 (Jónsson 1912–15 AII:124–7) (84 lines).

(e) 'Pétrsdrápa', an anonymous poem from the fourteenth century (Jónsson 1912–15 AII:500–8) (424 lines).

(f) 'Guðmundardrápa' by Einar Gilsson from the fourteenth century (Jónsson 1912–15 AII:397–404) (320 lines).

This makes a total of 1,438 lines.

As already stated, we will be looking for lines where, according to the classification given above (p. 107), light syllables seem to function metrically as if they were heavy. Obviously, we cannot take every breach of the old rules as evidence of change; we will have to allow for a certain amount of variation in the use of the metres.

Not only is it possible that poets varied in their versificatory skills, but also that a certain amount of deviation (*leyfi*) from the norm may have been used for artistic purposes, creating agreeable 'tension' in the rhythm. Indeed, since our knowledge of the rhythm is only indirect (as, we have no way of knowing exactly how the *dróttkvætt*-poems sounded in performance), our metrical schemes are only circumstantial guesses. What we find statistically most common may give false clues as to the inner structure of the *dróttkvætt*-form; and what seem deviants from the norm, from our point of view, may be quite regular or have served some purpose in the rhythm unknown to us. In order to get some idea as to how much deviation to allow for before drawing conclusions about linguistic or metrical changes, the first three items on the list of material above were chosen from periods when we have already assumed that the lengthening of old short vowels had not taken place.

In evaluating the evidence of the metrics, we must of course also keep in mind that any change we detect in the correspondence between linguistic forms and metrical function may have arisen from either a change in the language or from a change in the metrical rules. In the case of the *dróttkvætt*-metre, however, it would seem unlikely that the metrical rules could be changed in order to allow light syllables to fulfil the function previously held only by heavy syllables. Alternation between these two types of syllable appears to have been one of the basic characteristics of the metre, and a change in the rules of *dróttkvætt* giving light and heavy syllables the same value would seem to be nothing less than the abandonment of the basic principle on which the rhythm was based and the creation of a more or less new metre based on new rhythmic rules.

Let us start by looking at the older poetry. In the first three items on the list, there were twenty-six lines in all where the number of morae (counted in the way described above) is too low, and where a historically light syllable would have to be interpreted as heavy in order to make the line conform to the pattern. The total number of lines considered was 610, so that the percentage of lines potentially indicating a lengthening in light syllables is 4.3. In my investigation of 'Hákonarflokkur' by Sturla Þórðarson from shortly after the middle of the thirteenth century I found no lines which could be interpreted as showing signs of a lengthening. The total number of lines was eighty-four.

In the fourteenth-century poetry the results were the following: The total number of lines considered was 744. Of these, twenty-one had too few morae according to our system, and could therefore conceivably be taken to indicate that a lengthening had taken place. The percentage is 2.8, lower than for the poetry from the tenth and eleventh centuries.

Even though these statistics seem unequivocally to indicate that no change had taken place in the period between the eleventh and the fourteenth century, it is worth mentioning that practically all the 'deviant' examples from both before and after 1200 involve monosyllabic words. (There are a few cases, particularly in Egill's poetry, of disyllabics, or monosyllables that cannot be explained by cohesion; cf. below. But it seems that they may be discarded as insignificant on statistical grounds or as irregularities in the metre at the earlier stages.) For most cases, the assumption of heavy quantity for old light monosyllables gives the right number of morae. Typical examples are:

> ek bar sauð af nauðum (a *lausavísa* by Egill Skallagrímsson: 33.8)

where the short stem *ek* 'I' would seem to have to be taken as heavy to get a regular - - ᵛ - - ᵛ scansion, and:

> barðisk vel sá's varði (*ibid.* 8.3)

where *vel* 'well' will have to be taken as heavy. (It is assumed that the form *sá's* (contracted from *sá es*) is 'metrically unstressed' and therefore cannot carry an ictus.)[6] This might perhaps lead one to suggest that the monosyllables had already undergone a lengthening in the tenth century (if the poetry is authentic). But if we look more closely at the data, this becomes less plausible. In the examples from the oldest poetry ('Glymdrápa', Egill's *Lausavísur* and Sigvatr's 'Erfidrápa'), these light syllables are always followed by words beginning in consonants, and it has been suggested (cf. Craigie 1900:370) that such light monosyllables could carry a full ictus if they were followed by consonants. This would then be an instance of 'cohesion' between words similar to that which is commonly found in Latin and Greek poetry (cf. Kuryłowicz 1970:7; Allen 1973:25.). The sequences *ek bar* and *vel sá's* could be pronounced as one phonological 'chunk' creating a heavy consonantism following the short vowel, which made the syllable able to carry an ictus.

In the younger poetry, 'Guðmundardrápa' and 'Pétrsdrápa', the situation is not exactly the same, since out of the twenty-one examples apparently involving light syllables carrying a full metrical ictus, only fourteen are explainable as results of cohesion, two involve disyllabics, and five involve monosyllabics followed by vowels. The examples involving monosyllables followed by vowels are all from 'Pétrsdrápa'. They are:

> faðir gat *son* án sáði (2.3)
> brjóst ok *bar* inn löstu (4.3)
> sínum *vin* ok tínir (26.6)
> reistr of *kör* ok Kristum (54.3)
> kemr [*or* kemur] í *stað* at styðja (48.4)

It seems that in these lines the italicised forms would have to be taken as heavy in order to get a regular scansion.

The two lines where light syllables in disyllabic words are apparently treated metrically as heavy are also from 'Pétrsdrápa':

> ótt til *grafar* dróttins (45.8)
> sonr gleði var sveinum (19.7)

In the first line, the word *grafar* would appear to need a heavy first syllable if the line is to have a regular scansion. In the second line, either the first word, *sonr*, must be taken as disyllabic: *sonur* (assuming that the epenthetic vowel which developed between a final *r* and a consonant had already appeared), with a heavy first syllable, or *gleði* needs to have a heavy first syllable.

In general, the examples which break the rules determining (we have assumed) the metrical function of long and short stressed syllables are too few for us to be able to assign any significance to them. It may be tempting to suggest that, because in 'Pétrsdrápa' short monosyllables seem to break the rules five times, while short disyllabics seem to break them only twice, there is a change under way with, perhaps, the monosyllables tending to lengthen earlier. However, we would want to get clearer statistical evidence before drawing any such conclusions; and we must remember that there were no examples to be found in 'Guðmundardrápa' where the old rules seemed to be broken (granted that a light monosyllable was allowed to carry the ictus when followed by a word beginning with a consonant), and that the vast majority of occurrences of old light syllables conform to the old rules.

The fact that all the examples of breaches of old rules come from 'Pétrsdrápa' and none from 'Guðmundardrápa' may also tempt us to suggest that there is a difference in the age of these poems. As was seen above, Jónsson dates both poems to the fourteenth century. It is, however, possible that 'Pétrsdrápa' is younger. Its oldest manuscript (AM: 621 4°) is (according to Stefán Karlsson of the Arnamagnæan Institute in Reykjavík) from the third quarter of the fifteenth century, and there seems to be no compelling reason to push the age of 'Pétrsdrápa' as far back as the fourteenth century. One might then say, if 'Pétrsdrápa' stems from the fifteenth century, as is well consistent with its manuscript preservation, that we see here the first signs of the change in the metrical function of old light syllables that was to become more evident in the sixteenth century. This is consistent with the fact that in the poem 'Rósa' (probably from the first half of the sixteenth century, and edited in *Íslenzk miðaldakvæði* 1.2), which, according to Jón Helgason (*ibid.*: 1.2:5), follows the old quantity rule, there are at least eight examples (in 1,064 lines) where old light syllables seem to carry full ictuses. These could be the first signs of the change in the function of old light syllables. It must, however, be remembered that the numbers of breaches in these poems are significantly lower than those found by Þórólfsson (1929a) in many other sixteenth-century poems.

4.3.2.2 *The evidence of 'rímur'.* Since very little skaldic poetry exists from after the period to which 'Guðmundardrápa' (and 'Pétrsdrápa') belong (roughly the fourteenth century) I will look for other sources of evidence after this point. We have just seen that the fourteenth-century skaldic poetry I have looked at does not show clear signs of a change having taken place in the prosodic system of the underlying language, so any evidence as to when the lengthening took place is still to come.

Fortunately for us, another genre of poetry, which arose (probably) in the fourteenth century, can be used as evidence about the prosody of the language. This poetry was the *rímur* 'rhymes', a type of literature which was to flourish in Iceland right down to the present century. The *rímur* are usually considered to be of mixed origin (Þórólfsson 1934:35–51; Craigie 1952 I:XII–XVIII). The metres, which are quite varied, derive many of their peculiarities, such as alternative end-rhyme and the number of lines to each verse (normally four), from foreign folk ballads, but other features, such as the use of alliteration, are of native Icelandic origin. Furthermore, the poetic language is a direct inheritance from the skaldic poetry. The most common and basic, and probably the oldest, of the *rímur*-metres is the *ferskeytt* (meaning etymologically 'four-cornered') metre. A typical example is the first stanza of 'Ólafs ríma Haraldssonar', which is among the oldest specimens of this genre, dated about 1350–70:

> Ólafr kóngur örr ok fríðr
> átti Noregi at ráða
> gramr var ei við bragna blíðr
> borinn til sigrs ok náða

As can be seen, the alliteration follows the same principles as in the *dróttkvætt*-metre. There are two *stuðlar* in the first line of every pair, and one *höfuðstafr* in the beginning of the second line: *Ólafr/örr/átti* and *bragna/blíðr/borinn*. The main innovation, compared to *dróttkvætt* and other older Icelandic poetry, is the number of lines and the nature of the rhyme: alternating end-rhyme.

A look at the stanza cited above will give us some idea about the rhythm of the *ferskeytt*-metre. In the first line we see that there is a regular alternation between heavy stressed syllables and light (metrically) unstressed ones. We can scan this line on the same principles as those we used for the *dróttkvætt*-lines:

$$\acute{-}\ \smallsmile\ -\ \ -\ \smallsmile\ -$$
> Ólafr kóngur örr ok fríðr

This looks very much like a *dróttkvætt*-line except that one (in this case heavy) syllable has been added at the end. But the second line is of the same length as a *dróttkvætt*-line, counted in morae:

átti Nóregi at ráða

(We assume that there is a liaison to avoid hiatus between *Noregi* and *at*.) The third line scans exactly like the first:

gramr var ei við bragna blíðr

and the last line scans:

borinn til sigrs ok náða

It is worth noting that in the stanza quoted above, two light syllables can be treated like one heavy. If, for example, we analyse the odd-numbered lines into three feet, each with three morae, we see that these three morae can either be covered by one heavy stressed syllable followed by a light, giving a regular trochee as in *átti*, or by three light and/or unstressed ones, like *borinn til*. What is most important for us is that in 'Ólafs ríma Haraldssonar', and the other *rímur* from the oldest period, it seems to be a rule that if, for example, a line starts with a disyllabic word with a light first syllable according to the old rules, a third syllable follows before the start of the next foot. This means that a light disyllabic word like *taka* could not form a trochee, and a third syllable had to be added. This is why in lines like:

Hildings taka þá helgan dóm ('Ólafs ríma Haraldssonar' 62.1)

we get an unstressed *þá* 'then' after *taka* in order for a full foot to be formed. The form *taka* alone is not sufficient, as are *Hildings* and *helgan*. The temporal adverb is not strictly necessary for the meaning of the sentence, and if *taka* could have formed a regular trochee, the poet might have written:

Hildings taka helgan dóm

which is a perfectly normal line after the first syllable of *taka* has been lengthened.

Obviously, lines like the one just constructed are the sort of things we will be looking for as evidence that the lengthening of old light syllables had taken place. If, for example, we find a poem where it seems to be regular that forms like *bera* or a sequence like *bar ek* function as trochees, that is, without a third syllable following within the same foot, we will be tempted to assume that a lengthening of light stressed syllables had taken place when that poem was composed. To look for evidence of this sort I have studied the following *rímur*-material from the fourteenth to the sixteenth century:

(a) 'Ólafs ríma Haraldssonar' by Einar Gilsson (the author of 'Guðmundardrápa'; cf. above) from about 1350–70 (260 lines).

(b) 'Skáld-Helga rímur', from about 1400. The first forty stanzas were investigated, giving a total of 160 lines.

(c) 'Skíðaríma', from about 1400–50. 100 stanzas were investigated, giving 400 lines.

(d) 'Króka-Refs rímur', from the latter half of the fifteenth century. The first 102 stanzas were investigated, giving a total of 408 lines.

(e) 'Ólafs rímur Haraldssonar', composed after 'Rauðúlfs þáttur', from about 1550 (referred to below as 'Ólafs rímur B'). All the 126 existing *ferskeytt*-lines were investigated.

(f) 'Pontusrímur' by Magnús Jónsson prúði, composed in the years 1564–6. 696 lines were investigated.

Before I look at the evidence given by these data, I would like to make a few further remarks about the rhythm of *rímur*.

It seems that the rhythmical rules of the *ferskeytt*-metre were not as strictly based on quantity as the rules of the *dróttkvætt*-metre seem to have been. It is quite common in *ferskeytt* for a stressed heavy syllable forming an ictus to be followed by two (or even more) unstressed syllables, so that instead of trochees we get dactyls. Examples of this are:

Fimm hefir köngur kristnat lönd ('Ólafs ríma Haraldssonar' 4.1)

and

grams fyrir merkit væna (*ibid.* 38.2)

In both these lines, the first syllable is heavy and, consequently, only one syllable has to follow it in order for a regular foot to be formed; but in both cases two light syllables follow. Since this sort of thing is quite common, it seems that, in contrast to the *dróttkvætt*-metre, the number of 'morae' in each line was not fixed. This is quite an important difference from the metrical point of view. Our hypothesis concerning the *dróttkvætt*-metre is that its rhythm was fundamentally based on quantity. We could get heavy and light syllables distributed over the line in remarkably many ways, for example:

In this type of rhythm, as we have seen, it is perhaps not appropriate to speak in terms of feet, but rather in terms of bars, as in music. Two bars can be linked together, one final note in the first bar being tied over the bar-line to a note in the second bar. The two latter types of lines can be represented as respectively:

In the rhythm of *rímur*, however, stress seems to have played a more important role. The fact that two metrically unstressed (usually short) syllables could quite regularly follow the stressed long one, without disrupting the rhythm, shows that it was not crucially based on the number of syllables or the length of the line measured in morae, but rather that the basic or most central unit in the *ferskeytt*-metre was probably the foot with its ictus (*Hebung*) which could be formed by one heavy stressed syllable or two light (that could be said to have served as a 'disyllabic matrix' for the metrical ictus, cf. above, p. 136) and its drop (*Senkung*), which could be one or two (or perhaps even more) light and unstressed syllables. The fact that the rhythm of the *ferskeytt*-metre seems to have been basically different from that of the *dróttkvætt*-metre does not perhaps matter a great deal to us; but it is worth keeping in mind, when we consider and evaluate the evidence of the *ferskeytt*-metre, that only a relatively minor change was needed in the rules to allow light stressed syllables to function as full ictuses. All that had to be done was to remove from the metrical rules a restriction forbidding a light stressed syllable to carry the ictus by itself. A change allowing for the same thing in *dróttkvætt* would probably have been much more drastic, since it seems that the whole rhythmic structure of the metre was based on quantity alternations. It seems, therefore, that when a change is detected in the relation between metre and language as far as function of quantity is concerned, such a change in *ferskeytt* has a greater chance of being caused by a change in the metrical rules than a similar change in *dróttkvætt*.

Turning back to our *rímur* material, we may observe that the same cohesion principle as we saw in *dróttkvætt* could make a light monosyllable able to carry an ictus if it was followed by a word beginning with a consonant. Examples of this abound in the oldest, as well as in the younger, *rímur*. This means that lines like the following:

> að þinn leiður lymsku drengr ('Króka-Refs rímur' 1, 68.3)
> þat var mest af prýði ('Ólafs ríma Haraldssonar' 31.2)
> innan hol sem kista ('Skíðaríma' 14.2)

must be ignored as evidence concerning lengthening in the light syllables and were probably quite regular before the quantity shift.

What we will be looking for, then, are examples where sequences like $VC^1 \# \# VC_0$ or VC^1VC_0 function as whole feet. Assuming that the metre was unchanged, such examples can be taken as signs that the originally short syllables had lengthened. We will be interested to know when the light syllables lengthened and whether they lengthened at different times in monosyllables and polysyllabics.

In 'Ólafs ríma Haraldssonar' there was only one possible example of a light syllable having to carry an ictus in order to get a regular scansion:

þér innit framar hóti (32.2)

Here, it would seem most natural to assume that the pronoun *þér* is an unstressed upbeat, which is quite common in *rímur*, and if this is so, the three remaining disyllabics will each have to form a foot by itself, including *framar* which has a light first syllable. The reason why *þér*, which has a historically heavy syllable and could therefore carry an ictus if stressed, is probably to be taken as an upbeat and ignored in the scansion of the rest of the line, is that *innit* carries the alliterative *höfuðstafr*, which matches two word-initial vowels in the preceding line, and it seems to be a rule that such *höfuðstafir* can only be preceded by unstressed upbeats. It seems, then, that *framar* breaks the rule that an ictus can only be carried by a heavy stressed syllable or jointly by two light. One example in 260 lines, however, seems far too little to be of any significance.

In the 160 lines from 'Skáld-Helga rímur' (from about 1400), no examples were found where it is certain that the old rules were broken.

In the next item on the list, the first 400 lines of 'Skíðaríma', from the first half of the fifteenth century, seven exceptions to the old rules were found. Three of these involve old light monosyllables preceding words beginning in vowels:

það er hvorki skrum né skjal (7.3)
Ofrligt er um örleik þinn (26.3)
hann Leifi kvað ei liggja á (37.3)

In these three lines, the words *það*, *er* and *kvað*, respectively, will have to carry the ictus if a natural scansion is to be obtained. The other four examples involve disyllabics:

úr máta stór og *mikil* er (13.3)
Ísungs *synir* utar í frá (81.3)
eru margir meiri en þú (95.3)
Á Íslandi *eru* margir menn (96.1)

Here, the first syllables of the words *mikil, synir* and *eru* (twice) will have to carry the ictus if a natural scansion is to be obtained. Seven examples out of 400 lines may not seem statistically impressive, and they will probably have to be dismissed as not significant.

To test this, we may look at the data from a slightly different angle. In a special survey of the first 160 lines of 'Skíðaríma', I counted the overall occurrence of old light first syllables of polysyllabics in metrically stressed position, that is, within the ictus. Light first syllables of polysyllabics occurred twenty-five times in this position. In twenty-four of these instances the light quantity of the first stressed syllable was compensated for by the presence of an extra syllable in the same foot, that is, a disyllabic like *taka* was followed by an unstressed word like *það* in order for the foot to be filled. Therefore only once in the twenty-five instances was there no compensatory syllable.

For the monosyllables, the comparable figures were not quite as convincing, and I took a bigger sample of 400 lines. In these 400 lines I found fifty-nine instances of light monosyllables occurring under metrical stress in the middle of lines (we will later come to the behaviour of old light monosyllables at the end of lines). Three of these occurrences are those mentioned above where a word beginning in a vowel follows, and the rules we have set up seem to be broken. Looked at in this way they do not seem to harm our model. But a closer look at the data might arouse suspicion. We note that in forty-one instances light monosyllables are followed by a word beginning with a consonant and only followed by one syllable before the beginning of the next foot, as in the line cited above:

innan hol sem kista (14.2)

When these forty-one instances and the three we have already labelled as breaking the rules are added together, we see that forty-four times out of fifty-nine the light quantity of a monosyllable is *not* compensated for by the presence of a third syllable within the same foot, and only fifteen times do light monosyllables occur as the first syllables of trisyllabic ictuses. If we were to say that the instances where monosyllables carry an ictus when followed by a word beginning in a consonant are breaches of metric rules, we would come up with a situation where old light monosyllables break the old rules in forty-four instances out of fifty-nine. In that case, one might wonder whether the old monosyllables had already become heavy and the instances where they occur in trisyllabic feet are of the same sort as in:

Fimm hefir köngur kristrnað lönd ('Ólafs ríma Haraldssonar' 4.1)

Here a heavy stressed syllable (*Fimm*) is followed by two light syllables within the same foot. To this hypothesis one must first make the objection that it is already quite common in the oldest *dróttkvætt*-poetry for light monosyllables to function as if they were heavy when followed by a word beginning in a consonant, whereas it seems to be an exception if they do so when followed by a word which begins in a vowel. This would be difficult to explain if the hypothesis were correct; it seems that at the earlier stages there was some rule which allowed light monosyllables to carry the ictus when followed by a word beginning with a consonant, and it seems unlikely that this derived from the fact that light monosyllables had more quantity when preceding a word beginning in a consonant. The discrimination against old light monosyllables when followed by words beginning with vowels seems to indicate that they were linguistically different from heavy ones. Another way of trying to see whether this hypothesis is likely to be true is to compare the function of old light monosyllables in 'Skíðaríma' to their function in some other poem which dates from a later period, when we have reason to believe that a change had taken place in the metrical function of old short stressed syllables. 'Pontusrímur' (see below) are considered by Þórólfsson (1934:292–3) to be composed after the quantity shift had taken place, and we will consider a sample of 140 lines from this poem. A different statistical pattern emerges here from that of 'Skíðaríma'. In the 140 lines examined for this purpose, old light monosyllables occurred twenty-one times metrically stressed in the middle of lines. In twenty instances their light quantity was not compensated for by the presence of a third syllable and would therefore have to be taken as carrying the ictus by themselves. The ratio for 'Pontusrímur' is, then, 20:1, whereas the comparable ratio for 'Skíðaríma' is 44:15. Similarly, in 'Pontusrímur', the number of times an old light syllable carrying an ictus was followed by a consonant was eight, whereas it was twelve times followed by a word beginning with a vowel. The comparable ratio for 'Skíðaríma' is forty-one times followed by a word beginning with a consonant and three times followed by a word beginning with a vowel. The difference between 41:3 and 8:12 is so substantial that it seems reasonable to assume that a change had taken place in the interval between the composition of 'Skíðaríma' (in the first half of the fifteenth century) and that of 'Pontusrímur' (around the middle of the sixteenth century). Since, in 'Skíðaríma', an old light monosyllable, seemingly carrying the ictus, was followed only three times by a word beginning with a vowel, it seems that there was a restriction against it which later was relaxed.

In 'Króka-Refs rímur', which are considered to be from the latter half of the fifteenth century, two examples were found where an old light monosyllable seemed to carry the ictus when followed by a word beginning with a vowel, and four examples where an old light first syllable of a polysyllabic seemed to fill an ictus. The total number of lines examined was 408, and when this is compared to the three monosyllables and four disyllabics that seemed to break the rules in the 400 lines of 'Skíðaríma', we will have to assume that no change had taken place.

When we turn to the next item on the list, 'Ólafs rímur B', which are considered to be from about 1550, we seem to detect some change. Only 126 *ferskeytt*-lines are preserved from those *rímur*. They were all investigated with the results that four examples were found of old light monosyllables seemingly carrying an ictus when followed by words beginning with vowels, and twelve examples were found where a first light syllable in a polysyllabic needed to assume the status of a full ictus before a natural scansion could be obtained. When we consider that the number of lines is only 126, approximately one third of the material from each of 'Skíðaríma' and 'Króka-Refs rímur', this seems to indicate a change; we would have to multiply the figures from 'Ólafs rímur B' by three to compare them with those of 'Skíðaríma' and 'Króka-Refs rímur', making the figure for monosyllables twelve, and the one for polysyllabics thirty-six. The comparable figures for 'Skíðaríma' and 'Króka-Refs rímur' were three and four, and two and four respectively. These figures indicate, though perhaps not conclusively because of the poverty of the data, that a change was taking place or had already taken place about 1550.

It will have been noticed that the number of exceptions to the old rules involving polysyllabics is considerably higher than the number of exceptions involving monosyllables. This might lead one to suggest that a lengthening had affected polysyllabics earlier and more regularly than monosyllables. But it is doubtful whether any such conclusions can be drawn from these data, since, in general, the incidence of polysyllabic words is greater. (In a randomly-chosen prose text of twenty-three lines, I counted 146 polysyllabic words, but only ninety-one monosyllables, and in fourteen stanzas from 'Ólafs ríma Haraldssonar', I counted 145 polysyllabic words, against 111 monosyllables. In both cases, unstressed

words like prepositions and conjunctions, which are mostly monosyllables, were included.) These figures, then, do not allow us to assume that
there was any time interval between the changes of the metrical function
of old light syllables, according to whether they occurred in mono- or
polysyllables.

We have already looked at the evidence of 'Pontusrímur'. In the main
sample of 696 lines (the first and eleventh *ríma*) twenty-two examples
were found of old light monosyllables carrying an ictus, and forty-one of
historically light first syllables of polysyllabics. Although these
proportions are not as great as those we have from 'Ólafs rímur B', they
undoubtedly show that the old rules no longer prevailed. If we look first at
the polysyllabics, we see that in 696 lines we get forty-one examples of
light syllables functioning as heavy. That means that there is one breach
of the old rules in approximately seventeen lines (41:696); in 'Ólafs rímur
B' there is one breach of the old rules per approximately ten lines
(12:126). Both of these figures show a significantly higher incidence of
breaches of the old rules than the figures for 'Skíðaríma' and 'Króka-Refs
rímur', where there is one breach for approximately 100 lines
(4:400 and 4:408 respectively). It seems, then, relatively safe to assume
that the old light polysyllabics had a different function in 'Ólafs rímur B'
and 'Pontusrímur' from that in the fifteenth-century poems, 'Skíðaríma'
and 'Króka-Refs rímur'. The same can be said about old short
monosyllables. Here we have, in 'Pontusrímur', one breach for
approximately every thirty-one lines (22:696), and a similar ratio shows
up in 'Ólafs rímur B' (4:126); but in 'Skíðaríma' there is one breach for
approximately 133 lines (3:400), and one for approximately 200 lines in
'Króka-Refs rímur' (2:408).

4.3.2.3 *The last feet of untruncated lines.* From the investigation of the
evidence of *rímur* metrics so far, it seems clear that around the middle of
the sixteenth century there occurred a change in the metrical function of
old light syllables, so that the restrictions against their occurrence in place
of a monosyllabic ictus in a trochee were relaxed. Forms like *tala, vera,
bar ek* etc. are now allowed to form a full foot, something they could not
do before. This was investigated earlier by Þórólfsson (1929a,
1934:291–4) with similar results. Þórólfsson took this as evidence that
lengthening took place in the old light syllables around the middle of the
sixteenth century (at least in the dialects represented by the poems in
question), in other words that the change was a linguistic one. But one

cannot of course exclude the possibility that what took place was simply a change in the rules of the metre. I have already mentioned that a relatively small change was needed in the metrical rules for *rímur* to allow for this change. The old condition for a syllable to be able to carry the ictus by itself was that it was stressed and not light. (There were even exceptions to the quantity condition, in that a light monosyllable could carry the ictus if followed by a word beginning with a consonant.) All that had to be done to allow for the change that we have detected was for the condition concerning quantity to be removed. If this was the case, there is no need to assume that the change that took place about 1550 was the linguistic lengthening of short vowels. Indeed, it may be just as likely that the change was simply a change in the metrical rules (cf. Kjartansson 1971). If we look at the last feet of untruncated lines (lines ending in disyllabics, i.e. trochees), we see that the old restriction concerning the length of the stressed syllables in this metrical position seems to have prevailed much longer. Stefán Karlsson (1964:10–11, fn. 12) notes that, in the whole of 'Pontusrímur', old light disyllabics occur only ten (or nine) times as the last feet of untruncated lines. The total number of untruncated lines is 1,213, which gives us about one breach in every 120 lines. This seems a considerable consistency in distinguishing between old light and heavy stressed syllables in disyllabics, and is difficult to explain if no linguistic difference is assumed to have prevailed between these two types of syllables. Karlsson also shows that in a *rímur* poem from the first half of the seventeenth century (composed in 1643, according to the only existing manuscript), 'Egilsrímur Skallagrímssonar' by Jón Guðmundsson, a similar rule is maintained. Only in about 1 per cent of lines ending in disyllabic forms is the first syllable light according to the old rules. In these *rímur*, as well as 'Pontusrímur', there seems to be no restriction against old light syllables carrying the ictus by themselves when they occur in a non-final position in the line, but the fact that old light disyllabics hardly occur as last feet of untruncated lines in these poems is difficult to explain if no distinction was made in the metrical rules between old heavy disyllabics (*hestur, óska*) and old light disyllabics (*taka*). As long as a distinction was made between the metrical function of these two types of syllable, one must, it seems, assume that some relatively simple linguistic feature existed in terms of which the metrical rules were defined. It makes no difference which aspect of the metrical rules is based on this distinction; as long as a distinction is made somewhere in the metrical rules it must be assumed that some linguistic difference existed. The sixteenth-century change may then have been simply a change in the metrical rules as far as 'Pontusrímur' are concerned, since the author, Magnús Jónsson prúði, seems to be fairly consistent in distinguishing between the two types of syllables when it comes to deciding which words are eligible as the last feet of untruncated lines.

We might, then, want to say that the lengthening in old light syllables did not take place until the seventeenth century at the earliest. However, if we look more closely at the data investigated by Þórólfsson (1929a), this statement becomes less attractive. We have noted that a relatively minor change was needed in the metrical rules for *ferskeytt* (and other related metres) for old light stressed syllables to get the same metrical value as old heavy ones; but I have also suggested that such a change in the metrical rules for *dróttkvætt* would have been more drastic. It is interesting that the poet Hallur Ögmundsson (who, according to Þórólfsson, was one of the first to show signs of a change in the function of old short syllables in his poetry) breaks the old rules of the *hrynhent*-metre, which was a version of the *dróttkvætt,* developed in the eleventh century (Þorolfsson 1929a:40–4). Not only are there several examples where it seems that old light syllables in non-final position in the metrical line must be taken as heavy in order for a natural scansion to be obtained, but, more strikingly, there are quite a few instances of old light disyllabics functioning as last feet of the lines, which as we have seen, seems in general to be the most conservative position as regards distinction between two degrees of quantity of stressed syllables. Þórólfsson (1929a:51) also notes that Einar Sigurðsson (1538–1626) breaks the old rules in *dróttkvætt* (and another old metre, *fornyrðislag*). If the sixteenth-century change was a metrical one, it must, then, have been a change not only in the rules for the *rímur*-metres, but also in the rules for the old *dróttkvætt* and *hrynhent* (as far as they were still in use). It may seem a strange coincidence that changes should be made in all these metres at the same time. Why should the poetic conventions be changed so drastically in the sixteenth century?

We have here the following puzzle. A partial change takes place concerning the metrical function of old light syllables. The question is: Was it a linguistic change or merely a change of metrical rules? If, on one hand, it was a linguistic change, then why did the two types of old stressed syllable (heavy and light) still have different metrical value in some positions in some metres? On the other hand, if the change was metrical, then, apart from the question of why it took place, it may seem a remarkable coincidence that more or less all metres were affected by the same sort of change at the same time.

It is interesting to note that, whereas Einar Sigurðsson breaks the old rules concerning the metrical function of old light syllables in *dróttkvætt* and other old metres, he maintains them in the last disyllabic foot in *rímur* and other younger types of poetry. These younger metres were all intended for singing (or chanting), and the fact that the old distinction was only maintained in chantable metres may partly resolve our paradox. If the sixteenth-century change was a metrical change partly caused by a lengthening in old light syllables, it is possible that it was still not permitted that these old light syllables be stretched in singing or chanting, as for example in the *rímur*, assuming that the last feet of untruncated lines typically occurred on long notes in the appropriate tunes. In other words, we do not have to assume that because these old light syllables did not occur in the last feet of untruncated lines which were intended for singing or chanting, they had not lengthened at all. It is conceivable that for some reason they were not suited to being stretched in singing. It is conceivable that there was still some difference between the prosodic contour of the first syllables of, for example, *tala* and *lúka* in the 'stretchability' of the vowels, although the difference was not so great as to forbid the old light syllables from functioning as ictuses in the middle of lines. Only when it came to stretching the syllable in final position in a line in singing was a difference detected between old light and old heavy syllables. It is characteristic of many of the tunes to which the *rímur* were chanted, that they have long notes in the position of the last ictus of even-numbered lines (which are always untruncated in simple *ferskeytt* and many other *rímur*-metres). A typical tune, transcribed in a 4/4 rhythm by Þorsteinsson (1906–9:871), is the following:

And a typical tune in a 3/4 rhythm is the following (Þorsteinsson 1906–9:873):

Vatns - dæl - ing - ar   veita' ó - spart

veg - far - end - um   bein - a,

elsk - a   heið - ur, hefð og   skart og

hrund - ir eð - al stein - a.

Both these tunes show that the last feet of untruncated lines are long in singing, and it is to be expected that if there were any restrictions on the occurrence of old light syllables, these should be the positions where they were most consistently forbidden.

I will not try to give a conclusive solution to our puzzle here, since a much more detailed investigation of the data is needed than can be done in the context of this study, I shall merely state what I think is likely to have been the course of events and comment on possible ways of trying to solve the problem of the dating of the lengthening in old light stressed syllables.

It seems likely that the change seen in the sixteenth-century poetry is a consequence of a gradual lengthening in old light stressed syllables, most typically by a lengthening of the vowel, but possibly also by a lengthening of consonants in some cases. This lengthening was, however, not so great as to make it possible to use the old light syllables to carry the long notes that characterised the last ictuses of untruncated lines in metres that were intended for singing, such as *rímur* and some other metres, mostly of foreign origin. In other words, my answer to the question whether the lengthening of old short vowels took place in the sixteenth century is 'yes, to a certain extent, but not completely'. The old light syllables had lengthened, at least in certain dialects, but a difference in their prosodic contour from that of the old heavy syllables could still be detected. I am suggesting, then, that the lengthening in old light syllables and the change in their metrical function was a gradual process.

The idea of a gradual lengthening fits in well with the fact that the disappearance of the 'discrimination' against light syllables in the last feet of untruncated lines seems to be gradual. As we have already seen, there was one light disyllabic last foot for approximately 120 lines in 'Pontusrímur'. A similar ratio (1:125) holds for 'Egilsrímur' (1643) (Karlsson 1964:22). In 'Olgeirsrímur danska' by Guðmundur Bergþórsson (from 1680) the ratio is 1:47. In 'Brávallarímur' by Árni Böðvarsson (from 1760) the ratio has reached 1:12, and in 'Númarímur' by Sigurður Breiðdfjörð (from 1833), it is 1:5.6.[7] These figures clearly show that it gradually becomes more natural to have old light syllables functioning as ictuses of the last feet of untruncated lines, until there is no restriction against it.

It is perhaps worth noting that the last foot of untruncated lines can only be used as evidence about disyllabics; we have no evidence concerning monosyllables. For all we know, they may have lengthened earlier than the disyllabics, but we have no evidence for this, one way or the other.

Another point that should be made about the progress of the lengthening in old light syllables is that it probably progressed at different speeds in different dialects. Þórólfsson (1929a:79) suggested that it was an innovation which spread from the west, Hallur Ögmundsson being from there. Karlsson (1964:23) points out that this does not accord with the fact that Jón Guðmundsson í Rauðseyjum, the author of 'Egilsrímur', who was also from the west, is still distinguishing between heavy and light syllables in 1643. A thorough investigation of poetry from the sixteenth and seventeenth centuries is obviously necessary before any conclusions can be drawn as to the geographical progression of lengthening in old light syllables.

Before concluding this subsection, a few comments concerning the relation between the lengthening of vowels in monosyllables and polysyllabics are in order. I have already mentioned (4.3.1) two alternative models, the 'overnight hypothesis' and the 'conspiracy hypothesis'. Both these models are based on the assumption that changes are abrupt (cf. note 4). We set up a choice between lengthening of vowels in all short syllables at the same time ('overnight') or in two steps ('conspiracy'). One might now say that such a distinction is now irrelevant as we have abandoned the idea of abrupt lengthening. There may seem little point in distinguishing between two subparts of a change which perhaps takes about two centuries to be completed. If the whole change were a gradual move from two to one degree of quantity in stressed syllables, the fact that vowels of monosyllables tended to lengthen earlier than vowels of disyllables might be considered of little significance.

When discussing a conspiracy or a single change, we talked as if it was quite clear what 'single change' meant. It is worth considering what conditions must be fulfilled by something in order that it may be called a 'single change'. It has become increasingly clear that linguistic innovations can take a long time to spread; the changes are typically *gradual*. It is immediately apparent that, depending on one's point of view, 'gradual' can be used to refer to linguistic changes in different ways (cf. Wang 1969). There are at least three senses in which phonological changes can be *gradual* (and, logically at least, the opposite: *abrupt*). One can say that a phonological change is *phonetically gradual*, meaning that phonetic (allophonic) changes that can be said to underlie the structural changes take some time to develop. This change can proceed 'gradually' either in the speech of one speaker or in the speech of a community. Another dimension along which graduality can be measured is the *interindividual dimension*; one can grade the speed by which some innovation spreads from one individual to another, for example according to class or geographical location. A third dimension is the *vocabulary* of the language. It is possible that some changes are more regular in some parts of the vocabulary than others, and that it takes some time for the change to reach all forms of the language (cf. Krishnamurti 1978). Indeed, it is common for some special parts of the vocabulary never to be affected by the change; they become exceptions to synchronic rules (cf. Ralph 1975:132–62). When we maintain that the lengthening of short vowels was a gradual change, we might do well to clarify which of these senses of 'gradual' is meant. The answer is that it most probably was so in all three senses. If we assume that the lengthening was connected with the stressedness of the syllables, it is, firstly, very likely that it was phonetically gradual, even to the extent that individual speakers gradually lengthened their originally short stressed vowels as they got older. It is, secondly, quite likely that the innovation gradually spread from one geographic area to another, and perhaps also from one class to another. Thirdly, it is quite possible that the vowels lengthened earlier in one part of the vocabulary than in others, and the change was thus 'lexically gradual'. The nature of the lengthening is such that it very probably would have proceeded gradually. Most importantly, it did not produce any clashes in the system, since quite early, perhaps in the thirteenth century, the distinctive function formerly carried by vowel length began to be taken over by qualitative differences; from that point of view the length of segments was redundant and speakers were free to vary it. There was thus no hurry to restore order to the minor irregularity created by variation in the length of vowels and correspondingly in syllabic quantity. The phonetic nature of the change (the phonetic environments for the linguistic change, one might say) is also such that it can easily be conceived as progressing gradually. The only reason to introduce the factor of abruptness is the assumed structural innovation made by speakers when they start making generalisations about the length of stressed vowels according to environment; when, ideally, we have one generation (one speaker) having a more or less regular distribution of length without having strict phonological rules for it, followed by another generation (another speaker) with an 'underlying' phonological rule (or rules) accounting for it. (This is what H. Andersen (1973) calls 'abductive change'.) But of course the spread of this innovation can still be gradual on the interindividual (dialectal) parameter.

If the change was thus gradual in almost every sense of the word, it may be pointless, as we have already suggested, to speak in terms of a distinction between a single change or a conspiracy as far as the lengthening in monosyllables and polysyllabics is concerned. There is, however, nothing wrong with talking about two gradual changes, one beginning earlier (or having an earlier 'centre of gravity') than the other, even though the second change may have started before the completion of the other one.

It is also profitable to think of new generations, as it were, making different phonological generalisations at different times. For example: (i) all stressed vowels are short in front of two or more consonants; (ii) all stressed vowels are long before one (or no) consonant in monosyllables; (iii) all stressed vowels are long before single consonants in polysyllabics. If these 'generalisations' arise at different times, they can be called three different changes or at least three stages in a single change. This is essentially what our 'overnight' vs 'conspiracy' distinction is based on. Regrettably there is no clear evidence as to whether there was any difference in time between the beginnings or 'the centres of gravity' of the two lengthenings, but the question itself is clear. It is another question, different from the gradualness question, how much time is required between signs of the beginnings of potentially separate changes, and, perhaps more importantly, how far two events should differ in nature, causes etc. for them to be called separate changes. I will return to the question of conspiracy in §5.5.

4.3.3 The environment p, t, k, $s+v$, j, r. We have seen (§2.4) that there is an exception to the length rule in Modern Icelandic, in that in front of two-consonant sequences, of which the first member is p, t, k or s and the second v, j or r, vowels are long, whereas the general rule is that vowels are short before two or more consonants. It was suggested that this was due to the fact that the p, t, k, s + v, j, r-sequences are syllabified differently from other sequences of two or more consonants. It was proposed that the forms *vekja* (with a long vowel [vɛːcʰa]) and *vakna* (with a short vowel [vahkna]) should be syllabified *vek$ja* and *vakn$a* respectively, and that the difference in syllabification could either be explained as a consequence of a strength hierarchy in the consonants (v, j, r being 'weak' in that they have a tendency to stand near the vowel (nucleus) of the syllable they belong to) or by a syllabification rule based on some sort of distinctive feature classification of the consonants (for example, making v, j, r the only underlyingly voiced fricatives in Modern Icelandic). In this section I will look at this problem from the historical point of view.

Since forms like *vekja* 'wake up' (trans.), *vökva* 'to water', *akri* 'field' (dat.), *setja* 'to put', *þrisvar* 'three times' etc. show, in Modern Icelandic, long reflexes of old short vowels, we must assume that a lengthening of vowels took place in front of p, t, k, s + v, j, r-sequences at some stage.

It is interesting to see what function these forms had in the older poetry, that is, whether their first 'syllable' functioned as heavy or light. Apparently they functioned as heavy. In the poetry of Sigvatr Þórðarson (from the eleventh century; see Jónsson 1912–15 AI:223–75), for example, several forms of this sort fill the last foot of the line in *dróttkvætt*, which as a rule is only filled by disyllabic forms with heavy first syllables (e.g.: *frændsekju styr* VEKJA ('Flokkur um Erling Skjálgsson' 7.4; Jónsson 1912–15 AI:246) and *Hét sá er fell á* FITJUM ('Bersǫglisvísur' 4.1; Jónsson 1912–15 AI:252)). This also seems to be the case in *rímur* poetry from the fourteenth and fifteenth centuries. The *vekja*-type forms (as we may call them in this discussion) have the same function as other forms with two consonants following the vowel, that is, there are several examples where their first syllables carry the ictuses of trochees. It is the case, then, that the sequences V + {p/t/k/s} + {v/j/r} have the same metrical status as other sequences of vowels plus more than one consonant.

Before going any further we will note that the fact that these forms function as heavy in the metre seems to suggest that the segments *j, v* (and *r*) had, from the point of view of the metre, the same phonological status as other consonants. It seems that it is wrong to regard them (at least in this environment) as semi-vowels, as has often been done in the case of *j* and *v* for the earliest stages of Icelandic (cf. Noreen 1923/70:44–5). If *j* and *v* had been semi-vowels (or 'glides'), presumably definable as non-syllabic vowels, they would most properly have been analysed in forms like *setja* as the first components of rising diphthongs following the consonant, that is, *setja* would consist phonologically of a sequence CVCVV or CVCSV (S = semi-vowel), something like /setia/, /ia/ being a rising diphthong. If it were the case that *j* and *v* were non-syllabic vowels in Old Icelandic (eleventh- to fifteenth-century) one would expect the first syllable of the *vekja*-type words to function metrically as a light one, having a stressed syllable with only one consonant following the vowel. But this is not the case. (I will return briefly to the problem of the phonological status of semi-vowels in §6.5).

The metrical function of the *vekja*-type words, then, seems to group them with 'long-stem' disyllabics as far as prosodic structure is concerned. (There are no monosyllables ending in a *v* or a *j* following *p, t, k* or *s*, and words like *akr* 'field' with an *r* following a consonant word-finally became disyllabic in the thirteenth or fourteenth century by the rise of an epenthetic vowel between *r* and the preceding consonant.) But this does not correspond with the situation in Modern Icelandic, where the forms show reflexes of a vowel lengthening of the same type as in 'short-stem' words. It seems that the *vekja*-type words changed groups, so to speak, having been 'long-stem' disyllabics in Old Icelandic, joining the old 'short-stem' disyllabics in the quantity shift. It would be gratifying to be able to explain this.

Before considering this more closely I should point out that *a priori* there is more than one way in which a lengthening of vowels in front of *p, t, k, s* + *v, j, r* could be related temporally to the lengthening of short vowels in other environments. It is possible that before the lengthening of short vowels occurred, a split took place in the set of postvocalic consonant sequences, so that the *p, t, k, s* + *v, j, r* sequences came to provide a favourable environment for historical vowel lengthening, but the others did not. But it is also possible that the split in the postvocalic sequences took place after the historical lengthening of old short vowels had taken place. If this was the case, the change in the consonantal sequences simply created a new environment for a synchronically active lengthening rule. A third alternative is that the vowel lengthening and the change that caused the split in the postvocalic consonant sequences took place at more or less the same time. If the first of these alternative chronological orders of events is the right one, one could expect that before signs of the vowel lengthening showed up in the poetry, a change could be detected in the metrical function of the *vekja*-type words. That is, if for example some sort of reorganisation in the syllabic structure took place, making the syllabic structure of the *vekja*-words identical with that of *taka*, but different from that of, for example, *kasta*, this could conceivably show signs in the poetry in that *vekja* etc. could not function as trochees any more. I have found no signs of this in the poetry. We have, then, no external evidence as to whether a change in the prosodic status of *p, t, k, s + v, j, r* sequences took place before or after or at the same time as the lengthening of short vowels.

In the absence of direct evidence, we seem to be allowed the privilege of speculating freely about what happened. If we stick to the hypothesis set out in chapter 2 – that in Modern Icelandic stress determines syllabification, which in turn defines the scope of the length rule, and that stress 'caused' the lengthening of old short vowels – we can speculate about the development in the *vekja*-type words and the relation of syllabification and stress to the quantity shift.

The fact that the *vekja*-type words seem to have the same function as regular heavy disyllabics in the metrics before the quantity shift may be said to indicate that the concept 'heavy syllable in Old Icelandic' (as I have used it in the discussion of metrical function) was something quite different from the Modern Icelandic (necessarily heavy) stressed syllable. Indeed, it could be argued that the term 'syllable' should not be applied to the Old Icelandic unit at all. In this discussion I have simply used the term '(stressed) syllable' to refer to the stressed vowel plus all the consonants that follow up to the next vowel. (Of course, it has been implicitly assumed that a consonantal onset could be included in the syllable.) As is clear from the discussion of the concept 'syllable' in chapter 2, this use of the term is perhaps the least likely to have any appeal to linguists, since generally it seems that people tend to favour syllabification which maximises open syllables (cf. e.g. Pulgram 1970). The motivation for our syllabification of Modern Icelandic – extending the domain of the stressed syllable as far back as possible (final-maximalistic; cf. above) – was that by adopting such a syllabification we could account in a simple way for the distribution of several phonological phenomena, among them the length of stressed vowels. As far as we accept this motivation, we accept the stressed syllable as a linguistically significant unit in the phonology of Modern Icelandic. There is not the same motivation for the adoption of the final-maximalistic stressed syllable as a central unit in Old Icelandic. On the contrary, the metrical behaviour of the *vekja*-type words can be interpreted as evidence against it. If we assume that the metrical rules of *dróttkvætt* and *rímur* operated in terms of linguistic entities, that is, they were of the general form:

Linguistic unit X has metrical function F

and that the optimal relation between any linguistic entity and any metrical function was that X always had the same function, and conversely that F was always filled by the same entities, it would be natural for us to assume that the first four segments of *setja* as a sequence had the same linguistic status (or non-status) as the first four segments of *vakna*. The sequence of these four segments is what we have called a 'heavy stressed syllable in Old Icelandic'. But this 'syllable' must have been different from the Modern Icelandic stressed syllable. Our Modern Icelandic syllable is defined by stress, that is, the stress 'pushes' the syllable boundary as far back as allowed by phonotactic restrictions on the order of non-nuclear (consonantal) segments. If the unit utilised by the metrical rules was a final-maximalistic syllable defined in terms of stress, like the Modern Icelandic one, that syllable would have to be defined so as not to distinguish between the *vekja*-type words and other words having two consonants following the stressed vowel. But it seems highly unlikely that a stressed syllable for Old Icelandic could be defined as final-maximalistic without a distinction being made between *setja* on the one hand and *vakna* and *kasta* on the other, since then the syllable boundary would have to be pushed beyond the *v, j, r* of the *vekja*-type words. If a syllabification *setja, akri* etc. is unlikely to be valid for Modern Icelandic, it is even less likely to be valid for Old Icelandic since this could only be justified by assuming that the stress pushed the syllabic boundary of the stressed syllable even further 'to the right' in Old Icelandic than in Modern Icelandic. Indeed, as will be seen from what follows, it seems that the primary prosodic difference between Old and Modern Icelandic is that stress has come to play a more central role than it did before.

Although it seems unlikely that a linguistic unit of the same sort as the

Modern Icelandic final-maximalistic stressed syllable existed in Old Icelandic, it is possible that some phonological unit which, though different, could also be called a 'stressed syllable', did exist. It is, for example, conceivable that *setja, vakna* and *hestur* were all syllabified thus: *set $ja, vak $na, hes $tur*. In this case the change in syllabification from Old Icelandic to Modern Icelandic consisted in the movement of the syllable boundary one consonant to the right if not prohibited by phonotactic constraints of the type discussed in §2.4. This may well have been the case as far as we are concerned, but before setting up this syllabification for Old Icelandic it seems reasonable to demand that some independent justification be given for it, for example by showing that some phonological phenomena are more easily explained if such a syllabification is adopted. I have not found any purely linguistic phenomena which seem to demand such a phonological syllable for Old Icelandic. It is, however, interesting to note that if this syllabification is adopted, either at an abstract phonological level or on some lower phonetic level, one peculiarity in the metrical behaviour of heavy and light 'syllables' can perhaps be explained. I have already mentioned that it seems to be an exceptionless rule that the last feet of *dróttkvætt*-lines as well as untruncated lines in *rímur* had to consist of a long-stem disyllabic, like *kenna, hestur, láta* etc. The interesting thing is that when (particularly in *rímur*) the line was truncated (i.e. ended in a monosyllabic foot) there seems to have been no demand for that syllable to be heavy according to the old rules. These lines could just as easily end in light forms like *dag* and *tal*, as in heavy forms like *gest* and *rík* (cf. e.g. *Þórir lagði í kóngsins kvið* ('Ólafs ríma Haraldssonar' 51.1)). (In Greek and Latin poetry there is a similar phenomenon called 'indifference': the final syllable of a line can be either heavy or light; cf. Allen 1973:296ff.) This may seem strange given what we already know of the metrical function of heavy and light forms. We have seen that in the middle of lines old light stressed 'syllables', whether in mono- or disyllables, could not carry an ictus (except for light monosyllables when a consonant in a following word supported it by cohesion). But the last syllables of truncated lines certainly seem to have carried metrical stress, for example since they usually rhymed with other line-final syllables, and the question is why short syllables should be able to carry an ictus in this position but not others. If a syllabification like the one just mentioned is adopted, an explanation of this can be proposed. If we suggest that the condition for something being able to carry an ictus if the stressed vowel was short was that *the syllable was closed*, we could account for the metrical behaviour of old light monosyllables and the *vekja*-type words. We can suggest that the *vekja*-type words were syllabified thus: *vek*$*ja*, *ak*$*ri*, *kes*$*ja* etc. (i.e. had closed first syllables) and by virtue of that fact could carry the ictus. The same could apply to light monosyllables when they stood at the end of truncated lines; there was no way that *kvið* in front of silence could be syllabified other than *kvið*$. Disyllabic words standing at the end of (untruncated) lines, however, provided a following vowel so that if *tala* were to have occurred there, it would have given an open syllable: *ta*$*la*. When light monosyllables occurred in the middle of lines, we may suggest that their syllables were closed when a word beginning with a consonant followed, but open when a vowel followed. Thus, in this analysis, a sequence like *hol sem* would be syllabified *hol*$*sem* but a sequence like *böl á* would be syllabified *bö*$*lá*, when occurring in the flow of a poetic line. In this way *böl á* would have the same metrical function as *bera*, which would be syllabified *be*$*ra*.[8] This only accounts directly for the metrical behaviour of words having a short vowel in their first syllable. It says nothing about the syllabification and metrical function of forms like *dæma*, *sækja* or *óska*, which have long stressed vowels. But they cause no problems from the point of view of metrical function, since, however they are syllabified, they will end up with at least a 'bimoric' first syllable. The only forms that seem to be problematic for this sort of analysis are those with a vowel preceding a hiatus or a word boundary, such as *búa* or *bú*, which are treated metrically as light in the oldest *dróttkvætt*-poetry. But these forms are problematic anyway, since (as we have seen) there seems to have been some doubt as to the phonetic duration in vowels in this environment in Old Icelandic, and their phonological status was probably somewhat exceptional (see Benediktsson 1968).

It might be said that this explanation, if correct, would contradict what I have been saying above about the nature and causes of the quantity shift changes. I have suggested that the lengthening and shortening of Old Icelandic vowels was connected with a phonetic unit (a production unit) called the stressed syllable. If a phonetic unit of this sort is to be used to explain the lengthening of /a/ both in *tak* and *taka*, it will have to give the same environment in both cases, and this can best be done, it seems, by assuming that the syllabification was final-maximalistic, as in the case of the later phonological Modern Icelandic syllable. Also in forms like *óska* 'to wish', the shortening of the vowel can be explained only by taking into consideration the second consonant following the vowel; this seems to be crucial, because in the closed syllable *ós* 'estuary', no shortening takes place. This can be done if the phonetic syllabification we use is final-maximalistic. I may seem to have led myself into a self-contradiction: I suggest one syllabification to explain the quantity changes and another to explain the metrical behaviour of linguistic forms of the same language at more or less the same time. A conceivable way out of what might seem sinful opportunism is to say that these two syllabifications are of a different nature. I have assumed throughout that there could be at least two different types of syllables: phonetic and phonological. A way of defining the difference between these two concepts is to say that for something to be a phonological syllable, it has to play a central role in the phonology of the language, for example, figure in some phonological rules or account for phenomena that otherwise would look puzzling. In that respect the stressed syllable in Modern Icelandic would be a phonological unit. A phonetic syllable, however, can be looked on as a performance unit, occurring only in the actual production of speech without necessarily being used in accounting for structural phonological relations. The sort of thing I mentioned in trying to explain the nature of the changes in the duration of vowels would then have been, at the time of change, a phonetic unit of this sort (and then later, after having become 'responsible' for phonological regularities, it became a phonological unit). We might, then, want to say that the syllabification I have just suggested to explain the metrical behaviour of old short monosyllables was not a phonetic but a phonological syllabification at this stage. In that way the two syllabifications could perhaps have co-existed before the quantity shift; we could use the phonetic syllabification to explain the rise of the changes in quantity, but the phonological one to account for the metrical behaviour of old heavy and light forms. This is far from convincing, however. I have already mentioned that there is very little, if any, linguistic justification to be found for the 'final-minimalistic' phonological syllabification in Old Icelandic. There is no evidence that the first three segments of *tak* on the one hand and *taka* on the other behaved differently in Old Icelandic, nor are there any signs of, for example, the *t* of *kjöt* 'meat' and *jötni* 'giant' (dat.sg.) (syllabified according to the suggestion being considered: *kjöt$, jöt$ni*) showing a common difference from the *t* of *jötunn* 'giant' (nom.sg.), allegedly syllabified *jö$tunn*. So, if this syllabification was phonological, it has not proved its existence by phonological consequences, and adopting such a phonological syllabification without justification goes against our principles.

Is there, then, a way of using the 'open' (or 'final-minimalistic') syllabification to explain metrical behaviour while still retaining the idea that the quantity shift had something to do with the existence of a final-maximalistic phonetic production unit? If we believe in the explanation of lengthening using the final-maximalistic syllable, we seem to be forced to admit that the 'open' syllabification was neither phonetic (because then we would not be able to explain the quantity changes in the way proposed) nor phonological (because we have no independent arguments for its existence). We may seem to be left with no choice but to give it up. But there may still be a solution. It is logically possible that this syllabification only existed for metrical purposes; in other words it was imposed on the language only when it was used in poetic performance. In fact I have already suggested a kind of 'abuse' of the language in poetry. I suggested that the sequences *ek bar* and *vel sá's*, linguistically consisting of two different words, could by cohesion be taken metrically as compounds, so that a sequence of vowel + two consonants was obtained, and that a sequence like *böl á* could be taken to form one 'metrical word', so that conditions arose for an 'open' syllabification. If we are able to believe that a sequence of two words could behave metrically as one, there seems to be little to prevent us from being able to believe that a special 'metrical syllabification' could be imposed on the language when it was used in poetry. In this way we could maintain this syllabification as defining poetic performance units and use it to explain the metrical behaviour of some linguistic forms, without having to assume that it had any significance as an abstract phonological entity or was identical to 'every-day' performance units. In this way we could save the idea that the quantity changes were connected with a syllabification of a different sort. This is of course still opportunism with respect to syllabification, but at least it is not self-contradictory.

We may leave as an open question what sort of phonological syllabification should be postulated for Old Icelandic. Indeed, it could have been something similar to the metrical syllabification just mentioned, or something still different. There may even be no reason to assume that any phonological syllabification prevailed in Old Icelandic if no phonological phenomena need to be explained in terms of it. (This is rather unlikely, however, since it is probable that phonotactic rules could most easily be stated in terms of syllabification.)

It is perhaps worth emphasising at this point that although I have suggested that there was perhaps a difference betwen the actual, let us say, 'every-day syllabification' and a 'metrical syllabification', that does not mean that the arguments I have put forward about the analysis of the language, based on metrical function, are invalid. I am by no means suggesting that the language could be used in almost any way in poetry. The 'metrical syllabification' must, of course, have been defined in terms of the more abstract linguistic norm; it was, according to my assumptions, basically a division of the text into special production units which could fill the functions demanded by the metre.[9] Just as the 'every-day production units' heed the structure of the underlying linguistic forms, so also do the 'poetic production units'. It is therefore perfectly legitimate to use metrical function to make inferences about the phonological structure of the language. It is a fact that *tala* had a different metrical status from that of *dæma*, and it is reasonable to ascribe that difference to a linguistic difference in the vowels, most likely length.

The 'every-day' phonetic syllabification I have proposed as the phonetic basis for the evening-out of the quantity of stressed syllables was then different from another phonetic syllabification used in poetic performance. The 'every-day' maximalistic syllabification generated by stress can be assumed to have gained ground gradually, causing the old short vowels to lengthen. We could then ascribe the cause of the metrical change in the sixteenth century just as easily to an increased prominence of the new stressed syllable as to increased length of the old short vowels. The relative conservatism in the function of old light syllables in the last feet of untruncated lines can then be seen as a resistance of old short vowels against a syllabification leaving them without any consonantal arrest or support in a very prominent position in the metre.

4.4 Conclusion

I have been trying to formulate a description of the quantity situation before and after the quantity shift in terms of syllabification. If these hypotheses bear some relation to the truth, it becomes natural to look upon the quantity shift as being basically *the rise of the final-maximalistic stressed syllable as a central unit in the phonology of Icelandic*. I am suggesting, in other words, that the basic difference between the prosodic structure of Old Icelandic and Modern Icelandic is that in the latter the stressed syllable plays a more central role in the phonology.

The final outcome was, then, that the length of vowels became (via the syllable) defined by the stress pattern. Before the shift, length was paradigmatically free, and long or short vowels could combine more or less freely with a heavy or a light following consonantism, without any limitations imposed by stress or syllabification. I have suggested that phonetic stress was, in slightly different ways, the cause of both the lengthening and the shortening changes.

As I have already said, we do not have to assume that the change from the Old Icelandic to the Modern Icelandic structure took place in one great leap. There was probably a long period of instability. However, when the phonetic alternations had become sufficiently regular, a phonological reorganisation could take place as an innovation made by new speakers confronted with the previous generation's output, data which could be accounted for by rules of the type described in chapter 2. For the words with $p, t, k, s + v, j, r$ following the vowel, a final-maximalist syllabification triggered by the stressedness of the syllable encountered a constraint which prohibited syllable-final sequences where the consonants v, j, r followed p, t, k, s, so the syllable was only extended far enough to include the 'strong' consonants p, t, k, s. This meant that for the forms concerned the domain of the length rule only came to be a vowel followed by one consonant, so the vowel became long.

I have suggested that the phonetic change had begun not later than in the sixteenth century, but the fact that poetry from the latter half of the seventeenth century and even from the eighteenth century shows discrimination between old heavy and light 'syllables' seems to indicate that the new structure was not stabilised until much later, perhaps as late as the beginning of the eighteenth century. It is, furthermore, quite likely that the change progressed at different speeds in different geographical areas.

It seems natural for a change like this to progress gradually, since it did not lead to any clashes in the system. It seems that as early as the thirteenth century the original long and short vowel systems started developing separately, so that qualitative differences gradually took over the distinctive function formerly carried by length. Once these qualitative differences had developed, the way was clear for a reorganisation of the prosody. But there was still no hurry either; only perhaps a relatively unstable tendency acted to bring about the change.

When the change was completed and order restored to the former 'chaos' concerning the length of stressed segments and the quantity of syllables, it can be called a major 'event' in the history of Icelandic.

NOTES

1 It will have been noticed that the term 'syllable' is here used in the maximal sense discussed above. This does not mean that the same syllabification principles are valid for Old Icelandic as Modern Icelandic (see below).

2 The Icelandic text is as follows (in a standardised orthography): 'Þat er leyfi háttanna, at hafa samstǫfur seinar eða skjótar, svá at dragisk fram eða aptr ór réttri tǫlu setningar, ok megu finnask svá seinar, at fimm samstǫfur sé í ǫðru ok enu fjórða vísuorði, svá sem hér er.'

3 The original text: 'Nú skal sýna svá skjótar samstǫfur ok svá settar nær hverja annarri, at af því eykr lengð orðsins.'

4 Clearly it is an oversimplification to state an 'overnight hypothesis' and a 'conspiracy hypothesis' as the only two possible alternatives, since in actual fact linguistic changes need time to take place. It seems that the lengthening of short vowels both in monosyllables and in disyllabics took quite a long time to be completed, and this is probably also true of the shortening of long vowels. It may turn out that the difference between a single change or a conspiracy will be neutralised because of the 'gradualness' of the change(s). At this stage of the discussion, however, it seems profitable to make the simplifying assumption that the changes were or could have been more or less abrupt.

5 True, it is suggested by Sigmundsson (1970) that confusion in the spelling of intervocalic consonants (like *berra* for *bera*) that occurs in fourteenth- and fifteenth-century texts stems from changes that were taking place in the quantity structure. It is quite possible that spellings like these represent sporadic lengthening of consonants.

6 In this whole discussion on metrics, a few complications are left out concerning the metrical function of heavy and light syllables. For example, it seems that verbs could be 'metrically unstressed', and thus long verbal stems could function as light (metrically unstressed) as well as heavy. Another ambiguity in metrical function of linguistic forms is to be found in compounds, especially proper names like *Ólafr* (*Áleifr*), which could, it seems, either have a metrical function ‿ ‿ , or ‿ ‿ , or even ‿ ‿ . Although these facts may make it necessary to make some qualifications to my statements concerning metrical rules, it does not affect the main concern here; that is, whether it seems that old heavy and light stressed syllables had different metrical functions.

7 The figures for 'Olgeirsrímur', 'Brávallarímur' and 'Númarímur' were obtained by a special survey. The material investigated was: 'Olgeirsrímur': *Rímur* no. I, II, IV, V, VII, VIII, IX, XI and XIII ('Olgeirsrímur', 1:1–47), 1,360 untruncated lines, 29 breaches. 'Brávallarímur': *Rímur* no. I, III, IV, VIII ('Brávallarímur', 1–67), 572 untruncated lines, 47 breaches. 'Númarímur': The first *ríma* ('Númarímur', 7–20), 168 untruncated lines, 30 breaches.

8 It is perhaps worth considering whether these phenomena could be explained using Lass' (1971) idea of looking at boundaries as obstruents. One can, for example, say that word boundaries are like obstruents in that a consonant intervening between them and the preceding vowel will close a syllable. One can say that a word-final consonant will have to belong to the same syllable as the preceding vowel, since the word-initial sequence C # is not permissible in most languages. It seems to me, however, rather drastic to assign to the end-signals of words a phonological status similar to that of regular segments. For one thing, boundaries have a very peculiar distribution. I would like, then, to find more positive evidence before using this interesting idea to explain metrical behaviour.

9 Actually, thought along the lines that emerges from these speculations may prove to be fruitful in phonological theory in clarifying aspects of the relation between phonology and phonetics. The actual production can be seen as 'putting the words to the music'

(Donegan & Stampe 1978:29). The norm (the convention), or the structured language system, would here be the words, and the phonetic flow would be the music. There may occur cases of tension between the phonetic flow and the structure of the norm. Phonological change can on occasion be seen as aiming at resolution of that tension.

5 Explaining the changes

5.1 Introductory

In this chapter I will turn my attention more closely to the problem of what caused the changes discussed (question (c) on p. 121). 'Why did change X take place?' may seem a pointless question, to judge from the often-quoted remarks of prominent linguists: 'the causes of sound change are unknown' (Bloomfield 1933:385); 'The explanation of the cause of language change is far beyond the reach of any theory ever advanced' (Harris 1969:550). However, a question that is never asked is rather unlikely to be answered, and if we hope sometime to be able to say something about the causes of particular changes and to make statements about the causes of language change in general, we will obviously have to put some effort into trying to find at least tentative answers to questions like the one just put forward.

It will be useful to start by considering in general what sort of sensible answer we can expect to get to this question. We will, for example, have to form as clear an idea as we can about what can possibly be meant by the notion 'cause of a linguistic change'. Closely related to this, we will have to consider what is meant by a phrase such as 'a valid explanation in historical linguistics'. We will have to have some ideas about what conditions a piece of historical linguistics must fulfil in order to be able to call it a valid explanation, since, presumably, a part of an explanation of some specific historical change will be a statement about its causes.

5.2 Explanation

5.2.1 Explanation in synchronic linguistics. I should like to start by making some comments on the term 'explanation' in linguistics in general, and then turn to its possible uses in historical linguistics. In recent years questions of methodology and the nature of explanations in synchronic linguistics have received a great deal of attention (see e.g.

Botha 1971 ; Derwing 1973 ; Cohen 1974; Langendoen 1976; Lass 1976a: especially 213–20). The reason for this is that, probably more than in most other subjects, not only can it be a matter of dispute how to explain linguistic phenomena synchronically – that is, what sort of theoretical machinery is needed – but it is also a matter of dispute what there is to explain. Obviously, there is no room here for a thorough discussion of these matters, since almost total confusion seems to reign, but I will try to clarify some points which may be relevant to what I have to say about Icelandic.

One point that may be relevant is what we might call the question of depth of explanation. Chomsky (1965) distinguishes between what he calls 'descriptive' and 'explanatory adequacy'. This distinction has to do with the dichotomy between universal and particular grammar (on the psychological side: 'linguistic competence' and *'faculté de langage'*). Chomsky's point seems to be that a theory is 'explanatorily adequate' in so far as it 'explains' facts about particular grammars in terms of a universal grammar. This implies that linguists are concerned with at least two types of activities, (i) describing particular languages by writing grammars for them, and (ii) describing what are the common features of all grammars by writing a Universal Grammar and relating it to particular grammars. If we look at this in terms of explanation, we could say that Chomsky's point is that facts about particular languages are explained by particular grammars, but facts about particular grammars are in turn, in some sense, explained by Universal Grammar. We seem, then, to be able to talk about explanations on at least two levels; that is, one can explain *facts about languages* by writing particular grammars and one can explain *facts about grammars* by writing Universal Grammar. (Obviously there is a famous question lurking behind this one: What explains Universal Grammar?)

Another question is, of course, what actually constitutes an explanation in linguistics. I will deal with this by trying to form some idea as to what, in general, could be called an explanation of some phenomenon, and compare this to what we might call explanations in the context of linguistics. I will not try to give a review of the literature on this very central problem in the philosophy of science, but rather make an attempt to express my intuitions about matters related to it, which to some extent are influenced (in a positive or negative way) by my reading of, for example, parts of Popper (1968), Bach (1974) and Lass (1976a:213–20).

In a sense, one can say that an explanation is simply *a higher-order description of an event or state of affairs.* This seems to make some sense if we look at a simple example. We may observe a simple fact, say, that John has a pain in his toe. We have described a state of affairs. We can find an 'explanation' for that state of affairs by observing that there is a splinter stuck in John's toe. Evidently, this 'explanation' is simply a description of another state of affairs, that state of affairs being that a splinter in John's toe irritates his nerves so that he feels pain. If we can believe that the presence of the splinter is related to the pain, we may accept this as a valid explanation. We might stop there and say that we have explained the fact that John has a pain in his toe, but we may be more curious and search for a deeper explanation. Here, we can go in different directions. We might want a more detailed account of the relation between the fact that there is a splinter in John's toe and the fact that he feels pain. In that case we might enter on the activity practised by neurologists, who try to describe in more detail how irritation of nerves causes sensation of pain. We might not be interested in that problem, however, but rather we might want to explain the state of affairs as a result of which John has a splinter in his toe. We could do that by observing, for example, that he has just walked barefoot on a wooden floor. We can describe that fact and in that way 'explain' the state of affairs that John has a splinter in his toe. That might arouse our interest in knowing more about how the splinter got into John's toe by describing in more detail what sort of movements John made when he walked on the floor, and what state the floor was in. In so doing we might observe some facts that arouse our curiosity further, and carry on finding new explanations, which turn out to be simply descriptions of some new states of affairs. Each state of affairs can be said to be explained by a more penetrating description in which new facts are brought out. In this definition, then, a description of facts on a deeper level of observation, call it level n, is an explanation of facts observed at a more shallow level, level $n-1$. Each explanation gives rise to new puzzles, and this can go on indefinitely, unless perhaps ultimately we could reach a state where we have explained all phenomena, in which case we might have reached God, which (who) is perhaps a state of affairs which (who) cannot be explained by another state of affairs. In case we are not looking for God, we might only want to go a certain distance on this infinite (or ending in God) ladder of explanations; the limit at which we stop is determined by things like our intellectual capacities, the amount of time we have on our hands and the degree to which our curiosity is aroused. We may stop at the observation that John has a splinter in his toe and just take that for granted, or we might be more curious, which could, given enough time, energy and ingenuity, lead us to the forefronts of several sciences (neurophysiology, physics etc.).

To go back to Chomsky's descriptive and explanatory adequacies, we could, as I said before, say that a grammar (for Chomsky meaning also 'competence') for a particular language, being a description of the system (or lack of system) behind the sentences of that language, 'explains' the corpus of the sentences of that language. It is, in Chomsky's terms 'a theory of the language'. On a deeper level, Universal Grammar (being 'systematically ambiguous', meaning also *faculté de langage*) can be said to explain particular grammars; that is, it can tell us, in part at least, why the grammars of particular languages are the way they are. In describing Universal Grammar we find a basis for (perhaps only partial) explanations of particular grammars. If we are curious enough, we could of course ask ourselves why Universal Grammar is as it is. This is a question which we will not discuss here for obvious reasons.

A third problem that arises in this context (in addition to the question of the depth of explanations and the question of the essence or nature of explanations) is the question of what linguists should explain. Some would say that they should explain 'all systematic linguistic phenomena, including those dealing with the use of language', as Langendoen (1976:690) puts it. Others would say that the scope of linguistics is more narrow, that only some regularities observed in linguistic behaviour should be dealt with (the 'narrow scope' view; cf. Langendoen *loc. cit.*). It is, for example, possible to study what people say without studying why or in what context they say it. Another question pertaining to the scope of linguistics is the question of *reality*. Some linguists would maintain that they are describing 'psychologically real competences' of speakers, others would say that they are dealing with 'social reality', and still others do not commit themselves as to the relation of their models to any sort of reality. Obviously there is no room here for a detailed discussion of these matters. In fact we can form a general idea of the concept 'explanation in linguistics' without having solved the realism problem, or having sorted out in detail which aspects of people's linguistic behaviour we would want to reserve as a home ground for linguists. Of course we will not, in this framework, be able to sort out *particular instances* of explanations as good or bad without having formed an idea of what there is to be explained, but a general concept can be formed and particular applications envisaged without our having resolved these basic questions.

What is essential for the usefulness of my concept of explanation as a 'higher-order description' is that it is always possible to find a reference point for the description or explanations given. This is only too easy for realists, since the descriptions would always make claims about *reality* (states of affairs in the real world), mental or social according to the point of approach. Others might resort to a more abstract level for reference and talk about a 'logic of language' having a similar ontological status as that sometimes assigned to logic and mathematics. What is essential is that we have some means of knowing whether the descriptions or explanations given are true or false, good or bad.

It may seem that my concept of explanation as a higher-order description cannot cope with what could perhaps be called the relatively modest and realistic point of view that grammars do not have to describe reality – psychological or social. It is sometimes suggested that it is sufficient that grammars generate all the forms of the language under investigation (for example, by enumerating recursively all the sentences and giving them 'structural descriptions') without demanding at the same time that the derivations represent any reality. But it is doubtful whether anything that might be called 'non-realist grammar' is conceivable within linguistics as a science of human language. Even the concept of grammar just mentioned is realist in the sense that it has a 'real' point of reference in the corpus of sentences that it aims at generating. The neutrality with respect to the reality of the derivations and structural analyses is then only a function of the limited explanatory aims of the theory. Judgements about the value of explanations given within this framework will still have to be made, but in terms external to the principle of linguistics.

In a grammar aiming at a description of psychological or social reality, my concept of explanation seems to be easy to work with. Such a grammar will, for example, make claims about the existence of some entities or relations in the minds of speakers of the language. These claims will be either true or not true, and 'all' that has to be done is to check whether these entities are there or not. Similarly, a linguist wanting to describe a 'social reality' would make claims as to the existence of some linguistic social institutions or norms that would have a similar ontological status to things like 'national hero' or 'marriage', and it would be a question of truth or falsity whether such things as the linguist describes existed or not. The testing of explanations in the framework of 'non-realist linguistics' would by no means be as simple as this. In fact my concept of explanations as 'higher-order descriptions' may seem to be of no use here.

In order for there to be a description, one must assume that there is something to describe. Since no reality is assumed for the analyses given by the grammar, my concept of explanation may seem absurd. In such a 'non-realist' framework a new problem arises, however: the one of evaluation of grammars. If there is no reality to limit the number of ways we can generate a set of strings, there seems to be no way we can say that one account is better than the other. All analyses are equally good or bad. Most scientists would find this rather uncomfortable, if only because there would be no way to show that one theory is better than another. A famous attempt at solving this problem is Chomsky's (1957) suggestion that an 'evaluation measure' should be built into theories of this sort and could evaluate differing hypotheses within the framework. But if there is no external reality or point of reference in terms of which the evaluation measure can be defined, it can only be defined in terms of the system within which it is supposed to operate, for example by working out a simplicity measure. One might, for example, suggest that the explanation which uses fewest symbols (presumably defined in some clear way) is the simplest and therefore the best one. But different theories will have different primitive concepts, and there is no guarantee that an explanation which is simple in one formalised theory will be simple in another, if it is translatable into that theory at all. If different theories choose different explanations, we are then faced with the task of choosing between different theories if we still want to have one rather than many valid explanations. But choosing between theories poses exactly the same problems as choosing between different explanations within a theory. We will have to ask on what grounds we can evaluate different theories. If this is possible at all, it would have to be done within a meta-theory which incorporates an evaluation measure able to discriminate between different theories. But it is difficult to see how such a meta-theory can be chosen other than by a still higher evaluation measure, incorporated into a meta-meta-theory, because how else do we know if we have picked the right way of choosing between different theories? Evidently, this evaluation hierarchy is infinite, if we do not have some referent against which to test our theories and evaluation measures. The point is that, in order to save such analyses as those mentioned above from meaninglessness, a point of reference must be assumed against which the analyses are projected and from which they derive their meaning. Such a referent might be some metaphysical reality, like an absolute notion of 'simplicity' or 'harmony', against which the different theories are evaluated. Some might say that this is better than the premature claims made within realist theories. However, others might find a mentally-real competence, or a socially-real language system, or even an abstract 'logic of grammars', less outrageous than the idea of some universal principle of simplicity or 'world harmony'. And of course we may note that if some 'world harmony' is assumed, against which a theory of language is ultimately to be tested, it is no longer 'non-realist' in a wider context.

If we say that a 'valid explanation of the phenomenon X' will mean something like a 'true description of the context in which the phenomenon X exists', assuming that there is some reality or truth that we aim to describe, we may still ask how we *know* that we have given a correct description of the phenomena. More often than not, the 'deeper states of affairs', which we describe and connect with the more observable phenomena, those we want to explain, are not directly observable. How can we, then, know whether we have described them correctly, whether our explanations are valid or not? According to Popper we will perhaps never know whether our descriptions are true. The best we can do is to limit the number of descriptions that *may* be true: '*Only the falsity of the theory can be inferred from empirical evidence ...*' (Popper 1968:55; emphasis his). This can be done, according to Popper, by testing the predictions made by the proposed theories. If we have proposed some unobservable state of affairs to prevail, it may have some more-or-less logical consequences in that it predicts some other phenomenon which may be observable. If these predictions are contradicted by observable facts, our theory is wrong. Popper suggests that the difference between scientific and non-scientific explanations is that the scientific ones must be refutable. Irrefutable explanations and theories are unscientific, according to Popper. For an explanation to be refutable by observable phenomena, it will have to be formulated in such a way that its empirical consequences are clear, in that predictions about some phenomena which should be observable can be deduced from it in some logical way. This is closely related to the concept of law; the explanations will have to be predictive laws (the laws being, in our terms, quantified descriptions of the relations between phenomena or states of affairs). If we go back to the example of the splinter in John's toe and his sensation of pain, the explanation we proposed for the fact that John had a pain in his toe was the fact that he had a splinter. This is not a law, it is only a hypothesis about a particular state of affairs or event; it does not have the all-quantifier in it, it does not make predictions. In order to make this explanation refutable in Popper's terms, it would have to be turned into something like this: 'Whenever a person has a splinter in his toe, he or she feels pain.' And if we find a person who has a splinter in his toe, but still does not feel any pain, our law is refuted. In Popper's framework, one instance is enough to refute the law. But the important question is: Would this mean that our explanation of the pain in John's case is invalid? I think not. In explaining the fact that John had a pain in his toe, it was assumed that there was a connection between two facts, so that John would not have had the pain if the splinter had not been there. This may or may not be true. But the truth of that statement about John's case does not depend on whether we find some other person who does not have a pain although he has a splinter in his toe. So, if we take a valid explanation to be a true statement about a state of affairs, the falsity of that statement, which is made about one state of affairs, cannot be proved by showing that it does not hold for another state of affairs, perhaps similar, but slightly different. The point is that our explanation is not a predictive law. We may be right in assuming that there was a connection between John's pain and John's splinter without making a predictive statement that every time a person has a splinter in his toe he will feel pain.

Popper's suggestion that something qualifies as a science only if it can form refutable theories, theories that make general predictions about things other than those observed, seems to me to impose an unnecessarily strict constraint on the definition of science. There is more to science than mere theory-making and theory-refuting. Description of what are assumed to be the facts is surely a quite legitimate scientific activity, if not more important than theory-making. It may well be the case that basically, our descriptions of simple facts have a common core with predictive general theories. (The particular descriptions are, in essence, hypotheses about particular states of affairs. This certainly seems to be Popper's view (cf. Popper 1968:27–9).) But there is a very important difference between a hypothesis about a particular state of affairs and a predictive law. Predictive laws claim that the descriptions they incorporate are valid for more cases than the ones to which they originally applied. But it is impractical to form laws unless we can be fairly sure that we have taken all relevant factors into consideration. There may be a connection between the splinter and the pain, but there may also be other conditions necessary for a person to feel the pain. To admit that there may be other things at work is not to say that it is scientifically invalid to make the assertion that there is a connection between the splinter and the pain.

It seems perfectly sensible to say that the fact that John has a pain is 'explained' in a technical sense by the fact that he has a splinter in his toe and that we can call this a 'scientific explanation' (although it is admittedly not a very 'deep' one). But explanation in this sense is evidently not a law, and that means that the validity of our explanations cannot be tested by Popper's method. There may thus seem to be a conflict between my concept of a scientific explanation and Popper's criterion for scientificality. My explanations are not refutable by Popper's simple method, but I would maintain that they are empirical claims and in theory testable against the 'real' state of affairs. But in order to be able to test the explanations, one will ultimately have to 'see' the real states of affairs, to compare the theories to that reality; and in many cases our perceptual apparatus, both natural and man-made, is not up to the task of making these direct observations. In the absence of direct observations we can only make more or less plausible guesses. It is only when we move from the stage of claims about particular, more-or-less isolated pieces of reality, which can be said to be true or false hypotheses about particular phenomena, to the stage of forming predictive laws, which can be falsified by counterexamples, that Popper's method can help us. It seems to be an unreasonable puritanism to maintain that only the quantified laws are scientific statements.

5.2.2 Explanation in historical linguistics. I will now turn to historical linguistics and consider what could be called a 'valid explanation' on that principle. We have already seen that the question of what counts as a valid explanation is closely connected with the testability of the truth of explanations. Hypotheses in a mentalistic synchronic grammar or a grammar purporting to explain some social reality, it was said, should in theory be testable against the presupposed reality. It was also seen that a 'non-realist' synchronic theory would need some (perhaps more metaphysical) point of reference for its explanations in order for it to be saved from vacuity. To try to put historical linguistics in the same perspective, I will consider what sort of reality hypotheses of language change should be tested against, or in general whether they can be tested against any reality; that is, whether historical linguistics is an empirical science.

It was mentioned that the reality assumed could either be a mental reality in individual speakers, or a social reality; that is, synchronic linguists can claim to describe the competences of speakers or the linguistic systems of communities. (I will, for the moment, ignore the possibility of assuming a more abstract ontological status for linguistic systems.) It may be equally difficult actually to test hypotheses about social reality and hypotheses about mental reality, but it is theoretically possible in both cases; some sort of a reality is claimed to exist, and the aim is to describe it.

With regard to what historical linguistics should aim at describing, it is evident that it could not be defined simply as the mental reality of speakers. It is, for example, difficult to see how such a thing as Grimm's Law can, in any sense, ever have been mentally real to any speaker. If historical linguists are committed to mental realism, they will obviously have to look, not at the competences of speakers in isolation, but rather compare the competences of speakers from different times and describe the differences between them. But it has been argued, most notably by Weinreich, Labov & Herzog (1968:156), that this is not enough, that one should 'abandon the individual homogeneous idiolect as a model of language' in order to be able to 'suggest a more intelligible mechanism of transfer [of linguistic innovations]'. What seems to be the main thesis of their paper is that if linguists are to understand language change, they cannot limit their scope to the competences of individual speakers, but have to be able to look at the linguistic systems of communities and to study variation between speakers, for example according to age or social stratification. Not only this, but the theory will have to allow for a conception of 'competence', not as homogeneous, but allowing for variability, for example accounting for the switches that speakers often make between styles or registers, according to context etc. Part of what historical linguists have to do, then, is describe the language systems of social groups and individual competences, seen as fluctuating systems, and they then have to compare different language systems, both social and individual, from different times and places. But even though a historical linguist could make true statements about different language systems and describe the differences between them, that would not be enough. Statements like: 'In Old Icelandic, vowel length was free, but became context-determined in the sixteenth or seventeenth century', seem to lack something. Such statements merely describe correspondences between two stages in the history of the language in question: Where we have X at stage A, we have Y at stage B. Even a sophisticated model like that proposed by Weinreich, Labov & Herzog is not adequate if it merely compares one fluctuating system with another. Historical linguists have claimed that for something to be an explanation in historical linguistics, it must do more than describe the situation before and after some change, and must say something about the relation between the two stages (cf. e.g. H. Andersen 1973; Jeffers 1974:236). For example, we want to know *why* the change took place, and also *how* it took place. This is where the concept 'cause of a linguistic change' comes into the picture.

The most obvious way to look for what we might term 'causes of a change of some linguistic form' is to consider closely the context in which the form occurs before or at the time the change takes place. This could be not only the purely linguistic or systematic context of the form, but also, as stressed by Weinreich and his collaborators, the wider social and cultural context. Still another part of the context of a linguistic form is, of course, the phonetic medium, describable in terms of articulatory processes and acoustic laws. This last part is of particular importance when phonological changes are studied. If all these aspects of the content are studied closely, we may be able to find some factors which can be said to have in some sense 'caused' the change.

In these reflections on the notion 'explanation in historical linguistics' it has been assumed that there is some reality which the historical linguist should be trying to describe. In other words, we have assumed that the discipline is in some sense an empirical one. But one may well wonder whether this is necessarily so. It is theoretically possible to write synchronic grammars without making any claims about psychological or social reality, and it would seem possible to approach historical linguistics in the same way. One might then say that when there is no external or empirical evidence about what happened, one will choose a descriptive model without claiming that it represents the facts. But obviously this would lead to the same problems of restricting the number of plausible explanations as we have seen in synchronic linguistics. Another factor that makes it less attractive to think of historical linguistics as a metaphysical discipline is that it seems, perhaps somewhat paradoxically, that facts concerning historical changes are often more easily established than facts about unconscious mental processes and structures. Indeed, it seems always to be assumed by historical linguists that they are trying to find out what really happened, and the things they are trying to describe are, to them at least, in some sense real. A historical linguist would get strange looks from his colleagues (not to mention other more normal people) if he were to say: 'I am not interested in knowing what really happened in the history of language X, I am only wondering what is the most beautiful (= simple) picture of what might have happened.' This statement seems fairly representative of the type of historical linguistics which does not claim to be trying to describe some reality, in other words, a non-realist historical linguistics.

I am not, needless to say, claiming that considerations of simplicity, for example, are illegitimate or worthless in historical linguistics. Indeed, it is considerations of simplicity that prevent us from postulating complexities in development that are not directly evidenced by data. We would not, for example, want to explain a correspondence between [ɑ] at stage A and [æ] at stage B as representing two changes [ɑ] ⟶ [e] and [e] ⟶ [æ], if there is no external evidence to the effect that this happened. Also, simplicity is at the centre of old-established conventions in historical linguistics like the comparative method. The use of the simplicity arguments in these instances is based on the policy (often called Occam's razor) that, until proven wrong, it is best to assume that things happened in a simple way.

If we now try to summarise what would qualify as an explanation in historical linguistics, we seem to come up with a rather complicated concept: An explanation in historical linguistics makes claims about at least two different, synchronically defined stages in the history of some language (i.e. the linguistic systems of communities and/or competences of individual speakers at these stages), and it also makes claims about correspondences between the systems at the two stages. Furthermore it makes claims about the relation of particular forms at the first stage which show changed reflexes at the second stage to factors in the context of those forms, in such a way that we can say that the context in some sense explains why the change took place. The explanation may also have to make more specific claims about how the change took place; in other words how the 'cause' is related to the change and the result.

5.3 The term 'cause' in historical linguistics

I am trying to move gradually closer to what is supposed to be the main theme of this chapter, namely the 'explanation' of the Icelandic quantity shift. But I still have to make some general remarks, this time about the concept 'cause of a linguistic change'.

Closely related to the term 'cause', is the term 'condition'. The phrases 'cause of a change' and 'condition for a change' are often used to refer to the same thing. It seems to make some sense to say something like this: 'Under condition X, change Y will take place' or 'Under condition X, change Y can take place.' In statements like these it is assumed that there is some connection between the condition X and the consequence, the change, Y. We note that in the two conditional statements above, different claims are made. In the first, it is claimed that, given the condition X, the change Y *will* take place, but in the second, it is only claimed that, given the condition, the change *can* or *may* take place. In the latter it is only stated that the condition X is a *necessary condition* for the change, but it is not assumed that the change *will* take place. In the former statement, on the other hand, it is maintained that the condition X is both *necessary and sufficient* for the change to take place: given the condition, the change both *can and will* take place.

If we now put the term 'cause', as used in historical linguistics, into the perspective of necessary and sufficient conditions, it seems that it can only be used in a sense similar to that of 'necessary condition', and that we will never find sufficient conditions for linguistic changes. I am not saying, of course, that linguistic changes do not have sufficient conditions. The fact that changes occur must mean that, in some sense, there are sufficient conditions for their taking place ('sufficient condition' meaning in this context the surroundings that make it necessary for the change to take place). I am only maintaining that it would be too much to expect linguists to find all these sufficient conditions for all linguistic changes.

If it were true that for any change X it is possible to find sufficient conditions for it (i.e. there is no change Y such that it is theoretically impossible to find sufficient conditions for it), that would mean that it is theoretically possible to find sufficient conditions for all changes a given language is going to undergo. If there are no limits that discriminate against any language as far as this is concerned, it would be possible to find sufficient conditions for every single change that every single language is going to undergo. Thus, if it is in principle possible to find sufficient conditions for linguistic changes, it means that it is theoretically possible to predict every single change that every single language is going to undergo from here to eternity.

We are here faced with a problem common to all evolutionary sciences (evolutionary biology, genetics, history etc.), the problem of whether evolution can be predicted (cf. Scriven 1959). The question can be dealt with from two points of view. One can wonder whether it is *logically* possible to predict evolution. This is a philosophical problem, the answer to which probably depends on whether something like complete randomness exists. I will not try to solve this here. The other point of view is the more *practical* point of view of individual disciplines. In historical linguistics, as in evolutionary biology, it is not only linguistic factors which determine how linguistic entities evolve. There are always present other 'external' factors which confuse matters: 'the irregularity-producing factors lie outside their [i.e. the disciplines'] range of observation and are not predictable by reference to any factors within this range' (Scriven 1959:478). For language, these external factors are, for example, physical surroundings (it is possible for a language to die out because all its speakers die in an earthquake or some other natural catastrophe), but probably the most important 'irregularity-producing factor', as far as the evolution of language is concerned, is the human will (sometimes harnessed into currents of social laws and etiquette), which is in principle unpredictable from the point of view of linguistics. If historical linguistics is to be a branch of linguistics, working with more or less the same technical apparatus as other branches of linguistics, it is impossible to demand from it that it find sufficient conditions for linguistic changes and thus make them predictable. If linguistic changes are to be predicted, it requires knowledge of all sorts of things which have nothing to do with linguistics; in fact, historical linguistics would have to become a sort of theory of everything.

It seems, then, that if the term 'cause' is to have any meaning within historical linguistics, it certainly cannot mean 'sufficient condition'. It will have to mean something similar to the logical concept 'necessary condition'. In dealing with historical change, one can often find certain features which seem to be related to those features that change. For example, it has been noted that, in Germanic, stem vowels were fronted in forms where *i* or *j* followed the stem. The presence of a following *i* or *j* was a condition for the fronting of the vowel. Evidently, we are not talking about a sufficient condition, so that whenever a stressed vowel is followed by *i* or *j* (with some intervening consonants) it gets fronted. There are exceptions to this, not only in that in many languages *i*'s and *j*'s can follow stressed vowels without fronting them, but also in that there are quite a few exceptions to this in Germanic: Old Icelandic *staðr* place' (< *staðiz*) does not have a front *e* in its stem even though it was followed by an *i* at the time when the fronting of the stem vowel of *gestr* (< *gastiz*) took place. Many of these exceptions can be explained by more or less general features which interfere with the otherwise valid law, and the fronting did not have to take place. But the important thing is that we can say that if the *i*'s or *j*'s had not been there, the fronting would not have taken place. The presence of *i*'s and *j*'s was a necessary condition for fronting; there was a relation between the fronting and the presence of the *i*'s and *j*'s. It seems perfectly reasonable to use the term 'causal relation' to denote this. We can thus say that *i*'s and *j*'s caused fronting of preceding stem vowels.

So far, so good, but we have not gone far enough. If we simply state our definition of cause in terms of the concept 'necessary condition', we seem to have a rather wide definition. We may, for example, observe that a language will not change unless it is spoken (or used). Thus we can say that if language X had not been spoken, change Y would not have taken place. It is a necessary condition for change Y that the language X was spoken, and thus, according to our definition, the change Y was caused by the fact that X was in use. Of course this can be said to be trivially true, but no linguist would consider it a great achievement to be able to state this. Our definition of cause may thus lead to such, in a sense, absurd uses of the concept. But that may not be a bad thing. In reality, this is exactly the same thing as occurred in the above discussion of explanation. Explanations can be valid, but trivial. The explanation using the fact that language X was spoken to explain a change in that language is one of that type; it is perfectly legitimate, but it is very uninteresting. We are not surprised or enlightened (or amused) by this observation. It is only when we are surprised, when we experience some sort of revelation when faced with an explanation or a discovery of a cause (or causes) that we feel that our effort has been worthwhile. We can thus say that causes are more or less obvious, and explanations more or less interesting. Since our investigation is generated by curiosity, we will not want to discover what we already know, but rather look for new answers. Thus the number of projects that will be proposed in research will be greatly limited by this attitude of the researcher and his colleagues. The more interesting the discoveries, the better.

This is, however, still not enough to limit the use of the term cause in a way that seems desirable. It is not only that we want to be surprised by good explanations; we want to be sure that they are 'relevant' (cf. Hempel 1966:48). We would like to eliminate explanations like: 'The quantity shift was caused by the execution of Bishop Jón Arason.'[1] The question is how we can do this. The claim made by this explanation, referring it to our definition of cause, is that if Jón Arason had not been executed, the quantity shift would not have taken place. But, of course this cannot be tested; we will never know what would or would not have happened if Jón Arason had not been executed. So, on the grounds of our definition we cannot get rid of the hypothesis claiming that Jón Arason's death caused the quantity shift. This is, of course, intolerable. The commonsensical answer would be that the death of Jón Arason had nothing to do with the quantity shift. This is really an empirical claim. It is claimed that in reality the nature of Jón Arason's death and the nature of the quantity shift were such that they happened independently of each other.[2] And when we connect the fronting of stem vowels in Germanic with the presence of *i*'s and *j*'s we claim that the 'nature' of the fronting and the 'nature' of the *i*'s and *j*'s and their relation to the stem vowels were such that there was a connection. This is either true or not true. We find it likely to be true on various grounds. Our belief that this is so makes it sensible to claim that the *i*'s and *j*'s caused the fronting of stressed vowels.

It must be admitted that the concept of cause that is intended to emerge from this somewhat lengthy digression is far from being precise. Indeed, it has been maintained by philosophers like Hume that the causal relation exists only in the minds of people and is an (often misguided) interpretation of the relation or non-relation between two events (cf. von Mises 1951:151–62). There is, I feel, more to the causal relation than this. There are in reality some events that are connected to some other events in a way they are not connected to still others; in order to express this, human language, scientific as well as every-day, needs some concept.

In the belief that this is so and on the basis of the 'clarification' of the concept 'cause', suggested here, I will carry on happily in spite of the pessimistic comments quoted at the beginning of this chapter, implying that there is little hope of finding the causes of linguistic changes. If the meaning of the term 'cause' as a linguistic *terminus technicus* is restricted along the lines described above, there seems to be nothing wrong with applying it in historical descriptions.

5.4 The causes of lengthening and shortening

Let me now at last turn to the particular problem we have been facing and speculate about the cause or causes of the quantity shift. I have already suggested that it is not necessary to assume that the shortening of old long vowels in front of two or more consonants took place at the same time as the lengthening of short vowels in front of no more than one consonant.

Similarly, it is not necessary to assume *a priori* that the two changes had the same causes.

As far as the shortening of old long vowels is concerned, I have suggested that at an early stage there was a phonetic tendency to have underlyingly-long stressed vowels shorter than directly predicted by their underlying features, when they were followed by two or more consonants. I tried to make this plausible by postulating an articulatory unit, we can call it a phonetic syllable, which was delimited by stress. This unit, which we can assume was primarily a phonetic element, occurring in actual speech performance, was not necessarily central to the 'structure' of the language in the period we are discussing. (Presumably, unstressed phonetic syllables were different performance units, and probably different phonetic laws applied there. They may be left out of the discussion here.) Having assumed a phonetic unit, the stressed syllable, it will be assumed further that there was a tendency for all such units to be of approximately the same duration. Given these assumptions, it can easily be imagined that when a phonological form like *fátt* 'few' (neuter) – one syllable with a phonologically long vowel followed by a geminate, which was presumably relatively long in its phonetic duration – was pronounced as a phonetic stressed syllable, its vowel tended to be shorter than the phonologically identical vowel of the form *fát* 'confusion' which was followed by only one consonant. It can thus be imagined that the shortening of long vowels was originally initiated by a tendency of the long vowels to adapt to their phonetic surroundings. These phonetic surroundings were the stress and the following consonantism. The phonetic stress delimited the immediate context of the vowel, and when a part of the context was a long following consonantism (a geminate or a consonant cluster) the vowel was relatively short. At first, this shortening of the vowel was probably irregular and varied according to speakers, some speakers shortening the vowel more often and more regularly than others. This may also have varied according to dialect or class, and it should be easy to fit this sort of thing into a model similar to those used by Labov (1965) and Weinreich, Labov & Herzog (1968) for variation in American dialects.

At a later stage it can be assumed that the shortening of long vowels became more regular, until some language-learners picked it up as a 'full-fledged phonological rule' of the language and made the generalisation that all stressed vowels are short when occurring in front of two or more consonants. It is obviously a difficult problem to decide exactly at what stage a new rule like this one becomes, so to speak, an integral part of the phonology, so that all (or the majority of) the speakers have it as a 'regular phonological rule', as opposed to a more or less irregular phonetic alternation. Indeed it may be that it is theoretically unsound to make such a distinction, since it would seem that borderline cases will always occur, where it is impossible to decide whether to call something a low-level phonetic alternation or a regular phonological process. One might perhaps say that the problem is a pseudo-problem, created only by an unjustified dichotomy between phonetics and phonology. But it seems necessary, at least for practical purposes, to draw some distinction between completely phonetic alternations which are conditioned, for example, by the capacities of the speech organs or some physical laws of acoustics, and systematic phonological alternations which are defined by the rules of the grammar, and phonological rules which are language-specific and learned by speakers as part of the conventions of the language and not explainable in general phonetic terms.

In this context one may ask what, in the process I have been describing above, we should call 'the linguistic change', from the point of view of historical linguistics. Is it the appearance of the phonetic tendency to shorten long vowels in certain phonetic environments, or is it the actual incorporation of the phonological rule into the structure of the linguistic norm, or the change in the abstract 'competences' of speakers of the language? We are evidently faced with a situation which is reminiscent of historical structural linguistics, where there is a distinction between an allophonic change and the restructuring of the phonological system; the phonemicisation of previously allophonic differences. It was common among structuralists to claim that the only thing that mattered was the structural change: 'Phonetic change acquires significance only if it results in a change of the phonemic pattern' (Bloomfield 1933:369). This may be true to a certain extent, but as soon as it comes to asking questions of *how* and *why* (instead of only *what*) the phonetic drift becomes extremely important. If we only bother about structural changes, we may in fact end up comparing different synchronic stages without being able to explain their relation. A historical linguist should be just as interested in the phonetic aspects as the structural aspects of changes, and therefore there does not seem to be any justification for giving one aspect more priority than the other by singling it out as the change proper.

I have set forth a hypothesis concerning the cause and nature of the shortening of long vowels before two or more consonants. It could be said that I have proposed at least a part of an explanation of that part of the quantity shift. It is now reasonable to ask on what grounds we may think that it is valid; that is, do we have some evidence to support it? Part of the justification of our hypothesis is implicit in the above description of it. I have tried to give the explanation some plausibility by making it believable from the phonetic point of view. But if we start looking for other things that might corroborate it, the result will be disappointing. As said before, the testing of hypotheses like the one proposed is an empirical matter. Ideally, we would simply go out and see whether the hypothesis fits the facts. But the problem is that we do not have direct access to the details which would confirm or refute our hypothesis. We do not have access to speakers of Old Icelandic who show or do not show a tendency to have all stressed syllables of the same duration or have a more or less regular tendency to shorten long vowels in front of more than two consonants in stressed syllables. Nor do we know exactly what Old Icelandic stress was like. There may also have been other factors at work, like some laws of tonality, which, it is assumed, were the historical origin of the modern Norwegian and Swedish word tones. There are all sorts of things we would like to know, but do not. In the absence of relevant data, we can only make guesses which seem more or less likely to be true.

I will now turn to the question of what caused the lengthening of short vowels. I have already assumed that in Old Icelandic there existed an articulatory unit which I called the stressed syllable. I also assumed that there was a tendency to have these stressed syllables of approximately the same duration. On these grounds an explanation was proposed of why the old long stressed vowels were shortened before two or more consonants. Obviously, if we believe in these assumptions, we can use them to explain why the old short vowels lengthened. When a syllable like *fat* 'a piece of clothing', in which a short vowel is followed by only one consonant, was pronounced as a stressed phonetic syllable, we can look at the lengthening of the short vowel as resulting from the tendency to have all stressed syllables of the same duration. If the vowel was stretched, the quantity of the syllable could come to match approximately that of old heavy syllables like *fát* 'confusion' or *fatt* 'erect' (neuter).

It should perhaps be emphasised that I am not saying that the vowel was stretched *in order for* the syllable *fat* to get the same quantity as the heavy syllables; rather I assume that at the initial stage the lengthening was an automatic consequence of the stressedness of the syllable. This seems to be a reasonable assumption, given the close relation between

stress and duration which phonetic studies have shown to prevail in many languages. Obviously, it is possible to stretch a light syllable ending in a short vowel followed by one consonant in two ways; either the vowel or the consonant could be stretched. However, there are probably differences in the 'stretchability' of different segments; for example, it may seem to be easier to prolong the duration of vowels than that of stops. Other consonant segments, like nasals, would seem to be quite 'stretchable'. At the earliest stages of the lengthening of old light syllables, it is, then, quite possible that some syllables were lengthened phonetically by stretching the consonant (as must have been the case in many Swedish and Norwegian dialects), and it is also possible that both segments were sometimes stretched at the same time. Indeed, there are examples to be found which seem to reflect a consonant lengthening. One such is the adverb *fram* 'forward' which, when pronounced under stress in Modern Icelandic, has a long consonant and a short vowel, but seems to have had a short vowel and a short consonant in Old Icelandic. Furthermore, it has been suggested that lexical doublets in Modern Icelandic, one form showing a long consonant and the other a short one, for example *ramur –
rammur* 'strong' (Sigmundsson 1970:325), could derive from a stage of phonetic indeterminacy as to the length of the segments. It seems very likely that at the earliest stages of the phonetic lengthening of old short syllables, there existed forms in which a phonologically short consonant was stretched, but most likely a lengthening of the vowel was more common. When the lengthening in old stressed syllables became a part of the phonological system, the generalisation that was made by new speakers was probably that all stressed vowels were long before one consonant, but in a few cases, as in the form *fram*, restructuring took place in the lexicon so that the old short consonant was replaced by an underlying geminate.

5.5   A shift or a conspiracy?

In discussing the dating of the changes, and on various other occasions, I have touched on the question of whether the quantity shift was something which could properly be called a 'shift', or whether the term 'conspiracy' should be applied. Obviously, in order to be able to deal sensibly with such a question, we would have to give these two notions some clear meaning. One factor we have assumed would distinguish between the two notions is the timing of the events. If we have reason to believe that some complicated change took place in 'one stage' or over a short period of time, we would presumably tend to call it a shift or a single change, whereas if a number of changes taking place at different times 'conspire' to form a unified, simply statable result (cf. Lass 1974), we might want to call it a historical conspiracy. Another factor which will have some bearing on whether we call something a conspiracy or a shift is the cause (or causes) of the change (or changes). If we could say that a complicated change was caused by one single factor, we would tend to call it a shift or a single change, whereas if a number of changes forming a unified result (that result being apparently the only thing the changes have in common) are relatable to different conditions, or perhaps no prior conditions at all (the only reason for their taking place apparently being the result), we would tend to call it a conspiracy.

I have put forward hypotheses as to what caused the shortening of old long vowels and the lengthening of old short vowels in stressed syllables. I related both of these changes to stress, and we can say that in this respect the causes have a common element, and that consequently we should perhaps call the quantity shift a proper shift. However, the stress was related to the change in different ways. In the case of the shortening of old long vowels, one can say that the stress was not the most direct cause of the shortening, but rather the stress-pattern defined the context in which the shortening took place. I suggested that within the context of an articulatory unit which I called a stressed syllable the heavy postvocalic consonantism caused the long vowels to develop shortened allophones. In the case of old short vowels, however, we can say that the stress was a more immediate context for the lengthening, there being a close phonetic connection between stress and duration or quantity. We see, therefore, that the question of whether the same factors caused the shortening of old long vowels and the lengthening of old short ones cannot be answered simply with a yes or no. Even though the phonetic features most immediately connected with the changes are different – on the one hand a long following consonantism, and on the other, stress and a short following consonantism – a common factor lurks in the background, namely (according to my assumptions) a tendency for all stressed syllables to be of the same quantity.

One might perhaps object that this common factor is not a historically prior cause, as I claim, but simply the conspiratorial result of the two changes. Perhaps it is not justifiable to say that a tendency for all stressed syllables to have the same quantity was a part of the environment of the phonetic processes involved; we ought rather to say is that it was a consequence of the two changes that all stressed syllables came to have the same quantity. If this objection is valid, we could perhaps turn around and say that uniform quantity for all stressed syllables was the 'aimed-at result' of the changes (to borrow a phrase from Lass 1974:312), and it is not the case that the tendency to obtain the same duration for all syllables was a prior phonetic cause of the changes, but rather that it was the 'purpose' of the changes that all stressed syllables were to have the same quantity. One could then say that the uniformity of the quantity of stressed syllables was the 'final [orthogenetic] cause' (cf. Lass 1974:312, 333) of the changes. Looked at in this way the quantity shift seems to qualify as a historical conspiracy.

It seems, then, that the answer to the question of whether to call the quantity shift a conspiracy or a shift may depend (apart from the question of the dating) on whether the tendency for all stressed syllables to be of the same duration can be said to have been a relevant factor in the phonetic processes resulting in the systematic changes of vowel shortening and vowel lengthening. I have already suggested that this was the case, but one may of course wonder whether this is right. We can put the question like this: Is it more likely that what the two changes have in common is that they were partly triggered off by a common environment or that they aimed at the same result, which could then be called the 'final cause' of the change? One might say that the answer to this question will depend on what general view we have of linguistic change and its causes. If we look at language change as in general caused by phonetic and other factors present at the time of change or shortly before it, we would tend to favour the explanation which says that the changes were caused by a phonetic tendency to have all stressed syllables of the same duration. Another way of looking at language change is that it is in general, or sometimes, teleological: changes sometimes occur in order to attain some target, reachable in the (near or distant) future. If one accepts the latter as a more plausible view, one would presumably favour the conspiratorial explanation. Of course the two points of view are not mutually exclusive; it is possible to say that some changes are teleological and others mechanical; and indeed one can maintain that some (or all) changes are partly teleological and partly mechanical. (Perhaps one could say that 'structural changes' are teleological, introduced in order to restore order to some more or less chaotic situation created by mechanical phonetic tendencies.) Rather than embarking on the methodological questions which arise in a discussion of this sort, I will content myself with stating that, generally, it seems less likely that language change should have some predetermined purpose; consequently, an explanation requiring this assumption should be avoided if another explanation is possible. I will therefore assume that the lengthening of short vowels and the shortening of long vowels derive from a common phonetic element, namely a tendency to have all stressed syllables of the same quantity (the shortening of long vowels, of course, being more indirectly relatable to this tendency as a cause, the more immediate cause being a long consonantism following).

It should be emphasised that although it may seem that the term 'conspiracy' should not be applied to refer to the Icelandic quantity shift, that does not mean that it should not be applied to other phenomena. For instance the changes in English discussed by Lass (1974), which gradually, over a long period of time, 'aim at' eliminating vowel length as a paradigmatic feature, are much less amenable to a mechanistic explanation of the sort proposed here for the Icelandic quantity shift, because the changes forming the quantity conspiracy in English, culminating in Aitken's Law in Modern Scots, are much more formally heterogeneous and chronologically far apart than the Icelandic changes seem to have been. It seems that the term 'historical conspiracy' can be used to refer to the English changes, at least until a more satisfactory explanation presents itself to make the term superfluous.

NOTES

[1] Jón Arason was the last Catholic bishop in Iceland, executed in 1550.
[2] In actual fact one might find reason to deny this statement. Jón Arason was the leader of a strong opposition against Danish political influence. He was also, according to Þórólfsson (1929a), one of the last poets to follow the old tradition in the function of old light and heavy syllables. His social influence must have been considerable among opponents of Lutheranism and Danish power. He might, thus, have set a norm for a conservative variety of Icelandic retaining the old prosodic structure.

6 *Length and quantity in phonology*

As an epilogue to the discussion in the preceding chapters, I submit here some rather more general observations on the phonological status of duration. As a framework for the discussion I will assume the trichotomy between 'duration', 'length' and 'quantity' which was outlined in chapter 2.

6.1 Length

In general, in analysing segmental length phonologically, there is more than one option open to the linguist. These alternatives have been summarised by Lehiste (1970:43–4) as follows.

Length may be regarded as a feature of the segments of the language (most typically vowels, but consonants may also be analysed as long or short). In this analysis, some segments of the language are long, whereas others are short, much in the same way as, for example, some vowels are rounded and others unrounded. This feature can be 'distinctive' or 'non-distinctive' (in some sense) just as any other feature can be 'distinctive' or 'non-distinctive'. For length to be a 'distinctive feature' of a segment it is a necessary condition that there be at least two degrees of length in the segments, just as roundness is not said to be distinctive unless there are both rounded and unrounded vowels in the language. There may be other conditions for quantity to be phonologically 'distinctive', for example that the length of segments is not predictable by features in the environment.

Another way of analysing length is to assign it more or less the status of phoneme. Thus the difference between Old Icelandic *sat* 'sat' and *sát* 'ambush', for example, can be ascribed to the presence of a 'phoneme of length' in the latter. The pair could be transcribed like this: /sat/ vs /saːt/, where /ː/ is the length phoneme. Obviously this sort of phoneme has a peculiar status compared to other phonemes in that, for example, its phonetic realisation varies greatly, being (apart from the element of duration) completely determined by adjacent (preceding?) segments. It has been suggested that this peculiar status should be indicated by the name 'prosodeme' (Haugen 1949) or 'chroneme' (Jones 1962). This analysis would probably appeal only to the most abstract minded (pre-generativist) structuralists. It seems, for example, that there is something missing as far as the representation of the relationship between the length phoneme (chroneme or whatever) and the actual segment that is phonetically long. (See Haugen 1949 for a suggestion of an account of length and other 'prosodemes' (like tones) in terms of timing within the syllable.)

A third way of accounting for length is to derive it from higher-order units like syllables, or still larger units, even words (cf. Lehiste 1970:50ff). In this sort of analysis, the length of segments is determined by their position within these larger units, that is, their relation to other segments and their structural status in the unit. A very simple case of a system describable in this way would be one where vowels are long in open syllables, but short in closed ones. (Thus, every syllable, open or closed, would have the same quantity.) Questions of 'distinctiveness' may receive unclear answers in this sort of situation. This was reflected in the discussion above of whether it was vowel length, consonant length, or perhaps something else, that was 'distinctive' or underlying, in Modern Icelandic. A generative analysis of this situation would be one which left segments unmarked as to length at the underlying phonological level and then distributed it on the appropriate segments by a rule defined on the higher-order unit (the syllable or whatever).

One might, in this connection, wonder whether it would perhaps be improper to use the same term to refer to both types of length, derived and underlying. Would it, for example, be legitimate to use the same feature '[±long]' belonging to a universal phonological or phonetic alphabet to refer to both types of phenomena? Could one perhaps say – as Halle does (1959/71:61–2) when discussing palatal articulation, which is sometimes derived (or context-determined) and sometimes 'phonemic' or underlying – that we are dealing with different 'applications' of the 'same feature'? One could then say that the 'length feature' is in one case inherent in a segment and in another imposed by a phonological rule, and the difference would not be in the phonological concept of length (denoted by the feature [±long]) but in its function and place within the system.

For this question to make sense, a very big assumption must be made concerning the ontological status of phonological concepts, namely that phonological features are something positive, which can show up in different surroundings and which can always be the same thing. One might well wonder whether it would not be more sensible to look on phonological features as language-specific, having different meanings according to the systems in which they work. It can be said that a feature like [+high] has a different 'value', in the Saussurean sense, when it occurs in a system with two vowel heights than in one with three vowel heights. It is far from clear that there is something *positively the same* about the two instances of the height feature. Their phonetic (acoustic, auditory or articulatory) correlates may be similar in some ways, but that does not mean that their phonological 'content' (if any) is the same. One of the basic functions of phonological properties is to keep utterances apart, and their value or content will depend on the oppositional system in which they work. Trubetzkoy says (1958:60): 'Das Phoneminventar einer Sprache ist eigentlich nur ein Korrelat des Systems der phonologischen Oppositionen', and that 'in der Phonologie die Hauptrolle ... den distinktiven Oppositionen zukommt'. So, from the point of view of a phonology working with the concept of distinctive function, the main thing may not be the positive properties of distinctive features, but their opposition to other entities, and systems of oppositions are in principle either wholly different or wholly identical. Parts of these systems cannot be identical without the whole systems being identical.

So, if it is in principle the case that two different phonological systems have no entities which are exactly the same, then the feature [±long] will have as many values as the systems within which it operates. *A fortiori*, length in a system where it is predictable by rule will be a quite different thing from length in a system where it is free. It may, therefore, seem grossly misleading to use the same term for both. But if we recognise that 'length', 'highness', 'frontness' etc. may never mean exactly the same within grammars of two different languages, then we are in order. We do not assume that length and quantity in Old Icelandic were the same things as in Modern Icelandic, even though we use the same words to denote them.[1]

A fourth way of dealing with length is to analyse 'long' segments as clusters of identical segments. According to that principle the difference between *sat* and *sát* in Old Icelandic could be accounted for in such a way that *sat* would be analysed phonologically as /sat/ with a single vowel, but *sát* as /saat/ with a double vowel or vowel cluster. There are several things that have been listed as signs of this sort of underlying phonological structure. Trubetzkoy (1958:170–4) lists five phenomena (discussed below) which could be taken as indicating that a language analyses its long vowels as geminates.

If morphological boundaries can fall within a 'long' segment, as in Finnish for example, where there are paradigms like *talo* 'house' – partitive *taloa*, and *kukka* 'flower' – partitive *kukkaa*, Trubetzkoy (*ibid.*) suggests that long vowels should be analysed as geminates. The idea is that *a* + *a* in this case gives a long vowel, and that this analysis can be extended by analogy to other long vowels of the language. I am not sure that this is a very strong argument, although I may have used it when suggesting an analysis of long consonants in Modern Icelandic as geminates in chapter 2 (cf. p. 22). If, for independent reasons, it seems natural to analyse length of vowels as being, say, an 'inherent feature', it is difficult to see how, when two identical vowels are brought together by morphological rules, they can be analysed phonologically as anything other than long vowels. Trubetzkoy's argument is based on a 'free ride' principle: since a cluster-analysis seems to be appropriate in this set of cases, one might as well apply it to other cases, even though there is no independent motivation for it in these other cases.

A second indication of geminateness, Trubetzkoy suggests, is to be found when long monophthongs and diphthongs have a similar phonological status. That is, when long vowels and diphthongs seem to form a 'natural class' in that they can be represented as one in some phonological rules. He mentions (*ibid.*) a case in Central Slovak dialects, where there is a 'rhythmical law', according to which long vowels are shortened after heavy syllables. Long vowels and diphthongs contribute equally to the quantity of the syllable that is the environment for the shortening of the following vowel.

A third sign of the geminateness of long vowels is to be found, according to Trubetzkoy, when in phonological processes, long vowels (or syllables) have the same status as two short ones. The archetype of this sort of thing is the stress rule of Classical Latin, according to which stress falls on the second 'mora' preceding the last syllable; if the penultimate syllable was heavy (i.e. ended in a long vowel or was closed by a consonant), the stress fell there, but if it was short (i.e. ended in a short vowel), the stress fell on the antepenultimate syllable (cf. Allen 1969).[2]

Trubetzkoy's two remaining criteria are concerned with tonal or accentual variation within long segments. When there is a difference in tone or 'accent' at the beginning and the end of a long vowel, that, Trubetzkoy says, is a sign of 'Zweigliedrichkeit' of the vowel (pp. 172–3). A similar idea is proposed by Woo (1972:24–46), only here the geminateness of vowels is used to justify a particular analysis of the 'moving' tones of Mandarin Chinese. But Woo also mentions some other phenomena which according to her seem to support a geminate-analysis of Chinese long vowels independently of the tone phenomenon. There is a rule according to which in the absence of stress:

(a) long vowels (VV) become short (V),

(b) diphthongs (tend to) become monophthongs,

(c) a sequence of a vowel plus nasal becomes a single vowel (Woo 1972:35).

This could perhaps be taken to show that the second 'mora' of a long vowel and a segment following a short vowel have a similar status.

Although these criteria may seem plausible enough, it seems that one more criterion for showing that length is gemination of segments should be considered. Let us assume that in a hypothetical language 'long' vowels are geminates, and let us say that the canonical form for a syllable is CV(V) (C), that is, the syllable types that occur are CV, CVV, CVVC, CVC, and let us say that it has five basic vowels: *a, e, i, o, u*, which can combine to form vowel-geminates: *aa, ee, ii, oo, uu*. It could be said that a characteristic of this language is that it allows vowel-segments to combine to form long syllable nuclei. It allows sequences of two identical vowels, and so one might expect it to allow sequences of two non-identical ones; and granted that this is not prohibited by some other principles, the language should allow any combination of its five segments. In other words, we might suggest that one of the phonotactic principles of this language is something which says: *for every V there is a VV, where V is any vowel of the language*. We would expect the language to have not only vowel clusters (diphthongs) like *ai, ei, au*, but also *oe, iu, ui* etc., altogether twenty diphthongs. Of course, one might expect some of these vowel-clusters to be excluded by special phonotactic constraints, just as certain consonant-clusters are often excluded from certain positions in the syllable, but it seems that these should be regarded as exceptions to a general rule. It might turn out that many of the logically possible vowel-clusters could be disposed of as unfit either for articulatory or acoustic reasons, but one might still expect a vowel-geminating language to be rich in diphthongs.[3]

Another thing that would seem to follow from a geminate-analysis of long vowels is connected with this. If long vowels and diphthongs basically have the same structure, that is, two short vowels combined, one would expect, other things being equal, that the components of diphthongs get the same treatment as single short vowels, and each part of the vowel geminates should behave like a single short vowel. This could possibly be detected in historical changes like vowel shifts. If, in a system like the one mentioned above, *a* is fronted to *æ* by a context-free change, one would expect *aa* to go to *ææ*, *ai* to go to *æi* and *au* to go to *æu* etc. This criterion, of course, needs a historical perspective, which makes it a bit more difficult, but it has been used to demonstrate that Old English had a VV structure for its long vowels (Vachek 1959:446). Similarly, it is shown by Lass (1976a:94) that some generalisations concerning the great vowel shift in English can easily be captured by analysing long vowels as two identical vowels. For example, changes like that of *ee* (long *e*) to *ii* (long *i*) and that of *eu* to *iu* can be described as a single change of *e* to *i*.

To summarise, there are certain things that it seems should co-occur with vowel gemination, and these can be used as clues as to whether a language has geminates underlying its long vowels. It may be that none of these clues is conclusive, but when one or more of them is present, it can be taken as a sign that long vowels can be looked on as underlying geminates.

I have set up a distinction between four ways of analysing length: as an inherent feature, as a separate phoneme (prosodeme), as predictable or belonging to higher order elements, and as gemination. But it is conceivable that there exist systems with a mixture of more than one of these. In Lass (1974, 1976a) and Lass & Anderson (1975) it is assumed that a geminate-analysis can be combined with predictability of length in certain environments. In this analysis a lengthening rule can be stated simply as a gemination rule (and diphthongisation as epenthesis), and conversely, if needed, a shortening rule can be formalised as a deletion. This would seem to be an appropriate way of doing things, if there is good motivation for a geminate-analysis of vowels (or consonants), but there are still some synchronic processes at work, changing the 'length' of segments.

6.2 Types of correspondences between dichotomous systems

Lass (1976a:45) points out that there are basically two ways (with degrees of admixture) in which two dichotomous phonological systems, such as those split by length, can be related to each other. On the one hand, there can be corresponding pairs, so that there is a one-to-one function between the two systems, giving pairs where each phoneme from one system corresponds with one from the other. Lass calls this relation 'pair-based'. On the other hand, a dichotomous system can be split into two without there being a correspondence between any units in the subsystems. Here, the subsystems are opposed as wholes. All the segments of one subsystem have a property (or properties?) which members of the other subsystem do not have, but there are no segment-pairs which are kept apart only by the dichotomising feature. This sort of relation, Lass suggests, should be called 'set-based'. As an example of this type of dichotomy Lass takes the German vowel system, which has two sets of vowels, sometimes said to be distinguished by length, and sometimes by 'tenseness'. (Other conceivable examples are the vowel systems of Greek dialects discussed in Allen 1959.) Among the things that seem to justify a dichotomy in the German case is the fact that only vowels from one of the subsystems (the long or 'tense' ones) can appear in final stressed open syllables. In this type of situation it is appropriate to ask what makes some vowels, but not others, able to stand at the ends of final open stressed syllables. In principle one can look at this in two ways. Firstly, there seems to be some (perhaps phonetic) property of the vowels that makes them able to take up this position; a phonotactic constraint determining which vowels can stand in this particular position is stated in terms of some independently definable characteristic of the vowels. Secondly, one can say that the ability of the vowels to stand in this position is a property in itself. What the 'tense' vowels have and the 'lax' ones do not is the feature 'ability to stand in open final stressed syllables'. An obvious way to try to decide between these two alternatives is to see whether the two sets show a similar distinction in their behaviour in some other respects, whether some other phonological regularities (or irregularities) can be explained in terms of the 'tense/lax' dichotomy. In English, which has a similar distinction, there seems to be justification for a dichotomy independent of the positional argument, in that the vowels that can stand in open final stressed syllables show special behaviour with respect to stress-patterns (cf. Chomsky & Halle 1968:69 and *passim*; Lass 1976a:34). In this case it would seem desirable to abstract one 'phonological property' and use it as a common point of reference for the two (or more) phonological regularities. And then one might want to look for some phonetic property that could be used in giving substance to the 'feature' in question. Lass has shown that using the feature tense/lax, as Chomsky & Halle and many others do, amounts to nothing but inventing a cover term, since the feature seems to be phonetically empty, its 'phonetic correlates' having little or nothing in common but having been assigned to the feature 'tense'. Lass suggests that the 'tense' vowels of *boot, bite* etc. should be analysed as underlying vowel-clusters. Another way of accounting for the difference between the two sets of vowels is to emphasise a difference in the contact which the short ('non-tense', 'non-geminate') and the long ('tense', 'geminate') vowels make with following consonants (cf. Trubetzkoy 1958:176). This would bring us into the sphere of prosodic contours, and in that case the difference between *sit* and *seat* should perhaps be accounted for in terms of syllabic quantity, that difference in quantity or prosodic contour being derived from the characteristics of the vowels, or vice versa.

Pairing relations and set-based relations can theoretically be based on any sort of features. One can, for example, imagine a system where the feature 'rounded/unrounded' splits a vowel system into two subsystems, and there can, theoretically, be a one-to-one function between the two systems, based on the roundness feature. We are interested in cases where there seems to be some plausibility in assigning the dichotomising function to duration or length. Indeed, it is to be expected that the question of dichotomy in vowel systems arises in connection with length, since length has a very independent status as a variable in vowels. There seems to be very little in the way of markedness relations between length and other features that usually characterise vowels. Whereas we seem to be able to detect some general laws of naturalness (or markedness) of combinations of 'segmental' features like roundness, frontness and height (high back vowels tend to be rounded etc.), it seems to be much less obvious that length as a phonological entity combines more or less favourably with one vocalic feature than with others. True, the 'intrinsic duration' of high vowels is seen to be less than that of low (cf. Lehiste 1970:18–19), but that does not necessarily mean that high vowels are worse adapted than others for taking part in a length correlation as a phonological phenomenon. The fact that length seems to be easily combinable with other vocalic features makes it a good candidate for dichotomising vowel systems. It seems to be relatively easy to keep everything constant except the duration. That does not mean, of course, that length is always independent. As we have seen, in languages like

Icelandic and Faroese there seems to be a connection between diphthongál quality and length, and in standard German and Swedish there seems to be some connection between height and/or peripherality and duration (cf. e.g. Lass 1976a:46–9), but it is far from obvious that length can be said to be in some 'markedness' relation to other features as, for example, frontness/backness is to roundness.

It seems then, that the ideal function of length within vowel systems is to establish a paired relation between two isomorphic systems. By adding length to a system, one can get a set of pairs of long and short vowels. In this sort of situation where we have a pair-based relation, it is an open question how the length correlation should be accounted for phonologically. Whether it is looked on as an inherent feature, as context-determined in some way, or as gemination, one-to-one correspondence seems to be natural. But there is a connection between the question of the analysis of length and the question of the types of relations between dichotomous systems in that, in set-based dichotomies based on length, the most likely place to look for the 'underlying' place of length is within the segments themselves; it would be most likely to be an inherent feature. It would seem unnatural for a set-based dichotomy to be defined in terms of context-sensitive rules or gemination.

A set-based relation between a long and short vowel system seems to be theoretically impossible in analyses like the one proposed for Modern Icelandic in chapter 2, where length is assigned to vowels by a simple rule. Long and short (lengthened or shortened) pairs are automatically related by the rule of vowel length. It seems also rather odd to think of length as a prosodeme in the context of dichotomous systems in a set-based relation. A set-based length dichotomy is by definition such that there are no pairs kept apart only by length. So the 'prosodeme' would have to be something more than length. It seems that, basically, the plausible ways of analysing length in set-based dichotomies are either by geminate-analysis or by inherent feature-analysis. In the following I will try to show that a geminate-analysis is basically such that it fits only a pair-based dichotomy and that, consequently, an inherent feature analysis is the more appropriate in a set-based dichotomy, other things being equal.

If we have a dichotomy apparently based on length, but there is not a one-to-one correspondence between the two sets of vowels, it means that there are some vowels that do not take part in the correlation and/or that some other features go with the length, which make an additional (secondary) distinction between the two systems or potential pairs of vowels. If we wanted to analyse length in such a system in terms of gemination, we would face problems that do not arise in an inherent feature-analysis. In the first case, where there are vowels that do not take part in the correlation, we need to explain why certain vowels occur as geminates, but not others. If gemination of vowels is to be stated basically in terms of a principle of the sort mentioned above (p. 190), it would seem that we need to explain the non-occurrence of some geminates in terms of special phonotactic constraints. In an analysis giving length the status of an inherent feature this problem does not arise, since there is no reason to expect every vowel to have distinctive length even though some vowels do, any more than roundness/unroundness has to be distinctive in every vowel of a system where it occurs. In the second case, where there are other features that go with the length, the problem is different. Here, we are dealing with a situation where there are no pairs of long and short vowels having the same quality.

It is, of course, theoretically possible that there are some long and short vowels of which it can be said that they have more or less the same quality. But having already assumed that the relation between the subsystems is set-based, I will exclude this possibility for the purposes of this discussion. The fact that there are some pairs that are only kept apart by length could be taken as (some) indication that the subsystems are in a pair-based relation with secondary quality differences in some vowels. It is also possible that one is, in cases like these, dealing with subsystems in a 'mixed relation', having some pairs and the rest in a set-based relation. I am here, for the sake of the argument, only talking about clear-cut cases.

If we wanted to decide whether a system that on the surface seems to have a set-based dichotomy is analysable in terms of gemination, we would of course look for clues of the sort mentioned above. These clues might lead us to decide that a geminate-analysis is indeed appropriate, but I maintain that we have thereby automatically claimed (or should have claimed) that the relation between the two systems is fundamentally pair-based. Assuming that there is some logical difference between a geminate-analysis and an inherent feature-analysis, it seems that this should be so as a matter of theory. If a long vowel is analysed as a sequence of two identical vowels, one is in fact claiming that a long vowel is not one unit, but two: [aː] is 'really' not a single long vowel but two segments occurring together. As I have said before, in slightly different words, it seems that the fact that a vowel has two parts should lead us to expect that it can be split up and each part can occur independently of the other. So if we have a nucleus like /aa/ we would, granted that the language has single segment (short) nuclei, expect /a/ also to occur, and vice versa. But this would evidently lead us to expect a pair-based system, where there is a set of double syllable nuclei and another set of single nuclei in one-to-one correspondence.

We can put the matter in a slightly different perspective like this: if we have on the surface a dichotomous system, where there are no qualitatively identical pairs of long and short vowels, that is, the dichotomy seems to be set-based, there are two options open for an analysis in terms of geminateness. Either one can say that each vowel, long or short, has its own quality, and the difference between the long and the short vowels is that the long ones only occur as geminates and the short ones only occur as non-geminates. There seems to be no way of capturing this other than by stating, for each vowel quality, whether it is geminate or not. But then, of course, the question arises whether a geminate-analysis of this sort is not actually equivalent to an inherent feature-analysis. If two or more ways are possible for analysing length phonologically, one would like them to have different empirical (in the Popperian sense) implications. (One would, in other words, like them to be more than 'notational variants' of the same concepts.) If the prediction of the geminate-analysis that the same segment can occur either single or geminated is taken away from it, as in the above hypothetical example, the distinction geminate-analysis and feature-analysis will move closer to emptiness and the grounds for making the distinction weaken. The other way to deal with a surface system that seems to have a set-based dichotomy is to invent an abstract geminate-analysis. One can, for example, account for two vowels, say [a] and [aː], both occurring in some language, in terms of geminateness, by setting the long one up as a double and the short one as a single instance of the same vowel by abstracting. This could be done by setting up an abstract entity, which is either underlyingly back (as [aː]) or non-back (as [a]) or perhaps, being an abstract entity, unmarked with respect to backness. The surface forms would then be derived by a rule (or a set of rules) adjusting the backness of the surface segments. But evidently what is being done here is that pairing is being introduced into the abstract system: [a] and [aː], not being a pair distinguished only by length on the surface, are made such by analysing them as, respectively, a single and a double instance of the same phonological element.

The foregoing has, I hope, shown that to claim that length,

dichotomising a vowel system into two subsystems, should be analysed as gemination of vowels implies (or should imply as a matter of principle) that the relation between the two subsystems is fundamentally pair-based. But it has also shown another very important thing, namely the influence that allowing for abstractness has on the way phonological phenomena can be analysed. If one has a system that on the surface appears to have a set-based dichotomy and seems therefore not suitable for a geminate-analysis, it can be made amenable to such an analysis if a certain amount of abstraction is allowed. Given the possibility of abstraction, all sorts of ways open up for analysing systems as something other than what they seem on the surface. It becomes possible to relate vowels of different surface qualities to the same underlying quality, based on gemination vs non-gemination, as in the example above. As usual, when abstract analyses are proposed, this should be justified by some regularities that can be captured if the abstract analysis is adopted. For example, if long vowels behave like sequences of two segments with respect to some phonological phenomena, that may be used as an argument for an abstract geminate-analysis. But, of course, the abstraction will have to be evaluated as involving some 'cost'. Deriving a surface quality from a different underlying one, as in the above hypothetical example, seems a familiar enough process in generative phonology, and equipped with that, in fact suspiciously powerful, device one can account for qualitative differences between a pair of vowels differing in their underlying forms only in length (gemination). Systems where, on the surface, not all vowels take part in the long-short relation, as stated before, demand another type of solution in an abstract geminate- (by implication pair-based) analysis. Here, it seems most natural to account for the lack of pairing in terms of phonotactic constraints. For example, in a system where all vowel qualities except one appear freely as long or short, it may be plausible to set up a (perhaps independently motivated) phonotactic constraint prohibiting the occurrence of two instances of this particular vowel one after the other within one syllable. In this case the 'cost' of the phonotactic constraint will, of course, have to be measured against the 'gain' made in other parts of the grammar by analysing long vowels as geminates. It follows from this that the more constraints that have to be set up to prevent the otherwise predicted free occurrence of vowel geminates, the less plausible the geminate-analysis becomes, and the greater the other gains made by it will have to be.

From the foregoing it should be clear that allowing for abstractness in phonological solutions, leaving aside the question of the linguistic plausibility of abstract solutions in general, complicates the distinction we are discussing between geminateness or 'inherentness' of phonological length. Long and short systems that on the surface seem to be in a set-based relation and therefore suited for an inherent feature-analysis can, by abstraction, be made amenable to a geminate-analysis, which seems to imply a pair-based relation between the two subsystems.[4]

6.3 Diphthongs and long vowels

Up to now little attention has been paid to the relation between diphthongs and long vowels. I suggested that, other things being equal, a vowel-geminating language should be expected to be relatively rich in diphthongs, its basic principle being that vowels could combine freely to form vocalic nuclei of double length. I also mentioned Trubetzkoy's suggestion that if long vowels and diphthongs behave similarly, this could be taken as a sign that the language treats its long vowels as geminates.

Granted that a language analyses long vowels as geminates, it seems to follow that its diphthongs should be analysed as vowel clusters. (This is of course circular to the extent that Trubetzkoy's diphthong-criterion is used to establish the geminateness of the long vowels, but I will ignore that for the moment.) However, it is easy to find situations where such an analysis of diphthongs seems inappropriate. For example, if there is more than one degree of length of diphthongs, as in Icelandic which has an alternation between short and long diphthongs in forms like *dæma – dæmdi* 'to judge' (past vs pres.), or in Indo-European which is usually assumed to have had long diphthongs besides the 'normal' ones (cf. Allen 1976), it is not enough to state that a diphthong is simply a cluster of vowels. There would have to be added a distinction between, for example, 'short' and 'long' clusters.

According to my general belief that phonological entities are largely language-specific, I shall maintain that diphthongs can be different things in different languages. If diphthongs are to be analysed as vowel-clusters in languages that treat their long vowels as geminates, it seems that in languages that have length as a feature of segments (at some level, underlying or derived by rule), diphthongs should most typically be simply vowels with two qualitatively different stages, in other words moving vowels. This corresponds, in part at least, with H. Andersen's

(1972:18) distinction between 'sequential diphthongs' and 'segmental diphthongs'. 'Segmental diphthongs', according to Andersen's definition, are single segments 'whose central phase is acoustically heterogeneous in its temporal development'. A 'sequential diphthong' is a 'sequence of segments, usually forming part of the same syllable'. I will use these terms in the following, although I am not sure that I use them in exactly the same sense as Andersen. (It seems that some comments of Andersen's concerning 'phonetic and phonological diphthongization' may indicate that he considers that 'segmental diphthongs' cannot be phonemically (underlyingly) defined as such. I would not want to subscribe to this.)

It should perhaps be emphasised that I am not claiming that there is an if-and-only-if relation between length as a segmental feature and 'segmental diphthongs', or between length as gemination and 'sequential diphthongs'. I am saying only that, given one thing, the other is to be expected. A third type of diphthong should perhaps be added to the two mentioned above. These could perhaps be called 'combinatorial diphthongs'. An example would be the Modern Icelandic (except for south-eastern dialects) alternation between [ɔː] and [ɔi̯] [ʏː] and [ʏi̯], and [iː] and [ɪi̯] in forms like *bogi* [bɔi̯jɪ] vs *boga* [bɔːɣa] 'bow' (nom. vs acc.), *Hugi* [hʏi̯jɪ] vs *Huga* [hʏːɣa] a man's name (nom. vs acc.) and *stigi* [stɪi̯jɪ] (or [stijːɪ]) vs *stiga* [stɪːɣa] 'ladder' (nom. vs acc.). In the nominative forms of these words the voiced fricative following the vowel is palatalised by the following front vowel, but in the accusative it appears as a velar in front of a back vowel. When the palatal fricative meets the preceding vowel, a high glide appears, 'connecting' the vowel with the fricative. There seems to be good reason to analyse the morphemes in question as having underlying monophthongs and to account for the alternation accordingly, for example because the 'diphthongs' [ɔi̯], [ɪi̯] and [ʏi̯] do not occur in other environments, and [ɣ] does not occur before [ɪ]. We seem to have, then, a partial assimilation, where features deriving from segments that follow the vowel 'move into it' to make it diphthongal. Similarly in English, the diphthong in forms like *day* derives historically from a sequence of *æ* + palatal fricative, and while this process was still 'synchronically active', the form could perhaps be said to have a 'combinatorial diphthong' resulting from the concatenation of *æ* and *j*. It will of course have to be justified in each case that these 'combinatorial diphthongs' have a different phonological status from other, more 'deeply rooted' diphthongs.

An important question that I will not discuss here is that of the variation in the syllabic function of the two parts of diphthongs which gives rise to the distinction commonly made between 'rising' and 'falling' diphthongs. This should not invalidate the other comments made here about the nature of diphthongs.

If it is true that there are 'segmental diphthongs' with an internal movement of quality, it must follow that it is not necessary that phonological features like high, front and rounded always have whole segments as their domain. One can, then, have segments that are [−high] (or mid) at the beginning but [+high] at the end: [ei], or rounded at the beginning but unrounded at the end: [ɔa] etc. Although this fits rather badly with the general practice in using phonological features (cf. Chomsky & Halle 1968; Ladefoged 1971), it seems inevitable that such 'movements' in phonological quality within single segments should be allowed for. This sort of thing is by no means confined to vocalic diphthongs. There occur in languages in many parts of the world sounds that may be called consonantal diphthongs, for example pre- and postnasalised consonants [m͡b, n͡d, ŋ͡g, b͡m] etc. (cf. S. Anderson 1976). These sounds behave phonologically as single segments, but have a complex articulation, beginning as nasals, but ending as stops or vice versa. Anderson suggests that these, and nasals in general, should be treated as 'oral stops on which a nasal pattern is realized: if the stop is nasal throughout, we get the common primary nasals, while "contour" nasality patterns give rise to pre- and post-nasalized stops' (1976:343). Anderson also considers the possibility of treating affricates and labiovelars in a similar manner, but is rather doubtful whether this is appropriate. Anyway, the fact that both pre- and post-nasalised consonants occur and behave like single segments, seems to support the idea that diphthongs can be treated as single segments with changing articulation. What sort of formalism is needed for this is a different question which I will not discuss here.

6.4 Quantity

I have adopted Allen's (1973) distinction between length and quantity. There are several things that can be thought of as supporting a distinction between two phonological categories like these based on the phonetic variable of duration. I would like to make a few comments here concerning this, although I will have to leave many questions unanswered.

As is shown by Allen (1973:56–61), the concept of syllabic quantity is only relevant to what Fudge (1969) calls the *rhyme* of the syllable (cf. also Lejeune 1972:286). In traditional discussion of the length or quantity of syllables it is only the vowel and the following consonantism (if present) that are relevant. This is particularly clear in metrics where it is almost always the rhyme that is important. Thus *stal* and *sal* in Old Icelandic have the same quantity although they have different numbers of segments, whereas *stal* and *salt* have different quantities in spite of the fact that they have the same number of segments. The structure of the onset is irrelevant for the concept of syllabic quantity, apart from the relation there must of course be between the coda of a syllable and the onset of a following one.

This, among other things, leads Allen to reject a definition of quantity in terms of duration alone and to opt for a definition in 'motor' terms (cf. Stetson 1951), heavy syllables being defined as 'arrested' and light ones as 'unarrested'. The arrest of heavy syllables can either be made thoracically, with the result that the vowel is long, or orally by an 'arresting consonant' closing the syllable (Allen 1973:64). The obvious appeal of this theory stems from the 'phonetic sense' it seems to make in spite of the difficulty in substantiating Stetson's theory of syllables by experimental evidence (cf. Ladefoged 1967:20). But in a more abstract framework, other considerations may be brought forward. One might, for example, suggest that a certain amount of 'Stetsonism' is useful in accounting for the ontogenetic origin of linguistic constructs like syllables, while other elements may become more significant when the original phonetic condition for the emergence of the entity was obscured, for example by subsequent historical development (cf. Árnason 1978a). Here, formal or more indirect arguments may be brought into the discussion, since the unit originally close to the phonetic surface may have become 'phonologised'.

The basic significance of quantity as a phonological category would, it seems, not be in the functional (or systemic) sphere of concepts like distinctiveness, but rather in what might be called the organisational (or structural) sphere of the composition of the linguistic chain and the prosodic structure of the language. It is within that framework one will have to look for arguments in its support or disfavour. If there appears to be regularity in the pattern of segmental distribution, in that structural units of a set 'length' (for example measured in the number of units) seem to recur, this would seem to suggest the existence of our category. Thus, in Modern Icelandic, since the length of segments can be defined in terms of a unit larger than the segment and since that unit seems to be in some (not accidental) correlation with duration and stress, we are tempted to set up quantity in stressed syllables as a significant category in the organisational structure of the language. Similarly, since the Old Icelandic metrics seem to provide evidence of a distinction between at least two types of units, and since that distinction seems to be related to segmental length which in turn is likely to have had some correspondents in durational variation, we are tempted to set up a category of quantity with at least two values: heavy and light.

But there are other considerations relevant to the question of a distinction (in general theory or at the level of individual linguistic analyses) between length and quantity. The phenomenon of compensatory lengthening is only too common (cf. e.g. Allen 1973:52–3). In Proto-Nordic *ans- became ás-, and the disappearance of the nasal was compensated for by a lengthening of the vowel ($a > á$). This strongly suggests that some sort of unit of contour existed defining duration independently of segmental length, and we can say that the compensatory lengthening was a device to make the syllable conform to the quantity pattern of the language in spite of the loss of the nasal segment.

Support for a category of syllabic quantity would be found if there were cases where phonological processes or regularities seem to be definable in such terms. Lehiste (1970:50–1) reports on the system of length and quantity in Estonian. She says: 'Syllables may have three quantities. Short syllables contain a short vowel, which is followed by a short intervocalic consonant. Long syllables may contain either a long vowel followed by a short consonant, or a short vowel followed by a long consonant, or a long vowel followed by a long consonant . . . An overlong syllable contains at least one overlong sound – vowel, consonant, or both.' The quantity of the first syllable can be used in accounting for length relations in other syllables. Thus, the 'duration of the vowel of the second syllable . . . is inversely proportional to the quantity of the first syllable'; if the first (stressed) syllable is short (light, in my terminology), the second syllable has a so-called half-long vowel. Other phenomena of length and quantity are directly or indirectly related to the quantity of the first syllable as a part of what seems to be a complicated pattern of length and quantity structure, to be defined in the larger context of 'phonological word' in Estonian (Lehiste 1970:51). One may wonder whether the 'rhythmic law' in Central Slovak referred to by Trubetzkoy

(1958:170–1; cf. above) may also be accounted for in terms of syllabic quantity.

As we have seen, the relation between length and quantity could theoretically be of two types. First, syllabic quantity could be said to determine segmental length, as in the case of Modern Icelandic where the length of segments is predictable on the basis of stress, which as it were defines the quantity of the syllable as heavy. (It seems useful to maintain that length and quantity are two phonological categories because there are two types of regularity, although only in the case of length can there be talk of two values.) But the relation between length and quantity could theoretically be the inverse, so that quantity is determined by segmental length. This would be the case when, for example, segmental length is inherent, as seems to have been the case in Old Icelandic at some stage. Here length of segments forms the basis for the quantity of the syllable. It is also conceivable that the number of segments that form the syllable (or perhaps rather its rhyme) define its quantity, although here one might be able to say that the quantity of the syllable determines the number of segments permissible within it. In this type of situation other considerations would seem to determine which analysis to adopt, or of course the choice might be arbitrary and empirically empty.

In this connection one could make some further suggestions concerning the relation of quantity to the nature of segmental length as inherent, derived or geminateness, but it seems that theoretical speculations unsupported by further data would be rather pointless at this stage.

6.5 Length and quantity in Old Icelandic

Having briefly raised some general points connected with questions of how to analyse durational phenomena phonologically, I will now return to the Icelandic data and consider what sort of analyses are appropriate for the two stages of Icelandic that I have been concerned with in the earlier chapters of this study. I will start with Old Icelandic and then have a second look at the analysis of the Modern Icelandic data.

6.5.1 The status of length and quantity about 1200. To summarise briefly what was said in chapter 4, table 7 shows the probable vowel system of Icelandic shortly after 1200. Later in the thirteenth century, with the merger of short /ø/ and /ǫ/ into one phoneme, designated /ö/, and

of /øː/ and /æː/ into something represented as /æː/, the system had become something like that shown in table 8. The diphthongs at both these stages had the same 'prosodic' status as long vowels. This can be deduced from the fact that they, like the long vowels, in concatenation with a single following consonant, formed sequences that could function as monosyllabic ictuses in poetry.

TABLE 7. *Icelandic vowel system, c. 1200*

Short			Long			Diphthongs		
i	y	u	iː	yː	uː	ei	ey	au
e	ø	o	eː	øː	oː			
	a	ǫ		æː	ɑː			

TABLE 8. *Icelandic vowel system, c. 1250*

Short			Long			Diphthongs		
i	y	u	iː	yː	uː	ei	ey	au
e	ö	o	eː		oː			
	a			æː	ɑː			

If we now try to apply the notions described above to these data, we can ask what sort of analysis is appropriate for length in Old Icelandic. Should we analyse it as (i) an intrinsic feature of the vowels, (ii) gemination of vowels, (iii) a separate phoneme, or (iv) belonging to a higher-order element, say as a function of syllabic quantity? It should be relatively safe to exclude the last two alternatives. The last alternative seems to be inadmissible since there are minimal pairs distinguished by the length of vowels alone: *fat* 'a piece of clothing' – *fát* 'confusion', *lit* 'colour' – *lít* 'I look', *vel* 'well' – *vél* 'a trick' etc. It would seem rather far-fetched to set up different syllabic quantity types only to have this difference appear as a surface distinction between the vowels. All the more so since the short vowels that would characterise the light syllables in *fat*, *lit* etc. also appear in heavy syllables, as in *fatt*, *mitt* etc. The phoneme- (prosodeme-) analysis seems implausible on general theoretical grounds and because the diphthongs have long duration which it would seem unnatural to assign to an underlying length phoneme, since there are no short diphthongs. We are, then, left with an inherent feature-analysis or an analysis in terms of gemination.

If we start by trying to analyse the relationship between the two subsystems, the long and the short, we discover that it is not entirely clear whether it should be called set-based or pair-based. As far as limits on distribution are concerned, there seem to be no constraints except that, according to one theory, only long vowels and diphthongs can appear when no consonant follows (in stressed final open syllables and in front of hiatus). There are no forms like, *bu* or (disyllabic) *bua*, only forms represented in the standardised orthography as *bú* 'household' and *búa* 'to live'. According to Benediktsson (1968), vowel length is neutralised in these environments, and the phonetic duration varies. From a generative point of view, one would have to decide what to put in the underlying forms, long or short, and it seems that comparative evidence favours long vowels as the underlying segments in these positions. In Modern Icelandic the vowels of *búa* and *bú* have the reflex of Old Icelandic long /uː/, and in most cases these vowels can be traced back to what other comparative evidence suggests were Proto-Germanic long vowels. It is therefore possible that we have here a phonotactic constraint based on the long–short distinction. The diphthongs show the same behaviour as these 'long' vowels, that is, they can occur in stressed syllables without a following consonant, as in *hey* 'hay'. I have already mentioned the difference in metrical function between heavy and light syllables. There again, we had the long vowels and the diphthongs forming a class as opposed to the short monophthongs.

Looking at these facts we seem to have a good case for setting up a dichotomous system, but we may seem to have a rather poor candidate for a pair-based relation. True, we have (around 1200) correspondences like /i/ − /iː/, /y/ − /yː/, /u/ − /uː/, /e/ − /eː/, /o/ − /oː/, /ø/ − /øː/, but that is about all, unless we say that /a/ and /aː/ constitute a pair. There is no long phoneme corresponding to short /ǫ/ and no short one corresponding to /æː/, and there are no short diphthongs. (The lack of short diphthongs would, of course, not be strange in a geminate account of the system, the diphthongs being vowel clusters. I will come to this shortly.) Another factor that is relevant to the sort of relation that holds between the two systems is the amount of qualitative similarity between the members of the potential pairs /i/ − /iː/, /y/ − /yː/, /u/ − /uː/, /e/ − /eː/, /o/ − /oː/ and /ø/ − /øː/. We have seen that already in the thirteenth century the corresponding long and short vowels seem not to have been completely identical in quality. This is shown by a change that took place in the thirteenth-century spelling of the unstressed vowels /ɪ/ and /ʊ/, which, having been spelled *e* and *o* respectively, came to be identified with short /i/ and /u/ and spelled accordingly as *i* and *u*. This, according to Benediktsson (1962; cf. 1965:72–3), was caused by a lowering in the short stressed vowels /i/ and /u/ that brought them closer to corresponding in quality with the unstressed ones. It is further likely that the long vowels /eː/, /æː/ and /aː/, and perhaps /oː/, had started to diphthongise in the thirteenth century (cf. pp. 100–20). Both of these changes must have diminished the degree of 'pairedness' of the correspondence between the two subsystems, in that the difference between the members of the pairs /i/ – /iː/, /u/ – /uː/, /e/ – /eː/ and /o/ – /oː/ was now not based on duration alone. This discrepancy between the long and the short system was further increased in the thirteenth century by the above-mentioned mergers of /ø/ and /ǫ/ and /æː/ and /øː/. There was now no long segment corresponding to /ö/ (< /ø/, /o/), and the new /æː/ (≺ /æː/, /øː/) had no short counterpart.

Evidently, the answer to the question of what sort of correspondence prevailed between the long and short systems will depend on which stage we are talking about. The further down the time-scale we move, the more the relation comes to look like being set-based. And if what I said before about the connection between the sort of relation that holds between two subsystems of a dichotomous vowel-system and the analysis of length in terms of geminateness or as an inherent feature is correct, then the closer we get to the stage when the quantity shift started to have its effects, the less attractive becomes the geminate-analysis of length.

It seems, however, that around 1200 the case for a geminate-analysis is reasonably strong. As mentioned before, the place of diphthongs in the dichotomy, having the same status as long vowels, is natural in a geminate-analysis. The diphthongs would obviously be analysed as vowel-clusters and should therefore have a phonological status similar to the long vowels. Further, there is a considerable degree of correspondence between the long and short vowels, and the facts mentioned above as speaking against a pair-based geminate-analysis are mostly later than 1200. If we are willing to derive /a/ and /aː/ from the same abstract quality, by either a backing rule for the long variant or a fronting rule for the short variant or a two-sided rule, backing the long variant and making the short one non-back, then the main problems are the lack of a short version of /æː/, and the lack of a long version of /ǫ/. But there are good reasons to believe that both of these were present at slightly earlier stages.

It used to be common opinion that earliest Old Icelandic had a low front short vowel, the so called 'Umlauts-e' (derived from *a* by *i*-umlaut), often denoted *ę*, as distinct from original *e*. Benediktsson (1964:101) concludes that a distinction between *e* (<Germanic *e, i*) and *ę* (in my notation /æ/) (<a) did not exist around 1200. In the very oldest manuscripts, however, there are signs of a distinction in spelling between two *e*-sounds, which, according to Benediktsson, could be taken as indicating a distinction made in earlier (now lost) manuscripts and simply copied by the younger scribes. So it is possible that around 1100 there still was a short counterpart to the long *æ*. And if we assume that around 1100 the long and short subsystems (and the nasalised system postulated by the First Grammarian; cf. Benediktsson 1972:130–7) were in a pair-based (or triplet-based) correlation, one can perhaps expect this relation to survive a minor blow like the one of the merger of /e/ and /æ/, leaving a gap in the short subsystem. This gap could be, from the synchronic point of view, just an idiosyncrasy caused by a historical change, foreign to the pairing principle which was still valid in general.

In connection with the lack of a long counterpart to the short /ǫ/, it is even probable that in the first decades of the thirteenth century there still prevailed a distinction between a long /ǫː/ and /aː/ in some dialects. The former had arisen historically as a *u*-umlaut variant of long /aː/, just as /ǫ/ was created by the umlauting of short /a/; but in the early thirteenth century this long /ǫː/ disappeared, merging with /oː/ in many nasal environments (*nótt* 'night' <*nǫtt* Germanic <*nahtu* (the Germanic *a* is lengthened before the disappearing *h*)), but with the original /aː/ in other environments (*rákum* 'we drove' <*rǫkum*, <Proto-Scandinavian *rākumR*) (cf. Benediktsson 1965:61–2).

So, granted that the distinction between /ǫː/ and /aː/ prevailed up to about 1200 and that the merger of /e/ and /æ/ was not earlier than about 1100, it is not implausible to assume that the long and the short vowel systems around 1200 were fundamentally in a pair-based relation, even though they had been and were being affected by disruptive changes disturbing the pattern to some extent. If the relation between the long and short monophthongs was pair-based and the diphthongs behaved like long vowels, it would perhaps seem natural to assume that vowel length in Old Icelandic up to about 1200 was gemination of vowels (or cluster-formation, in the case of diphthongs).

One final point should be mentioned briefly in this connection – the number of diphthongs. In the vowel systems cited above, there are listed only three diphthongs: *ei, ey* and *au*. I have suggested that languages whose long vowels are geminates would tend to be rich in diphthongs. In the light of what has been said, it may seem rather little for a language with eight or more vowel qualities and a principle of vowel-gemination and cluster-formation to have only three diphthongs. In response to this criticism, it should be stated that these are not the only diphthongs that can or have been set up for the earliest stages of Icelandic. There are other sequences that have been analysed as 'rising diphthongs', beginning in a semi-syllabic *i*, usually denoted in the standardised orthography by *i* or *j*. These are *iu* (or *jú*) and *io* (*jó*) (both deriving from IE *eu*), *ia* (*ja*) and *iǫ* (*jǫ*) (arising from 'breaking' of *e*), and perhaps a fifth *iaː* (*já*) (distinct from *ia/ja*.) In addition to this, some comments made by the First Grammarian seem to suggest that he looked upon the Old Icelandic reflex of the Modern Icelandic labiodental fricative [v], when preceding a vowel, as a non-syllabic instance of /u/, since in listing examples of cases where a vowel 'gives up its nature and must then be called a consonant rather than a vowel' he cites the example *vín* 'wine' (MI *vín* [viːn]). By analogy, one should expect the First Grammarian to consider any combination of *v* (perhaps phonetically [w]) with a following vowel as a rising diphthong (i.e. he would consider *v* preceding a vowel to be a non-syllabic /u/). However, in other instances he seems to treat it as a consonant, so there is some ambiguity here (cf. Benediktsson 1972:154–5).

In general, it seems doubtful whether these 'rising diphthongs' can be used to argue for a geminate-analysis of length. It seems that, if they were diphthongs at all, their status was peculiar, not only in that they were 'rising' but also in that there seems to have been a distinction between 'long' and 'short' diphthongs of this type. Forms with *iu* (*jú*), *io* (*jó*) and *iaː* (*já*) as their stressed nuclei function metrically as heavy in poetry, but forms containing the 'breaking' diphthongs *ia* and *iǫ* function as light. The idea of short rising diphthongs /ia/ and /iǫ/ as opposed to long rising diphthongs /iuː/, /ioː/ and /iaː/, seems not to fit at all into the geminate length model. The only way a cluster of *i* + vowel can form a short nucleus in a geminate-analysis is if the *i* functions as a consonant, and becomes a part of the onset of the syllable. Similarly, the 'long rising diphthongs' would, within a vowel-clustering framework, be underlying 'triphthongs' /iuu/, /ioo/ and /iaa/, and would only conform to the canonical syllable structure (not allowing, in general, vocalic nuclei of more than two 'morae') either by shortening the second quality (by degemination) or by making the *i* consonantal and assigning it to the consonantal onset of the syllable. These problems would not arise if the 'rising diphthongs' were simply analysable as clusters of a consonantal /j/ + vowel, as seems to be appropriate for Modern Icelandic (cf. §4.3.3). This, however, is not without problems, since in poetry right down to the sixteenth century, (initial) *j* alliterates with vowels (Þórólfsson 1925:XXV–XXVI). In general, the whole problem of how to analyse the 'rising diphthongs' and the question of the phonological status of prevocalic *i* (*j*) and *u* (*v*) seems to be rather complicated historically and unsuited to a full discussion in the present context.[5]

Even though support for the geminate-analysis of length is not easily forthcoming from the 'rising diphthongs', this and/or the paucity of diphthongs does not ruin the case for such an analysis. We can still make a distinction that will help us to overcome this point. I suggested above that it could be said of a language classed as 'geminating', in that it allows every vowel to occur either singly or doubly and, ideally, should allow clusters of dissimilar vowels to form a relatively great number of diphthongs, that a part of its phonotactic principles was something like: *For every V there is a VV.* (This would mean that every vowel can combine with another vowel (as well as itself) to form a long vocalic nucleus.) If such a system were to exist (I am not sure that it does; Finnish may be close; cf. note 3), it could be said that the rule above would generate all the long–short vowel pairs of the language, as well as the diphthongs. Suppose a new vowel were to be added to this system; then the phonotactic principle above should allow for it to occur both as long and as short. (It is of course a different matter whether lexical items can be supplied to fill the spaces allowed for; there might be 'accidental gaps'.) Suppose, on the other hand, that things were to happen to this system so that it became impossible to apply the geminating principle in all cases. If, for example, there is a conditioned merger of two vowels x and y into z in the short subsystem, leaving xx and yy in the long one without counterparts, and creating a short z without a corresponding zz in the long system, this would mean that the principle stated above would not hold for all vowels. But it could still be valid for the rest of the vowels in the system and be kept with modifications as a matter of inheritance. One could say that the vowel system (looking back) is still geminating, but other forces have undermined the effect of the geminating rule; the generalisation can be said to be 'passive', or 'past-oriented' (cf. Anttila 1975).

If Old Icelandic about 1200 is to be analysed as having vowel length which is basically vowel-clustering (and gemination), it would have to be so as a matter of inheritance, and if we allow for that, the lack of symmetry between the long and short subsystems and the relative paucity of diphthongs can be looked on as a consequence of the 'passivity' of the gemination. When the umlauts produced new vowels in Proto-Nordic times, these did not combine with the old vowels and other umlaut sounds to form new diphthongs, and when mergers took place in one of the subsystems, reducing the number of vowels, this did not have to affect the other. The geminateness or clustering relation between the two subsystems could still hold within old established pairs, although new vowels appeared that did not take part in it and old ones disappeared leaving some vowels without correspondents. Thus the geminateness of vowel length (if it existed) was a matter of inheritance that still prevailed in spite of some unfavourable events. Evidently, the sort of things that happened to the old system were slowly obliterating the signs of the old pair-based relation and the geminateness of vowel length.

This is exactly what I will assume, namely that the geminate-character of vowel length that perhaps prevailed as far down as to around 1200, gave way to an inherent feature of length no later than in the thirteenth century. After the mergers and qualitative changes that we have described in this section and in chapter 4, it becomes more and more difficult to maintain that the systems are in a pair-based relation, and, proportionally, it becomes less likely that the length is analysable as geminateness.

Once geminateness was 'given up' and the inherent feature [±long] 'introduced' instead, length obviously had a completely different status within the system. If we imagine that length was an inherent property of some vowels, but not others, there is no strong reason to expect there to be pairs that are identical in everything but length. In formal terms, a feature like [±long] has a similar status to [±rounded], and there is no necessity for it to have a minimal distinctive function in every instance. There is now less reason to expect length to be superimposed on other features and that vowels that differ in length only differ in that respect.

6.5.2 The status of length as an inherent feature. I am gradually getting closer to a problem mentioned briefly above (§4.2.2.2), namely the status of length relative to other features in the Icelandic vowel system from the thirteenth century down to the time when the quantity shift was completed. Having assumed that length had become an inherent feature of vowels, the question arises what sort of a relationship prevailed between the length feature (responsible for the long duration of the appropriate vowels) and other vowel features. We may wonder whether some features of the long vowels or, conversely, some features of the short vowels are predictable from length vs shortness. Or might it be the case that length is predictable from some other feature(s)? Should one perhaps invent an abstract feature that can be used to predict both the length and some other features of the vowels (cf. Sigmundsson 1970)? Indeed, do we have to worry about this at all? Is length perhaps just a feature like any other with no special relation to other features? Is, for example, the relation between the positive value of length and diphthongal quality that probably prevailed quite early in the vowels /æː/, /ɑː/, /eː/ and /oː/ to be accounted for in the same way as the relation between roundness, height and frontness? An important point here is whether there really is any need to abstract and set up some hierarchical order of the features. Several things may have a bearing on this. To start with, the system is dichotomous. There are two facts that show this: (i) long vowels form heavy 'syllables' when combined with a single following consonant; these have a specific function in metrics; and (ii) only long vowels and diphthongs can appear (we assume) in a stressed position when no consonant follows. It seems that neither of these facts demands an abstraction of any sort or a statement of the hierarchy of features. The length is just there and can be used in accounting for these things. A more important question, perhaps, is whether some features are secondary, or 'redundant'. One can say, for example, that the diphthongal quality of the long vowels just mentioned is 'non-distinctive' if we have already distinguished the vowels in question from every other vowel in the system: /æː/ as a long, front, low, spread vowel, /ɑː/ as a long, back, low (perhaps rounded) vowel, /eː/ as a long front mid spread vowel and /oː/ as a long back mid-rounded vowel. But of course one may ask: Why not have it the other way around and 'predict' the length of these vowels from their diphthongal character? Or is there any reason to predict anything? There are two types of arguments, it seems, that could be put forward for an abstraction by which some features are in some sense secondary and predictable from some other underlying feature(s). There are considerations of formal simplicity of the sort just mentioned, namely, that one should use the fewest possible features to distinguish between all the vowels of the system and make the others predictable by rule. Although this type of argument is very widely used in modern linguistics, it is, I think, rather dangerous (cf. Árnason 1977b) for very important reasons. It is not, for example, clear what justification there is for assuming that simplicity in terms of an invented *formalism* can be used to justify a *linguistic* analysis. In other words, there seems to be no guarantee that the laws of the formalism of distinctive features and redundancy rules, which would be used in our case, can be used to make 'generalisations' that are *linguistically* significant (cf. Lass 1976b). Another similar type of argument sounds more linguistic: that some of the features actually characterising the vowels have a more central *function* than the other ones. They are *distinctive*, the others are *non-distinctive*. I have already mentioned the ambiguity of the term 'distinctive' (§2.2); we saw that in structural phonology, it is often used in a sense something like 'not predictable from other phonological features'. This argument is, then, similar in its effects to the formal argument above; it leads to a distinction between predictable and non-predictable features, only here it is assumed that the motivation for the abstraction is linguistic. The appeal is not to notational economy, but rather to the claim that the linguistic system is such that one feature is basic and the others derived from it. This would conceivably be reflected in the fact that speakers 'see' the phonemes in question, in our case /eː/, /æː/, /oː/ and /aː/, as basically long but having diphthongal qualities as secondary features (cf. Durand 1939). This sort of statement is basically a claim about facts, and is either true or not true. The argument, or perhaps rather the claim, seems to be purely linguistic and, in theory, independent of formal considerations, but the problem with it is of course the difficulty of verifying it (our old problem from §5.2.1).

The same type of arguments can be adduced for an analysis in terms of 'tenseness' as an abstract feature distinguishing between the long vowels and diphthongs on the one hand and the short vowels on the other. One may argue that it is formally simpler (true or false) to do this, or one may claim that in reality speakers 'saw' the two sets of vowels as different, but connected the difference with no specific phonetic characteristic, neither long duration nor diphthongal quality, nor anything else, but added these together and subsumed them under the term 'tense', or as is the common practice in contemporary Icelandic school-books, 'broad'.

I have to admit that I see very little evidence in favour of either of these alternatives. This is so because the possible difference in 'empirical predictions' (in a Popperian sense) made by the different alternatives are difficult to test from the synchronic point of view. If one were to say, for example, that length was basic, one would perhaps expect the secondary features (like the diphthongal quality of the non-high long 'monophthongs') to fluctuate. But since we are dealing with a historical ('ideal') stage, and there are no signs of a fluctuation of this sort in the spelling in manuscripts, we cannot test this. The only evidence we can produce is comparative, and this shows that at a later stage the qualitative differences between the vowels took over the function previously (perhaps) held by length. But this was a consequence of the quantity shift which we have already assumed to have arisen from causes that, strictly speaking, lie outside the context of relations between segmental phonological features. We can, of course, say that the lengthening and shortening processes eventually undermined the 'distinctive function' of the length feature, and once these processes began to have their effect, the length feature could no longer be central, but that does not tell us anything about the status of the length feature relative to other features before these changes began to have a serious effect on the system.

In spite of this uncertainty we can set up a plausible model of what happened. In the thirteenth century at the latest, the underlying nature of the length correlation changed from being that of gemination and cluster-formation (which was an inherited characteristic) to being a matter of an inherent feature of vocalic segments. In the period immediately after this, it is likely that length was a 'central' feature in the monophthongs (having perhaps a different status in the diphthongs), but gradually, as a consequence of the lengthening and shortening processes that later resulted in the quantity shift, the length feature lost its central status and the qualitative features assumed the distinctive role previously held by length.

6.6 The phonological analysis of length in Modern Icelandic; a brief reconsideration

Having dealt fairly thoroughly with length and quantity in Modern Icelandic in chapter 2, I will here make only a few final comments.

The basic conclusion was that the length of segments was predictable in terms of stress and syllabic structure. Stressed syllables necessarily have heavy quantity. In the perspective of the preceding discussion we may say that the relation between short and long vowels is pair-based: every vowel, diphthongal or monophthongal, has both a long and a short alternative. The appearance of length is largely limited to vowels, perhaps appearing as 'tenseness' or half length on consonants following a short vowel and preceding another consonant (as in *hestur* [hɛsːtʏr] 'horse'). (It may be added that it seems natural for length variation to be more or less limited to vowels, since vowels, as the most 'stretchable' segments, having maximally open articulation and more resonance than consonants, can more easily take length as an independent variable.)

As to the appropriate way to analyse length, it is impossible to say that the length rule can be formulated in terms of gemination, since long diphthongs are not geminated short diphthongs, nor are short diphthongs produced by deleting one mora of a 'full' (long?) vowel. What happens is that the segments, diphthongal or monophthongal, are stretched or shortened as wholes.[6] Thus it seems most plausible to look upon length in Modern Icelandic as a derived feature of the vowels (we can call it [+ long]) which indicates that the segment in question is relatively long in duration. It should be recalled that the fact that diphthongs can appear either as long or short is strong evidence in favour of my suggestion above that diphthongs can be single segments with movable quality, but are not necessarily clusters of vowels (cf. Lass 1974:339, fn. 9).

One point remains to be mentioned briefly concerning length in Modern Icelandic. It has been showed by Garnes (1974b) that there are, in spite of what I have said so far, slight differences in phonetic quality between the corresponding long and short allophones of vowels. For example the high vowels /i/ and /u/ are more diffuse when long than when short, and the diphthongs /εi/, /œy/, /ai/, /au/ and /ou/ are 'somewhat monophthongized' when short (Garnes 1974b:3). Perhaps the most important of these qualitative alternations is the slight diphthongal quality of the long variants of the non-high, non-low monophthongs /ε/, /œ/ and /ɔ/. Garnes (table 1) transcribes the long alternatives respectively as [eᵉː], [øœː] and [oᵒː], but the corresponding short ones as [ε], [œ] and [ɔ]. So, from the point of view of the short vowels, the long alternants have raised their first part, thus forming a sort of diphthong. None of this is very surprising, and no doubt the diphthongal nature of the long variants of the mid monophthongs has a quite different phonological status from the diphthongal quality of the underlying diphthongs. It is only to be expected that vowels with a long duration are susceptible to slight temporal variation in their quality, and we can see here the seeds of a diphthongisation similar to that which seems to have affected the long variant of old /a/ in Faroese (see §3.1).

Evidently, these variations of quality between the long and short allophones of the vowels are at a low level in the phonology. But it would be a mistake to dismiss them as 'purely phonetic' and therefore uninteresting from the linguistic point of view. The mere fact that these alternations seem to be regular makes them, in some sense at least, a part of the linguistic norm, and they cannot be said to be governed by general laws of a purely phonetic sort. But it seems difficult to say what their status is, relative, on the one hand, to 'firmly' established phonological processes like the length rule of chapter 2, and on the other hand to still more phonetic features of coarticulation etc. Indeed, there is probably one more type of process between the highly systematic level on which rules like the length rule and (morpho-)phonological processes like devoicing of /r/ in front of a voiceless obstruent (*vor* [vɔːr] – *vors* [vɔr̥s] 'spring' (nom. vs gen.)) exist and the level of phonetic processes of coarticulation etc. Many things that occur in 'allegro speech', can be shown (cf. e.g. Zwicky 1972; Dressler 1975) to be, to a certain extent, regular and dialect-specific. These things probably abound in every language. In Icelandic, we find alternative pronunciations, like *enskur* 'English': [ɛnˑskʏr], [ɛ̃skʏr]; clines as in *vinfengi* 'friendship' (a compound word): [vɪːnfɛiɲ̊ɟɪ], [vɪnfɛiɲ̊ɟɪ], [vɪ̃ṽfɛiɲ̊ɟɪ]; and, still worse, complete loss of stressed vowels as in *viltu* (*koma*) 'will you (come)': [vɪl̥tʏ], [vl̥̩tʏ], [l̥̩tʏ] (with a syllabic (in some sense) lateral fricative in the last two cases). And compare these four versions of *það getur verið* 'it may be' [θaːðj̊ɛɛːtʰʏrveɛːrɪð], [θaðj̊ɛɛːtʰʏrveɛːrɪð], [θaːjetʰʏrvᵉɛːrɪð], [hajⁱtʰʏrvɛːrɪð]. Only the last of these alternatives can be said to be really fast speech. (All of these pronunciations are my own.) It seems that these processes in Icelandic cannot be said to be wholly unsystematic and linguistically uninteresting. These four examples already indicate a very peculiar regularity, namely that reduction seems to be more liable to take place in syllables that are stressed (rather than unstressed) on the word level. We get reduction in the nasal following the stressed vowel in *enskur*, and a similar thing in *vinfengi*; in *viltu* and *getur* (of *það getur verið*) the vowels that appear in the stressed position in the word are affected more seriously than the 'unstressed' ones in faster speech – they can be completely deleted. This sort of thing, it seems, is difficult to explain as some sort of consequence of general phonetic laws of coarticulation etc.

It remains to be seen whether there is a genuine difference of kind between the three types of rules we have seen, the 'well-established' length rule, the quality variation between long and short vowels, and the reduction rules of fast speech (which, indeed, only reduce certain phonological forms and leave others more or less intact). If these are three different kinds of rules, it would seem to follow that there is much more complicated stratification in phonology than is usually implied in the literature.

Evidently this question of stratification in phonology is too important and complex to be dealt with adequately in this context. But, to return briefly to the relation of the rules of qualitative differences in the vowels to the length correlation itself, I would say this: It seems evident that the quality variation is dependent on the length variation, at least historically, and it seems to make little sense to imagine anything else from the synchronic point of view. In terms of rules and rule-ordering relations, the length rule 'feeds' the rules for quality alternation. But does that mean that the quality rules are of a different kind from the length rule (and the stress rule, and the syllabification principle proposed in chapter 2)? This is not at all clear. Indeed, one could imagine all these processes as one big cline of intrinsically ordered rules. The stress rule and the syllabification principle define the input to the length rule, which in turn defines the input to the rules accounting for the quality alternations. If that were the case, one would presumably say that all these rules belong to the same part of the grammar. However, one might still say that the quality-alternation rules are somewhat more 'phonetic-like' than the length rule. Is it then the case that all phonological rules are basically the same, but that there is a cline of 'phoneticness', in that some are more central to the system than others and some are closer to the actual acoustico-articulatory medium? In that case, where do the fast-speech rules fit in, since they are applied only in certain situations and in fact sometimes undo much of the 'work' of our more abstract rules (long stressed vowels etc)? Do *they* perhaps form a special part of the phonology, 'the fast-speech component'?

NOTES

[1] This whole discussion of distinctive features may seem somewhat high-flown and the assertions unsupported, but I wonder whether a belief in universal phonological features is any better supported. It seems that it is partly based on the (severely challenged; cf. Putnam 1971; Derwing 1973; Sampson 1978) assumption that children are equipped with a certain set of innate linguistic universals, among which are the phonological features, thirty or so (depending on your creed). It seems that these 'innate universals' would by nature have to be positive entities or concepts. But in actual language it seems that the features are more appropriately defined by their function within systems and largely negative. The only place where universality comes into the picture of phonological features is in the actual physical scales on which the features operate. But these universal scales are non-linguistic, rather physical surroundings within which every human language works. Some physical phenomena may be better suited for use in

language than others and are therefore used more commonly than others, perhaps even in every language. (See Sampson 1974 for arguments against the existence of a 'universal phonetic alphabet', using data concerning tones.)

2   Phenomena of a similar sort in Lithuanian are described by Kenstowicz (1970), and in West Greenlandic Eskimo by Pyle (1970), supporting what Kenstowicz and Pyle call 'sequence analysis' of length (which seems to correspond to Trubetzkoy's gemination). But Kenstowicz argues that other phonological regularities can be accounted for more easily in terms of a 'feature analysis' of length and suggests that both a 'sequence analysis' and a 'feature analysis' are needed for Lithuanian. Similarly, Pyle (1970) suggests that 'sequence analysis' and 'feature analysis' are both needed in a generative account of West Greenlandic Eskimo phonology. My unfamiliarity with the data prevents me from commenting on these phenomena, but I wonder whether an account based on a categorial distinction between length and quantity (cf. §6.4) might be fruitful, particularly in the case of Lithuanian.

3   It seems that Finnish is close to being a language of this kind. All vowels occur as long or short, and there seems to be good reason to analyse long vowels as vowel geminates. The monophthongs are of eight qualities: *a, e, i, o, u, y, ä, ö*, and there are seventeen diphthongs, each having two consecutive qualities that can be identified with one of the simple vowels (Fromm & Sadeniemi 1956:20–1). True, we are far from having the fifty-six theoretically-possible combinations of the eight monophthongs, which indeed is not surprising (what would a language do with sixty-four vowel nuclei?), but the prediction of a relatively high number of diphthongs is at least in some way borne out by the facts. Some of the theoretically-possible combinations of monophthongs into diphthongs are excluded automatically by a rule of vowel harmony, which demands that only front or only back vowels (with the exception of *i* and *e*, which stand outside the domain of the vowel-harmony rule) co-occur within the same word. This excludes diphthongs like: *aö, oä, uy, oy, ay* etc., altogether eighteen diphthongs. Of the thirty-eight remaining theoretically possible diphthongs, the following occur: *ai, au, ei, eu, ey, ie, iu, oi, ou, ui, uo, yi, yö, äi, äy, öi* and *öy*. It remains to be seen whether the absence of the other twenty-one theoretically-possible diphthongs can be stated naturally in terms of phonotactic constraints, perhaps of the same type that make initial clusters like *tk* uncommon in languages.

4   It should perhaps be noted, as must be evident from the discussion of abstractness, that the statements I have been making concerning the connection between geminateness of vowel length and 'pair-basedness' of relations between long and short vowel subsystems should not be interpreted in the spirit of if-and-only-if statements. It may be that the grounds for a geminate-analysis are so strong (apart from the question of 'pair-basedness') that one would accept considerable *ad hoc* constraints against V – VV pairs for every vowel quality. I am only saying that, other things being equal, one should expect systems with length as geminateness to have a pair-based relation between two subsystems.

5   For a suggestion for a phonological analysis of the semi-vowels see Benediktsson (1972:159–61) and references. Benediktsson suggests that syllabicity and length belong to the same underlying feature, that the rising diphthongs are clusters of a short vowel + long vowel and the first vowel loses its syllabicity because of its shortness as opposed to the length of the second vowel. Thus *jó* would be underlying /io:/, and *ei* (falling diphthong) would be underlying /ei/. It seems that this analysis is problematic in that it does not account for the difference of *já* and *ja* ('long' and 'short' 'rising diphthong').

6   This is shown in spectrograms I have made of my own speech (cf. also Garnes 1974b). Although the quality movement in short diphthongs is often not very noticeable in

listening, there is definitely a similarity in the movement of the vowel formants in pairs like *læs – læst*, which must be assigned to the diphthongal nature of the [ai]-sound. The short variant looks like a miniature of the long one.

Bibliography

Abercrombie, D. (1967) *Elements of general phonetics*. Edinburgh University Press

Aitken, A. J. (1962) 'Vowel length in Modern Scots', (mimeo). University of Edinburgh, Dept. of English Language

Allen, W. S. (1959) 'Some remarks on the structure of Greek vowel systems', *Word* 15:240–51

– (1965) *Vox Latina : a guide to the pronunciation of Classical Latin*. Cambridge University Press

– (1969) 'The Latin accent: a restatement', *Journal of Linguistics* 5:193–203

– (1973) *Accent and rhythm, prosodic features of Latin and Greek*. Cambridge University Press

– (1976) 'Long and short diphthongs: phonological analogies and phonetic anomalies', in Davies, A. M. & Palmer, L. R. (eds.) *Studies in Greek, Italic, and Indo-European linguistics*. Innsbruck: Innsbrucker Beiträge zur Sprachwissenschaft

Amundsen, S. (1964) 'Le vocalisme féroïen: essai de phonologie diachronique', *Fróðskaparrit. Annales Societatis Scientiarum Færoensis* 13:54–61

Andersen, H. (1972) 'Diphthongization', *Language* 48:11–50

– (1973) 'Abductive and deductive change', *Language* 49:765–93

Andersen, P. (1954) 'Dansk fonetik', in Blegvad, N. Rh. (ed.) *Nordisk lærebog for talepædagoger* 1. Copenhagen: Rosenkilde og Baggers Forlag, 308–53

Anderson, J. M. (1969) 'Syllabic or non-syllabic phonology?' *Journal of Linguistics* 5:136–42

– (1975) 'Principles of syllabification', *York Papers in Linguistics* 5:7–20

– & Jones, C. (1974) 'Three theses concerning phonological representations', *Journal of Linguistics* 10:1–26

– & Jones, C. (1977) *Phonological structure and the history of English*. Amsterdam: North-Holland (North-Holland Linguistic Series 33)

Anderson, S. R. (1969) 'An outline of the phonology of Modern Icelandic vowels', *Foundations of Language* 5:53–72

– (1972a) 'Icelandic *u*-umlaut and breaking in a generative grammar'. In Firchow, E., Grimstad, K., Hasselmo, N. & O'Neil, W. (eds.) *Studies for Einar Haugen*. The Hague: Mouton

– (1972b) 'The Faroese vowel system', in Brame, M. (ed.) *Contributions to generative phonology*. Austin: University of Texas Press, 1–21

219

- (1974) *The organization of phonology.* New York: Academic Press
- (1976) 'Nasal consonants and the internal structure of segments', *Language* 52:326-44

Anttila, R. (1972) *An introduction to historical linguistics.* New York: Macmillan
- (1975) 'Excpetion as regularity in phonology', in Dressler, W. U. & Mareš, F. V. (eds.) *Phonologica 1972. Akten der zweiten Internationalen Phonologie-Tagung.* Vienna, 5-8 September. Munich, Salzburg: Wilhelm Fink Verlag, 91-9.

Árnason, K. (1974) 'Beygingarlýsing veikra sagna', (mimeo). Reykjavík: University of Iceland
- (1975) 'Athugasemd um lengd hljóða í íslenzku', *Mímir, blað stúdenta í íslenzkum fræðum* 23:15-19
- (1976) 'A note on Faroese vowels', *Work in Progress* 9:58-63. University of Edinburgh, Dept. of Linguistics
- (1977a) 'Quantity in Icelandic: a historical and comparative study', PhD thesis, University of Edinburgh, Dept. of Linguistics
- (1977b) 'Preaspiration in Modern Icelandic: phonetics and phonology', in *Sjötíu ritgerðir helgaðar Jakobi Benediktssyni*, 20 July. Reykjavík: Stofnun Árna Magnússonar, 495-504
- (1978a) 'Palatalization in Modern Icelandic: a case for historicism in synchronic linguistics', *Lingua* 46:185-203
- (1978b) 'Quantity, stress and the syllable in Icelandic: formal vs functional arguments', in Gårding, E., Bruce, G. & Bannert, R. (eds.) *Nordic prosody.* Travaux de l'Institut de Linguistique de Lund XIII, Gleerup & Fink

Awedyk, W. (1975) *The syllable theory and Old English phonology.* Wrocław: Polska Akademia Nauk, Komitet neofilologiczny

Bach, E. (1974) 'Explanatory inadequacy', in Cohen, D. (1974), 153-71

Bannert, R. (1976) *Mittelbairische Phonologie auf akustischer und perzeptorischer Grundlage.* Travaux de l'Institut de Linguistique de Lund X, Gleerup & Fink

Basbøll, H. (1970-1) 'A commentary on Hjelmslev's outline of the Danish expression system' I, *Acta Linguistica Hafniensia* XIII:173-211
- (1974) 'The phonological syllable with special reference to Danish', *Annual report of the Institute of Phonetics, University of Copenhagen* 8:39-128

Bell, A. & Hooper, J. B. (1978) (eds.) *Syllables and segments.* Amsterdam: North-Holland. (North-Holland Linguistic Series 40)

Benediktsson, H. (1959) 'The vowel system of Icelandic: a survey of its history', *Word* 15:282-312
- (1962) 'The unstressed and the non-syllabic vowels of Old Icelandic', *Arkiv för nordisk filologi* LXXVII:7-31
- (1963a) 'The non-uniqueness of phonemic solutions: quantity and stress in Icelandic', *Phonetica* 10:133-53
- (1963b) 'The Old Icelandic enclitic 2nd pers. pronoun -þo', *Arkiv för nordisk filologi* LXXVIII:190-6
- (1964) 'Old Norse short *e*: one phoneme or two?', *Arkiv för nordisk filologi* LXXIX:63-104
- (1965) *Early Icelandic script as illustrated in vernacular texts from the twelfth and*

thirteenth centuries. Reykjavík: The Manuscript Institute of Iceland
(1968) 'Indirect changes of phonological structure: Nordic vowel quantity',
Acta Linguistica Hafniensia XI:31–65

– (1972) (ed.) *First Grammatical Treatise.* University of Iceland, Publications in
Linguistics I. Reykjavík: Institute of Nordic Linguistics

– (1977) 'An extinct Icelandic dialect feature: *y* vs *i*', in Elert, C.-C., Eliasson, S.,
Fries, S. & Ureland, S. (eds.) *Dialectology and sociolinguistics: essays in honour
of Karl-Hampus Dahlstedt,* 19 April. Acta Universitatis Umensis, Umeå
Studies in the Humanities 12:28–46

Bergman, G. (1973) *A short history of the Swedish language.* (2nd edition,
translated by Magoun, P. Jr. & Kökeritz, H.) Lund: The Swedish Institute
for Cultural Relations with Foreign Countries

Bergsveinsson, S. (1941) *Grundfragen der isländischen Satzphonetik.* Berlin:
Metten; Copenhagen: Ejnar Munksgaard

Bjerrum, M. (1964) 'Forsøg til en analyse ad det færøske udtrykssystem', *Acta
Philologica Scandinavica* 25:31–69

Bloomfield, L. (1933) *Language.* New York: Holt, Rinehart & Winston

Botha, R. P. (1971) *Methodological aspects of transformational generative
phonology.* The Hague: Mouton

Cathey, J. E. & Demers, R. A. (1976) 'On establishing linguistic universals: a case
for in-depth synchronic analysis', *Language* 52:611–30

Chapman, K. G. (1962) 'Icelandic–Norwegian linguistic relationships', *Norsk
tidsskrift for sprogvidenskap,* supplement 7. Oslo

Chen, M. (1976) 'Relative chronology: three methods of reconstruction', *Journal
of Linguistics* 12:209–58

Chomsky, N. (1957) *Syntactic structures.* The Hague: Mouton

– (1965) *Aspects of the theory of syntax.* Cambridge, Mass.: MIT Press

– & Halle, M. (1968) *The sound pattern of English.* New York: Harper & Row

Christiansen, H. (1946–8) *Norske dialekter.* Oslo: Johan Grundt Tanum

Cohen, D. (1974) (ed.) *Explaining linguistic phenomena.* Washington, DC:
Hemisphere

Craigie, W. A. (1900) 'On some points in skaldic metre', *Arkiv för nordisk filologi*
XVI:341–84

– (1952) *Sýnisbók íslenzkra rímna* I–III. (*Specimens of Icelandic rímur, with
introductions on the history, metres and language of rímur.*) London: Nelson

Derwing, B. L. (1973) *Transformational grammar as a theory of language
acquisition.* Cambridge University Press

Dobson, E. J. (1962) 'Middle English lengthening in open syllables', *Transactions
of the Philological Society,* 124–48

Donegan, P. J. & Stampe, D. (1978) 'The syllable in phonological and prosodic
structure', in Bell, A. & Hooper, J. B. (1978), 25–34

Dressler, W. U. (1975) 'Methodisches zu Allegro-Regeln', in Dressler, W. U. &
Mareš, F. V. (eds.) *Phonologica 1972. Akten der zweiten Internationalen
Phonologie-Tagung.* Vienna, 5–8 September. Munich, Salzburg: Wilhelm
Fink Verlag, 219–34

Durand, M. (1939) 'Durée phonétique et durée phonologique', in Blancquaert,

E. & Pée, W. (eds.) *Proceedings of the Third International Congress of Phonetic Sciences*. University of Ghent: Laboratory of Phonetics, 261–5

Einarsson, S. (1927) *Beiträge zur Phonetik der isländischen Sprache*. Oslo: A. W. Brøggers Boktrykkeri A/S

– (1945) *Icelandic: grammar, texts, glossary*. Baltimore: Johns Hopkins Press

Elert, C.-C. (1964) 'Phonologic studies of quantity in Swedish, based on material from Stockholm speakers', Uppsala: Monografier utgivna af Stockholms Kommunalförvaltning

Eliasson, S. (1978) 'Swedish quantity revisited', in Gårding, E., Bruce, G. & Bannert, R. (eds.) *Nordic prosody*. Travaux de l'Institut de Linguistique de Lund XIII, Gleerup & Fink

– & La Pelle, N. (1973) 'Generativa regler för svenskans kvantitet', *Arkiv för nordisk filologi* LXXXVIII:133–48

Eliot, T. S. (1942) 'The music of poetry'. Third W. P. Ker Memorial Lecture, presented at the University of Glasgow, 24 February 1942. Reprinted in *On poetry and poets*. New York: Farrar, Strauss & Giroux, 1957

Fromm, H. & Sadeniemi, M. (1956) *Finnisches Elementarbuch* 1: *Grammatik*. Heidelberg: Carl Winter – Universitätsverlag

Fudge, E. C. (1969) 'Syllables', *Journal of Linguistics* 5:253–86

Gårding, E. (1973) 'The Scandinavian word accents', *Working Papers* 8. Lund University: Phonetics Laboratory

– (1977) *The Scandinavian word accents*. Travaux de l'Institut de Linguistique de Lund XI, Gleerup & Fink. (A revised edition of Gårding 1973)

Garnes, S. (1973) 'Phonetic evidence supporting a phonological analysis', *Journal of Phonetics* 1:273–83

– (1974a) 'Quantity in Icelandic: production and perception', PhD dissertation, Ohio State University. Published 1976 as *Hamburger phonetische Beiträge* 18. Hamburg: Buske Verlag

– (1974b) 'Suprasegmental aspects of Icelandic vowel quality', (mimeo). Ohio State University

– (1975a) 'Perception, production and language change', in *Papers from the Parasession on Functionalism*. Chicago Linguistic Society, 156–69

– (1975b) 'The Nordic quantity shift: quantity vs quality', (mimeo). Paper presented at the Winter Meeting of the Linguistic Society of America. San Francisco, December

de Groot, A. W. (1926) 'La syllabe: essai de syntèse', *Bulletin de la Société Linguistique de Paris* XXVII: 1–42

Grundt, A. (1973) 'Open syllable lengthening in English: a study in compensatory phonological processes', PhD dissertation, University of California, Berkeley

Guðfinnsson, B. (1946) *Mállýzkur* I. Reykjavík: Ísafoldarprentsmiðja

– (1964) *Um íslenzkan framburð. Mállýzkur* II. (Edited by Ólafur M. Ólafsson & Óskar Ó. Halldórsson.) *Studia Islandica* 23. Reykjavík: Heimspekideild Háskóla Íslands – Bókaútgáfa Menningarsjóðs

Halle, M. (1959/71) *The sound pattern of Russian: a linguistic and acoustical investigation* (2nd edition). The Hague: Mouton

Hammershaimb, V. U. (1891) *Færøsk antologi* 1: *Tekst samt historisk og grammatisk indledning*. Copenhagen: S. L. Møllers Bogtrykkeri (Møller & Thomsen)

Hankamer, J. & Aissen, J. (1974) 'The sonority hierarchy', *Papers from the Parasession on Natural Phonology*. Chicago Linguistic Society, 131–45

Harris, J. W. (1969) 'Sound change in Spanish and the theory of markedness', *Language* 45:538–52

Haugen, E. (1949) 'Phoneme or prosodeme?' *Language* 25:278–82

– (1950) *First Grammatical Treatise : the earliest Germanic phonology*. An edition, translation, and commentary. *Language* Monograph 25, Baltimore

– (1958) 'The phonemics of Modern Icelandic', *Language* 34:55–88

– (1967) 'On the rules of Norwegian tonality', *Language* 43:185–202

Hempel, C. G. (1966) *Philosophy of natural science*. Englewood Cliffs, NJ: Prentice Hall

Hjelmslev, L. (1951/73) 'Outline of the Danish expression system with special reference to the *stød*', in *Essais linguistiques par Louis Hjelmslev* II. Travaux du Cercle Linguistique de Copenhague XIV (1973). Copenhagen: Nordisk Sprog- og Kulturforlag, 247–66

Hoard, J. E. (1971) 'Aspiration, tenseness, and syllabication in English', *Language* 47:133–40

Hooper, J. B. (1972) 'The syllable in phonological theory', *Language* 48:525–40

– (1976a) *An introduction to natural generative phonology*. New York: Academic Press

– (1976b) 'Constraints on schwa-deletion in English.' Paper presented at the International Conference on Historical Phonology. Ustronie, Poland, 17–20 March

Indrebø, G. (1951) *Norsk målsoga*. (Edited by Per Hovda & Per Thorson.) Bergen: A. S. John Griegs Boktrykkeri

Jakobson, R. & Halle, M. (1956) *Fundamentals of language*. The Hague: Mouton

Jakobson, R., Fant, G. & Halle, M. (1952) *Preliminaries to speech analysis*. MIT Acoustics Laboratories, Technical Report 13. Cambridge, Mass.: MIT Press

Jeffers, R. J. (1974) 'On the notion "explanation" in historical linguistics', in Anderson, J. M. & Jones, C. (eds.) *Historical linguistics* II: *Theory and description in phonology*. Amsterdam: North-Holland (North-Holland Linguistic Series 12b), 231–55

Jespersen, O. (1909/61) *A modern English grammar on historical principles* 1: *Sounds and spellings*. London: Allen & Unwin; Copenhagen: Ejnar Munksgaard

– (1922/49) *Modersmålets fonetik*. Copenhagen: Gyldendalske Boghandel – Nordisk Forlag (3rd edition 1949)

Jones, D. (1962) *The phoneme : its nature and use*. Cambridge : W. Heffer & Sons

Jónsson, F. (1912–15) *Den norsk-islandske skjaldedigtning* A1–11, B1–11. Udgiven af Kommissionen for det Arnamagnæanske legat ved Finnur Jónsson. Copenhagen: Gyldendalske Boghandel – Nordisk Forlag

Kahn, D. (1976) 'Syllable-based generalizations in English phonology', MIT dissertation. Reproduced by the Indiana University Linguistics Club, Bloomington, Indiana

Karlsson, S. (1964) 'Gömul hljóðdvöl í ungum rímum', *Lingua Islandica – Íslenzk tunga* v:7–29

Keller, R. E. (1961) *German dialects: phonology and morphology.* Manchester University Press

Keller, W. (1908) 'Die Akzente in den ags. Handschriften', *Prager deutsche Studien* viii:97–120

Kelly, J. & Kress, H. (1972) 'Icelandic: readings, grammar, exercises', (mimeo). Reykjavík: University of Iceland

Kenstowicz, M. (1970) 'On the notation of vowel length in Lithuanian', *Papers in Linguistics* 3:73–113

von Kienle, R. (1960) *Historische Laut- und Formenlehre des Deutschen.* Tübingen: Max Niemeyer Verlag

King, R. D. (1974) 'Can rules be added in the middle of grammars?' Reproduced by the Indiana University Linguistics Club, Bloomington, Indiana

Kiparsky, P. (1968a) 'Linguistic universals and linguistic change', in Bach, E. & Harms, R. T. (eds.) *Universals in linguistic theory.* London: Holt, Rinehart & Winston, 170–202

– (1968b) 'How abstract is phonology?' Reproduced by the Indiana University Linguistics Club, Bloomington, Indiana

Kisseberth, C. W. (1970) 'On the functional unity of phonological rules', *Linguistic Inquiry* 1:291–306

Kjartansson, H. S. (1971) 'Hljóðdvalarbreytingin, lítil athugasemd um heimildargildi kveðskapar', *Mímir, blað stúdenta í íslenzkum fræðum* 18:20–2

– (1974) 'Lengd íslenzkra sérhljóða', *Mímir, blað stúdenta í íslenzkum fræðum* 22:19–22

Krishnamurti, Bh. (1978) 'Areal and lexical diffusion of sound change: evidence from Dravidian', *Language* 54:1–20

Kuryłowicz, J. (1948/73) 'Contribution à la théorie de la syllabe', in Kuryłowicz (1973), 1:193–220

– (1970) *Die sprachlichen Grundlagen der altgermanischen Metrik.* Innsbrucker Beiträge zur Sprachwissenschaft, Vorträge 1

– (1973) *Esquisses linguistiques* i–ii. Munich: Wilhelm Fink Verlag

Labov, W. (1965) 'On the mechanism of linguistic change', in Kreidler, C. W. (ed.) *Report of the Sixteenth Annual Round Table Meeting on Linguistics and Language Studies.* Georgetown University Monograph Series on Languages and Linguistics 18. Washington, DC: Georgetown University Press, 91–114

Ladefoged, P. (1967) *Three areas of experimental phonetics.* Oxford University Press

– (1971) *Preliminaries to linguistic phonetics.* University of Chicago Press

Langendoen, D. T. (1976) Review of Cohen (1974), *Language* 52:690–5

Lass, R. (1971) 'Boundaries as obstruents: Old English voicing assimilation and universal strength hierarchies', *Journal of Linguistics* 7:15–30

– (1974) 'Linguistic orthogenesis? Scots vowel quantity and the English length conspiracy', in Anderson, J. M. & Jones, C. (eds.) *Historical linguistics* ii:

Theory and description in phonology. Amsterdam: North-Holland (North-Holland Linguistic Series 12b), 311–52
- (1976a) *English phonology and phonological theory : synchronic and diachronic studies.* Cambridge University Press
- (1976b) 'On generative taxonomy, and whether formalizations "explain"', *Studia Linguistica* xxx:139–54
- (1977) 'Internal reconstruction and generative phonology', *Transactions of the Philological Society*, 1–25
- & Anderson, J. M. (1975) *Old English phonology.* Cambridge University Press
Lehiste, I. (1970) *Suprasegmentals.* Cambridge, Mass.: MIT Press
Lejeune, M. (1972) *Phonétique historique du Mycénien et du Grec Ancien.* Paris: Éditions Klincksieck
Liberman, A. S. (1970) 'Reconstruction of Icelandic Prosody', *Science in Iceland* 2:37–42
- (1971a) 'Islandskaja prosodika. K fonologičeskoj xarakteristike sovremennogo islandskogo jazyka i ego istorii', (Leningrad)
- (1971b) 'Gibt es Silbenakzente im Isländischen?' (Griefswald) *Nordeuropa. Studien* 4:173–83
Linell, P. (1974) 'Problems of psychological reality in generative phonology.' Reports from Uppsala University, Dept. of Linguistics 4
- (1978) 'The interaction of stress and quantity in Swedish', in Gårding, E., Bruce, G. & Bannert, R. (eds.) *Nordic prosody.* Travaux de l'Institut de Linguistique de Lund xiii, Gleerup & Fink
Lockwood, W. B. (1955) *An introduction to Modern Faroese.* Copenhagen: Ejnar Munksgaard
Malone, K. (1952) 'The phonemes of Modern Icelandic', in *Studies in honor of Albert Morey Sturtevant.* Lawrence: University of Kansas Press, 5–21
- (1953) 'Long and short in Icelandic phonemics', *Language* 29:61–2
Marchand, J. W. (1973) *The sounds and phonemes of Wulfila's Gothic.* The Hague: Mouton
von Mises, R. (1951) *Positivism : a study in human understanding.* New York: Dover Publications
Mitzka, W. (1954) 'Die dänische und die deutsche Konsonantenschwächung', *Zeitschrift für Mundartforschung* xxii:65–87
Noreen, A. (1904) *Altnordische Grammatik* ii: *Altschwedische Grammatik mit Einschluss des Altgutnischen.* Halle: Max Niemeyer
- (1923/70) *Altnordische Grammatik* i: *Altisländische und altnorwegische Grammatik.* (5th edition.) Tübingen: Max Niemeyer. (4th edition 1923)
Ófeigsson, J. (1920–4) 'Træk af moderne islandsk Lydlære', in Blöndal, S. *Islandsk-dansk Ordbog. (Íslensk-dönsk orðabók).* Reykjavík: Verslun Þórarins B. Þorlákssonar; Copenhagen: H. Aschehoug (W. Nygaard), xiv–xxvii
Oftedal, M. (1952) 'On the origin of the Scandinavian tone distinction', *Norsk tidsskrift for sprogvidenskap* xvi:201–25
O'Neil, W. A. (1964) 'Faroese vowel morphophonemics', *Language* 40:366–71
Orešnik, J. (1971) 'On the phonological boundary between constituents of Modern Icelandic compound words', (Ljubljana) *Linguistica* xi:51–9

- (1972) 'On the epenthesis rule in Modern Icelandic', *Arkiv för nordisk filologi* LXXXVII:1–32
- & Pétursson, M. (1977) 'Quantity in Modern Icelandic', *Arkiv för nordisk filologi* XCII:155–71
Paul, H. / Mitzka, W. (1963) *Mittelhochdeutsche Grammatik.* (19th edition.) Tübingen: Max Niemeyer
Pétursson, M. (1972) Review of Liberman (1971a), *Phonetica* 26:89–128
- (1974) *Les articulations de l'islandais a la lumière de la radiocinématographie.* Paris: Librairie C. Klincksieck
Pike, K. (1947) *Phonemics: a technique for reducing languages to writing.* Ann Arbor: University of Michigan Press
Popper, K. R. (1968) *Conjectures and refutations: the growth of scientific knowledge.* London: Routledge & Kegan Paul
Prokosch, E. (1939) *A comparative Germanic grammar.* Baltimore: Linguistic Society of America
Pulgram, E. (1970) *Syllable, word, nexus, cursus.* The Hague: Mouton
Putnam, H. (1971) 'The "Innateness Hypothesis" and explanatory models in linguistics', in Searle, J. R. (ed.) *The philosophy of language.* Oxford University Press, 130–9
Pyle, C. (1970) 'West Greenlandic Eskimo and the representation of vowel length', *Papers in Linguistics* 3:115–46
Ralph, B. (1975) 'Phonological differentiation: studies in Nordic language history', *Nordistica Gothoburgensia* 8. Gothenburg: Acta Universitatis Gothoburgensis
Rasmussen, P. (1972) 'Oversigt over det danske udtrykssystems historie', (mimeo). Reykjavík: Bóksala stúdenta
Rischel, J. (1964) 'Toward the phonetic description of Faroese vowels', *Fróðskaparrit. Annales Societatis Scientiarum Færoensis* 13:99–113
- (1968) 'Diphthongization in Faroese', *Acta Linguistica Hafniensia* XI:89–118
Sampson, G. (1970) 'On the need for a phonological base', *Language* 46:586–626
- (1974) 'Is there a universal phonetic alphabet?' *Language* 50:236–59
- (1978) 'Linguistic universals as evidence for empiricism', *Journal of Linguistics* 14:183–205
Scriven, M. (1959) 'Explanation and prediction in evolutionary theory', *Science* 130:477–82
Sievers, E. (1893) *Altgermanische Metrik.* Halle: Max Niemeyer
Sigmundsson, S. (1970) 'Um hljóðdvöl í íslenzku', *Fróðskaparrit. Annales Societatis Scientiarum Færoensis* 18:320–32
Sigurd, B. (1955) 'Rank order of consonants established by distributional criteria', *Studia Linguistica* IX:8–20
Skautrup, P. (1944) *Det danske sprogs historie* I: *Fra Guldhornerne til Skånske lov.* Copenhagen: Gyldendalske Boghandel – Nordisk Forlag
Söderström, S. (1972) 'Om kvantitetsutvecklingen i norrländska folkmål', *Acta Academiæ Regiæ Gustavi Adolphi* LII. Uppsala: Lundequistska Bokhandeln
Sommerfelt, A. (1951/62) 'The development of quantity as evidence of Western European linguistic interdependence', in Sommerfelt, A. *Diachronic and*

synchronic aspects of language : selected articles. The Hague: Mouton, 81–6. (First published in *English studies today*, 1951)

Spence, N. C. W. (1965) 'Quantity and quality in the vowel system of Vulgar Latin', *Word* 21:1–18

Steblin-Kamenskij, M. I. (1960) 'The vowel system of Modern Icelandic', *Studia Linguistica* XIV:35–46

Stetson, R. H. (1951) *Motor phonetics.* Amsterdam: North-Holland

Taylor, J. E. (1973) 'A generative phonology of Faroese, utilizing unordered rules', PhD dissertation, Indiana University

Trubetzkoy, N. S. (1958) *Grundzüge der Phonologie* (2nd edition). Göttingen: Vandenhoeck & Ruprecht

Vachek, J. (1959) 'Notes on the quantitative correlation of vowels in the phonematic development of English', in *Mélanges de linguistique et de philologie.* Paris: Didier, 444–56

Vago, R. M. (1977) 'In support of extrinsic ordering', *Journal of Linguistics* 13:25–41

Vennemann, T. (1971) 'The phonology of Gothic vowels', *Language* 47:90–132
– (1972) 'On the theory of syllabic phonology', *Linguistische Berichte* 18:1–18

Wang, W. S-Y. (1969) 'Competing changes as a cause of residue', *Language* 45:9–25

Weinreich, U., Labov, W. & Herzog, M. I. (1968) 'Empirical foundations for a theory of language change', in Lehmann, W. P. & Malkiel, Y. (eds.) *Directions for historical linguistics: a symposium.* Austin: University of Texas Press, 95–195

Weinstock, J. (1975) 'Quantity and labialization in the Nordic languages: a historical interpretation', in Dahlstedt, K. -H. (ed.) *The Nordic languages and modern linguistics* 2. Stockholm: Almquist & Wiksell, 756–73

Wessén, E. (1945) *Svensk språkhistoria* 1: *Ljudlära och ordböjningslära* (2nd edition). Stockholm: Filologiska föreningen vid Stockholms Högskola
– (1960) *Våra folkmål* (6th edition). Malmö: Fritzes. (1st edition 1935)

Woo, N. (1972) 'Prosody and phonology.' Reproduced by the Indiana University Linguistics Club, Bloomington, Indiana

Zachariasen, U. (1968) 'Munurinn millum Suðuroyarmál og føroyskt annars í longdaruppfatanini av *p, t, k, s, +j, r* og *p, k+l', Fróðskaparrit. Annales Societatis Scientiarum Færoensis* 16:45–51

Zwicky, A. M. (1972) 'Note on a phonological hierarchy in English', in Stockwell, R. P. & Macaulay, R. K. S. (eds.) *Linguistic change and generative theory.* Bloomington: Indiana University Press, 275–301

Þórólfsson, B. K. (1925) *Um íslenskar orðmyndir á 14. og 15. öld og breytingar þeirra úr fornmálinu.* Reykjavík: Fjelagsprentsmiðjan
– (1929a) 'Kvantitetsomvæltningen i islandsk', *Arkiv för nordisk filologi* XLV:35–81
– (1929b) 'Nokkur orð um hinar íslensku hljóðbreytingar *é* > *je* og *y, ý, ey* > *i, í, ei*', in *Studier tillägnade Axel Kock.* Supplement to *Arkiv för nordisk filologi* XL:232–43. Lund: Gleerup
– (1934) *Rímur fyrir 1600. Safn Fræðafjelagsins um Ísland og Íslendinga* IX. Copenhagen: S. L. Møller

228　Bibliography

Þorsteinsson, B. (1906–9) *Íslenzk þjóðlög*. Copenhagen: S. L. Møller

Þráinsson (Thráinsson), H. (1976) 'Dialectal variation in Icelandic as evidence for aspiration theories', in Weinstock, J. (ed.) *The Nordic languages and modern linguistics* 3. Papers from the Third International Conference of Nordic and General Linguistics, Austin, Texas, 5–9 April, 533–44

- (1978) 'On the phonology of Icelandic preaspiration', *Nordic Journal of Linguistics* 1 : 3–54

LIST OF ICELANDIC WRITTEN SOURCES

See also Jónsson (1912–15) for sources of *dróttkvætt*-poetry.

'Bravállarímur', in *Brávallarímur eftir Árna Böðvarsson*. (Edited by Björn K. Þórólfsson.) *Rit Rímnafélagsins* VIII. Reykjavik: Rímnafélagið, 1965

First Grammatical Treatise (= Benediktsson 1972). See also Haugen (1950)

Íslenzk miðaldakvæði. Islandske digte fra senmiddelalderen 1.2–11. Udgivne for Kommissionen for det Arnamagnæanske legat ved Jón Helgason. Copenhagen: Ejnar Munksgaard, 1936–8

'Króka-Refs rímur', in *Króka-Refs saga og Króka-Refs rímur*. Udgivne af Pálmi Pálsson. *Samfund til udgivelse af gammel nordisk litteratur* X. Copenhagen: S. L. Møllers Bogtrykkeri, 1883

'Númarímur', in *Númarímur eftir Sigurður Breiðfjörd* (3rd edition). Reykjavík: Snæbjörn Jónsson, The English Bookshop, 1937. (First published 1833)

'Ólafs ríma Haraldssonar', in *Rímnasafn* 1 : 1–9

'Ólafs rímur Haraldssonar', in *Rímnasafn* 1 : 215–21

'Olgeirsrímur', in *Olgeirsrímur danska eftir Guðmundur Bergþórsson* 1–11. (Edited by Björn K. Þórólfsson & Finnur Sigmundsson.) Reykjavík: Landsbókasafn Íslands – Ísafoldarprentsmiðja, 1947

'Pontusrímur', in *Pontusrímur eftir Magnús Jónsson prúða, Pétur Einarsson og síra Ólaf Halldórsson*. (Edited by Grimur M. Helgason.) *Rit Rímnafélagsins* X. Reykavík: Rímnafélagið, 1961

Rímnasafn 1–11. *Samling af de ældste islandske rimer*. Udgivet for *Samfund til udgivelse af gammel nordisk litteratur* XXXV, ved Finnur Jónsson. Copenhagen: S. L. Møllers Bogtrykkeri, 1905–22

'Skáld-Helga rímur', in *Rímnasafn* 1 : 105–65

'Skíðaríma', in *Rímnasafn* 1 : 10–42

'Snorra Edda', in *Edda Snorra Sturlusonar*. Udgivet eftir håndskrifterne af Kommissionen for det Arnamagnæanske legat ved Finnur Jónsson. Copenhagen: Gyldendalske Boghandel – Nordisk Forlag, 1931

Index